Deleuze and Art

D1558832

Bloomsbury Studies in Continental Philosophy

Presents cutting edge scholarship in the field of modern European thought. The wholly original arguments, perspectives and research findings in titles in this series make it an important and stimulating resource for students and academics from across the discipline.

Deleuze and Art

Anne Sauvagnargues

Translated by

Samantha Bankston

Bloomsbury Academic
An imprint of Bloomsbury Publishing Plc

B L O O M S B U R Y
LONDON · OXFORD · NEW YORK · NEW DELHI · SYDNEY

Bloomsbury Academic

An imprint of Bloomsbury Publishing Plc

50 Bedford Square
London
WC1B 3DP
UK

1385 Broadway
New York
NY 10018
USA

www.bloomsbury.com

**BLOOMSBURY and the Diana logo are trademarks
of Bloomsbury Publishing Plc**

Originally published in French as *Deleuze et l'art* © Presses Universitaires de France, 2005, 2013

Paperback edition published 2018

This English Language translation © Bloomsbury Publishing PLC, 2013, 2018

All rights reserved. No part of this publication may be reproduced or transmitted in any form or by any means, electronic or mechanical, including photocopying, recording, or any information storage or retrieval system, without prior permission in writing from the publishers.

No responsibility for loss caused to any individual or organization acting on or refraining from action as a result of the material in this publication can be accepted by Bloomsbury Academic or the author.

British Library Cataloguing-in-Publication Data
A catalogue record for this book is available from the British Library.

ISBN: HB: 978-1-4411-7380-5
PB: 978-1-4742-6024-4
ePDF: 978-0-8264-3563-7
ePub: 978-1-4411-4915-2

Library of Congress Cataloging-in-Publication Data
Sauvagnargues, Anne, author.
[Deleuze et l'art. English]
Deleuze and art / Anne Sauvagnargues ; translated by Samantha Bankston.
p. cm. – (Bloomsbury studies in continental philosophy)
Includes bibliographical references and index.
ISBN 978-1-4411-7380-5 (hardcover : alk. paper) – ISBN 978-0-8264-3563-7 (ebook (pdf) – ISBN 978-1-4411-4915-2 (ebook (epub) 1. Deleuze, Gilles–Aesthetics. 2. Aesthetics, Modern–20th century. 3. Arts–Philosophy. I. Bankston, Samantha, translator. II. Sauvagnargues, Anne. Deleuze et l'art. Translation of: III. Title.
B2430.D454S2313 2013
701'.17092–dc23
2013015955

Typeset by Newgen Imaging Systems Pvt Ltd, Chennai, India
Printed and bound in Great Britain

Contents

List of Abbreviations

Deleuze's texts are cited with the following abbreviations that correspond to their original French titles and publication dates. Titles of published English translations of the texts are also provided below:

AO   *Anti- Œdipe* (with Félix Guattari) [*Anti-Oedipus*]. Paris: Minuit, 1972.

CC   *Critique et clinique* [*Essays Critical and Clinical*]. Paris: Minuit, 1993.

D   *Dialogues* (with Claire Parnet) [*Dialogues*]. Paris: Flammarion, 1977.

DR   *Différence et Répétition* [*Difference and Repetition*]. Paris: PUF, 1968.

FBLS   *Francis Bacon. Logique de la Sensation* [*Francis Bacon: The Logic of Sensation*]. Paris: Éditions de la Différence, 1981.

F   *Foucault* [*Foucault*]. Paris: Minuit, 1986.

ID   *L'Île déserte et autres textes 1953–1974*, Lapoujade ed. [*Desert Islands: And Other Texts 1953–1974*]. Paris: Minuit, 2002.

IM   *Cinéma 1. L'Image-mouvement* [*Cinema 1: The Moment-Image*]. Paris: Minuit, 1983.

IT   *Cinéma 2. L'Image-temps* [*Cinema 2: The Time-Image*]. Paris: Minuit, 1985.

K   *Kafka. Pour une littérature mineure* (with Félix Guattari) [*Kafka: Toward a Minor Literature*]. Paris: Minuit, 1975.

LS   *Logique du sens* [*The Logic of Sense*]. Paris: Minuit, 1969.

LW   Préface à L. Wolfson, *Le Schizo et les langues* [Trans. 'Louis Wolfson; or, The Procedure' in *Essays Critical and Clinical*]. Paris: Gallimard, 1970.

MP   *Mille Plateaux* (with Félix Guattari) [*A Thousand Plateaus*]. Paris: Minuit, 1980.

N   *Nietzsche et la philosophie* [*Nietzsche and Philosophy*]. Paris: PUF, 1962.

PS   *Proust et les signes* [*Proust and Signs*]. Paris: PUF, 1970.

PCK   *La Philosophie critique de Kant* [*Kant's Critical Philosophy: The Doctrine of the Faculties*]. Paris: PUF, 1963.

Pli   *Le Pli. Leibniz et le Baroque* [*The Fold: Leibniz and the Baroque*]. Paris: Minuit, 1988.

PP   *Pourparlers 1972–1990* [*Negotiations*]. Paris: Minuit, 1990.

QP   *Qu'est-ce que la philosophy?* (with Félix Guattari) [*What Is Philosophy?*]. Paris: Minuit, 1991.

RF   *Deux régimes de fous. Textes et entretiens 1975–1995*, Lapoujade ed. [*Two Regimes of Madness: Texts and Interviews 1975–1995*]. Paris: Editions de Minuit, 2003.

S   *Superpositions* (including *Richard III*, Carmelo Bene) [Deleuze's text, 'Un manifeste de moins,' trans. 'One Manifesto Less' in *The Deleuze Reader*]. Paris: Minuit, 1979.

SM   *Présentation de Sacher-Masoch* (including *La Vénus* à *la fourrure*, L. von Sacher-Masoch) [*Masochism: Coldness and Cruelty and Venus in Furs*]. Paris: Minuit, 1967.

SPE   *Spinoza et le problème de l'expression* [*Expressionism in Philosophy: Spinoza*]. Paris: Minuit, 1968.

SPP   Deleuze, *Spinoza. Philosophie pratique* [*Spinoza: Practical Philosophy*]. Paris: Minuit, 1981.

Translator's note: All citations in *Deleuze and Art* are my translations, unless otherwise noted.

Cartographies of Art

From Literature to the Image

One must proceed with caution when entering the complexity of Deleuze's thought, uncovering the entirety of his work step by step while noting the methods used in the art encounters that are found along the way. This introduction proposes to use the following method: to observe the status of art at its closest point of empirical function in the corpus in order to establish a dynamic cartography of problems and concepts as they appear, mapping their points of arrival and departure. Such a reading makes it possible to avoid abstract elaboration and releases art from certain perspectives and challenges by seizing precise tensions within the becoming of thought.

The first notable observation is quite clear; the importance of art bursts forth when merely looking at the chronological list of his publications. From a solely descriptive point of view, Deleuze devotes more than a third of his published works to analyses of art, not including the numerous articles that, in his typical fashion, he wrote in preparation for his longer works, articles that he does not always return to in later texts.[1] He conducts successive studies of the following art forms: literature (a novel, *In Search of Lost Time*, in 1964; a body of work, that of Kafka in 1975; a play by Carmelo Bene, *Richard III*; three plays by Beckett; and several articles on Zola, Tournier, Klossowski, Lewis Carroll, etc.), and also the paintings of Fromanger (1973), Francis Bacon (1981), classical and neorealist cinema, and a moment in the history of style, the Baroque.

Deleuze often devotes entire books to recent or even contemporary works of art, and he thus provides laborious critiques that never diminish his interest in art, even his stated interests. This is a new use of art, an encounter and exercise that turns out to be indispensable to thought. The way he uses artworks as a terrain for experimentation and validation allows us to capture the conceptual fabrication from the life of his philosophy. His manner of thinking about art and using art exceeds the explicitly aesthetic context of study and diffuses into the whole of his work. Even in the studies that do not explicitly thematize art, the analyses devoted to it are decisive. Making an inventory of these uses and observing their zones of variation should enable us to carve a path within this complex body of work.

A periodization of the question of art provides the necessary elements to establish the system's cinematics. When Colli and Montinari published the French translation of Nietzsche's complete works, Deleuze and Foucault wrote, "In fact, when a thinker like Nietzsche, a writer like Nietzsche, introduces several versions of the same idea, it goes without saying that this ceases to be the same idea."[2] The order of appearance of problems is first established longitudinally, whereby the interest in a cursory inventory of his entire work makes it possible to locate stable nuclei and zones of transformation that touch upon art. This examination provides a periodization that does not subject Deleuze's thought to chronology, or extend it into the realm of historical evolution, which he criticized so often. Periodization does not consist in privileging chronological order or restoring the genesis of thought. Rather, it aims to sketch a cartography; that is to say, a dynamic reading of the system that does not stop at static clichés, but looks to render the becomings of thought sensible. Without a doubt, Deleuze always claims to adhere to systematic thought, but systems do not stand still like static, timeless, homogeneous crystals around an invariant state of thought. Rather, they form mobiles that operate under the principle of exteriority, which Deleuze defines well for Foucault: a system always starts from the exterior, is defined by its external points of force, and not by intrinsic, internal consistency.

> This is a question of method in general: instead of going from an apparent exteriority to an essential "nucleus of interiority," we must conjure the illusory interiority in order to return words and things to their constitutive exteriority.[3]

A system must be defined by its challenges, impacts, appropriations, and external contacts, as well as its variations, wandering lines, speeds, and paces that are not at all homogeneous. Texts are freed from such determinations and gravitate toward concrete problems and textual references that they put into play. Sticking to a static conception of a system would end up eliminating the becomings of thought for the sake of teleology in the work; observing the kinetic transformation of concepts does not result in historical disintegration, but is interested in paths and discloses the concepts' movements. On top of not privileging an affirmative, or polemical method of enunciation that is always endogenous, it makes it possible to demand a method of exoteric exposition in accordance with the principle of exteriority: Deleuze moves from the privilege of literature to the political implications of art, then to the semiotics of creativity. These distinct moments can be broken down when they are considered as three different philosophies of art. These different stages or "plateaus" also define different, theoretical, practical lines of contextualization: which authors and which works ensure that which analyses respond to which problems and at which moment? The impact of an externalist method enables itineraries to be traced within the work, while taking the speeds and slownesses of the circulation of notions into account before proposing a cursory reading of them. It is not the case that a concept is reduced to its conditions of textual appearance or spatiotemporal coordinates, but it is not an autonomous event in the system, despite being created. A concept cannot be dissociated from the external circumstances of its constitution any more than it can be dissociated from the outcome of its movements and migrations, which produce movements or other considerations in the system.

Thus, it is necessary to move from a static, abstract concept of a system, which ignores chronology and contextualization, to a dynamic concept of a system whose problems map their successive variations. Additionally, the dynamism of the system must be correlated with its field of individuation and its intellectual and social contextualization. Concepts arise out of pragmatics and respond to challenges that are not necessarily theoretical, which comes back to what Deleuze and Guattari call "rhizomatic" logic, as we will see. This entails paying incredible attention to the apparatus of confirmed references so as to establish the concepts' components within the doctrines and authors with whom Deleuze converses. That is also important since Deleuze uses them in a way that is strange and problematic, which can be expected from a philosopher who propounds a theory of masks and creation, is constantly hostile toward the establishment of dogma, and as a result, is hostile toward the reification of doctrines in constituted knowledge. Nevertheless, nothing about Deleuze would be understood without methodologically reproducing his reference work, which is usually implicit and masked in his successive reformulations. And yet, Deleuze's work will not be transformed into a Harlequin's coat, even for the very philosopher who theorized that the practice of philosophy is the creation of concepts. Being interested in the irruption of the new requires locating the contour of a conceptual curve within the system, paying special attention to its point of entry, zone of dissipation, theoretical sectors that it puts into play, and the practical connections that ensue from it.

In sum, those are the preparatory parameters that are destined to facilitate the entry into Deleuze's contracted and living thought. It would also be mistaken to consider this periodization an absolute prerequisite for every systematic reading: apart from the fact that every periodization must be relative to the material it is handling—the proposed plateaus here do not at all exclude other divisions— the logical order of consistency often interferes with the historical order of the individuations of notions and their operative zone. Thus, we will first think about this entry into matter like we would a stretching exercise; it is less basic than it seems, and its pedagogical merit consists in facilitating or ameliorating the system's dexterity. The plateaus allow us to define at least three different stages, three states of variation within the system: from the first works up to *Difference and Repetition*, the question of art first passes through the privilege of literature. Deleuze launches a critique of interpretation and a logic of multiplicity with Guattari and the pragmatic turning point of thought that begins with *Anti-Oedipus*, which allows him to completely devote himself to the semiotics of the image and artistic creativity after *A Thousand Plateaus*. We do not propose to break down these three plateaus, but to locate the problematic tension that links them, following Deleuze from literature to the image.

A taste for literature

We will start by looking at the list of Deleuze's publications that focus on literary works and examine their defining features. Up until 1979 all of his writings that analyze art are dedicated to literature, demonstrating the predominance, primacy, and exclusivity of his literary interest, which demarcates the Deleuze's first theoretical phase of art. Beginning in 1980, after the intense period of collaborative work with Guattari, who literally caused Deleuze to *step outside* philosophy (Guattari was not a philosopher but a psychoanalyst engaged in militant activism), Deleuze begins to theorize nonliterary art. There is a definite trajectory that moves from the discursive toward the nondiscursive, affirming the theory of a periodization in Deleuze's philosophy. The break in this trajectory culminates in the question of interpretation, which is the object of intense criticism from the moment that Deleuze and Guattari meet.

Deleuze's first philosophical period, which is inspired by literature, is constructed on a plane of pure thought. In his second period, corresponding to his collaborative work with Guattari from *Anti-Oedipus* (1972) to *A Thousand Plateaus* (1980), Deleuze develops a semiotics that is capable of accounting for signs in the materiality of expression that is irreducible to linguistic signification. Then a third period emerges in Deleuze, which is dedicated to the sign and the image. These three periods form a truly definitive trajectory that addresses the status of the sign and its path from the realm of interpretation to force. His studies from the 1960s reveal a philosophy of signs that is naturally mindful of literary expression, where Proust and Nietzsche, Sacher-Masoch, Zola, and Tournier give the philosopher an opportunity to reformulate the image of thought. Beginning with *Anti-Oedipus*, Artaud and Kafka become heroes in the fight against interpretation, transforming the status of literature: "Experiment! Never interpret!" Deleuze gradually develops a program for a philosophy of signs that is irreducible to the linguistic sphere and the rules of language and linguistics: from that moment onward semiotics was strictly opposed to semiology, or semantics. In other words, every theory that subordinated the sign to linguistics was strictly opposed to semiotics.[4] Deleuze's interest in images, cinema, and painting corresponds to the logic of nondiscursive signs, a "logic of sensation" that pervades all of his works starting from the 1980s. *Francis Bacon, the Logic of Sensation* for painting, *The Movement Image* and *The Time Image* for cinema—these works meet philosophy head-on with the creative thought of art. The last philosophical period for Deleuze crystallizes around the problem of creativity in the arts, sciences, and philosophy. His semiotics of the image is of the utmost importance in this context. This is the project that we intend to explore here.

Even though Deleuze develops an interest in literature early in his philosophical career, this interest never wanes. It is necessary to understand that his semiotic theory does not at all imply a criticism of literature, or a diminution of its value. On the contrary, Deleuze maintains a passion for literature throughout his entire philosophical life. In 1947, two years after his very first text appeared in print, he published an introduction to *La Religieuse* by Diderot.[5] His last work in 1993, *Essays Critical and Clinical*, is also dedicated to a theory of literature and revisits (sometimes very old) articles that are connected and rearticulated by new texts (an article on Nietzsche also emerges, the first version of which dates back to 1963).[6] This attests to a constant interest in literature that did not diminish after he established a nonverbal semiotics. But it is in literature, on literature, and through literature that Deleuze encounters the problematic of nondiscursive art. This makes his transition from interpretation to semiotics in the 1980s all the more fascinating.

The way that Deleuze fulfills his interest in literature merits a detailed description: a brilliant inventiveness of method is used to develop his semiotics.

From *Proust and Signs* in 1964, which was the first version of a book that was reworked into two later versions in 1970, and then again in 1976—the product of 12 years of development—to *Kafka: Towards a Minor Literature*, which he wrote in collaboration with Guattari in 1975, Deleuze invents reasons to theorize about literature and offers striking methods for connecting philosophy and literature without confusing them or subordinating one to the other. The modifications to his work on Proust offer a good example of his unique practice of reexamination, creating a perpetual text that exemplifies the movement of his thought. The three consecutive versions that appear in 1964, 1970, and 1976 radically transform the original version, which is not so much renounced as expanded. The original version changes shape to some degree by branching out into an unpredictable series of solutions that correspond to the problems that Deleuze formulates in later works. Some of these formulations reappear unaltered in the cinema books; namely, to think beneath the irruption of a shock, to look for "a little time in a pure state." *Proust and Signs* is not the only text that is subjected to the shifting maturation of Deleuze's thought. *Spinoza: Practical Philosophy* and *Foucault*[7] meet the same fate in successive republications that contain supplemental additions, and these additions alone manage to restructure the original work. This is the specific mechanism that Deleuze uses in his book on Foucault in order to secure the thinker's status, which is built around this exact process of calculated variance. The stratification of Deleuze's published texts only becomes apparent when the reader simultaneously takes account of the specific changes that are animated across separate versions.

Next, the second singularity is the impressive practice of two-handed writing in Deleuze and Guattari's collaborative work. The first work that Deleuze coauthors with Guattari, before being modified and integrated into *Anti-Oedipus*,[8] according to the aforementioned method, addresses Klossowski's work, who was a painter, philosopher, writer, and who considered himself a "disjunctive synthesis." This picks up the notion of the disjunctive synthesis that Deleuze introduces in *The Logic of Sense* and demonstrates the importance of its practical application. Accordingly, a synthesis, for Deleuze, is not a return to the One, but a disjunctive differentiation that proceeds by bifurcations and transformations, and not by fusion and identity of the same. This differing and nonconjunctive synthesis is applied practically in Deleuze and Guattari's singular, collaborative writings, and it not only changes the status of the text but also its construction. His collective work with Guattari creates a theory of systems that includes literature (*Rhizome*, in 1976). Their analysis of Kafka's works the year prior provides the first example of this systemic theorization and introduces the exploratory method they use to study the political implications of literature.

The practice of collective and impersonal writing ultimately results in the theory of a "collective assemblage of enunciation." This concept, which appears in *Kafka*, corresponds to two dramatizations that Guattari outlines: the assemblage transforms the notions of "structure," "system," "form," and "process" by increasing the formally articulated nature of the system or structure in a pragmatic process that opens onto "heterogeneous" elements. This means that the assemblage acts in accordance with the protocol of semiotics, which is not exclusively intellectual, discursive, or linguistic, but consists of coexisting signs that are diverse, heterogeneous, biological, political, and social. Secondly, such an *assemblage* is deemed an assemblage of *collective enunciation* when it involves the demarcation of a nonsubjective, impersonal mode of literary creation beyond the individuated instances of enunciation that privilege linguistics or stylistics, and is thus not reducible to the author, or to individual genius.[9] Literature must no longer be considered the matter of an exceptional individual, revealing his or her personal memories and other "dirty little secrets," but should be considered a collective enterprise that explores social becomings. This is what constitutes minor literature, which strives toward a clinical critique and a symptomatological definition of literature.

In addition to this method of a philosophical return, of a true "continued" writing, a collective writing that alters the status of literature, Deleuze introduces a kind of editorial symbiosis with *Sacher-Masoch: An Interpretation* in 1967. He does so by grafting two different writing forms together into a single volume, philosophy and literature, which are not necessarily written in concert with one another. Symbiosis, which is borrowed from animal ethology, serves as a model for pursuing the concept of disjunctive synthesis in living domains. The model of symbiosis is used through the introduction of a heterogeneous graft or connection between disparate series. Deleuze applies this concept to his description of Proust's homosexuality and the seductive courtship between the wasp and the orchid (a heterogeneous animal and vegetal series), which, paradoxically, are joined together in the reproductive mechanism of the orchid. Leaving Proust, the capture of the wasp and orchid, or collective becoming (the becoming-wasp of the orchid, and the becoming-orchid of the wasp), does not merely serve to describe a new method of literary process that is produced "between" Deleuze and Guattari. In this case, symbiosis describes the unpublished techniques that Deleuze uses when he adjusts philosophy and literature to one another without mixing them or hierarchizing them, but conserves their disjunctive difference and their necessary encounter. This coexistence between literature and philosophy contrasts with the traditional preface or postscript, the erudite commentary which illuminates the text that it frames.

Sacher-Masoch: An Interpretation juxtaposes two works of comparable length: Masoch's novella "Venus in Furs" and Deleuze's preceding essay "Coldness and Cruelty." It serves as a true "introduction" to Sacher-Masoch, providing an opportunity for a republication of his works. Masoch, less than Sade, attracted the attention of those who were interested in the relationship between literature, desire, and normality, including Bataille, Klossowski, and Foucault. Deleuze does not simply offer a springboard for an appreciation of Masoch in order to correct the injustice that led to his works being thrown into oblivion at the same time that his name took on its current meaning, nor does he want to recreate an interest in masochist literature that was already sparked by sadist literature. Deleuze is neither a preface writer, nor a commentator; on the contrary, he claims to produce a critical space that cannot be reduced to an exegesis of internal sense or external commentary: this is what defines a clinical critique. Deleuze reveals the methods of this practice by choosing *Superpositions* as the title of a text he wrote with the dramaturge Carmelo Bene.[10] Once again, the text does not serve as a postscript, and in this case Deleuze's text follows Bene's text. The book *superposes* Bene's play "Richard III" on "One Manifesto Less," written by Deleuze. The title of Deleuze's text is borrowed from Bene and demonstrates why the dramaturge holds his attention. Philosophy does not add an additional sense to the force of literature; it is not "one manifesto *more*." It does not provide theoretical instructions for a piece of writing that would remain opaque without it. On the contrary, philosophy uses dramaturgical shock to introduce its own philosophical response, which is motivated by the writer's own work.

The critique proposed by Deleuze does not set out to add *more* commentary, but cuts out a commentary from *less*. In this instance, the clinical site is redoubled by the fact that Bene's play is itself a reprise or doubling of *Richard III* by Shakespeare, but a reprise or doubling that is an intentional excision, allowing literature (Bene), like philosophy (Deleuze), to write alongside great works while transforming them. Therefore, creation follows from surgical amputation. Critical admiration involves a relationship with tradition that is characterized by subtractive tension and contraction, resulting in a kind of active, improvisational reprise or doubling, and not a passive canonization. That is why critique has been known to exercise a *minoritarianism*, which does not reinforce a masterpiece's immutable, cultural standing and major ruling position, but actually *invalidates* the masterpiece in order to grant it continued life, which means that it becomes while being transformed. It is better to mishandle a masterpiece in an act of laudatory experimentation than it is to reify it in the hopes of keeping it intact in an illusory state of immutability. The subtractive position also develops the definition of minor literature and allows the critique to be conceived as an encounter, through vital neighborhoods and vicinities, like a literal clinic, or way of life. Such spaces circulate between the works in question, determining the encounter and vitality within the exchange between philosophy and literature.

In *Quad*, published in 1992, Deleuze follows Beckett's "Quad and Other Plays for Television" with an extraordinary essay entitled "The Exhausted," which should be read for its faint voice and succinct rhythm, like a dense text of poetic thought. Differing from *Superpositions*, this book appears under Beckett's name, and Deleuze—with considerable tact—fades away and disappears under the author's name. The search for a "co-adaptation of two forms," literary thought and philosophical thought, is conducted on the formal plane through a material superposition of discourses that do not forfeit their impermeable singularities or their decisive intersections. This exercise exemplifies the disjunctive encounter that Deleuze and Guattari theorize in their collective writings on literary works. A beautiful example of this encounter appears in *Rhizome*,[11] which is a true discourse on the method of impersonal writing. From 1964 to 1993, Deleuze pursues this philosophical quest with and about literature, this *clinical critique*. The appearance of his first essay that is explicitly about literature appropriately pertains to Sacher-Masoch, and this essay is developed in his last published work, *Essays Critical and Clinical*, focusing on the "problem of writing,"[12] which appears in the first chapter on "literature and life." There is much in Deleuze's thought that follows from a reflection on literature, which is characterized by its continuous force, its urgency and redevelopment, and its innovative use of resources.

From literature to semiotics

In a remarkable trajectory, the writings from 1972–80, which are years of capture and collective writing with Félix Guattari, years where the status of writing undergoes encounters and transformations, are followed by a series of publications that Deleuze writes independently at different times. This trajectory signifies the maturation and urgency of a theory of nonliterary art, a semiotics of art. Art is no longer limited to literature: painting and cinema make appearances. Deleuze becomes involved in producing a precise logic, taxonomy, and classification of images and signs without reducing them to statements. Semiotics requires a philosophy of art that is not reducible to the order of signification and discourse. Deleuze calls "Ideas" complexes of sensation that are not reducible to discursive signification, but that stimulate thought. These images do not say anything; they give rise to thought. Semiotics seeks to express a sensorial experience (auditory, visual) of the given of a problem that produced the image, without translating it into discursive language, and without reducing it to models of interpretation, imaginary analogy, or symbolic correspondence.

How does Deleuze move from literature to semiotics? He does so by deepening the status of signs in his theoretical work and in the practice of collaborative writing with Guattari, which grants him freedom to move from the intellectual status of the sign to its ethology, its vital environment, and its material effectiveness. The sign is no longer indebted to a hermeneutics of sense which deciphers signifying procedures, but belongs to a logic of forces that captures art and creates an image from a composite of affects and percepts. The ethology of the affect creates a path from *The Logic of Sense* to *The Logic of Sensation*. These two works by Deleuze frame his collective work with Guattari, from *Anti-Oedipus* (1972) to *A Thousand Plateaus* (1980); they are signified by an investigation of politics and madness, social and psychic norms, or in other words, sociology and psychology. The two books are conjoined in a single title, *Capitalism and Schizophrenia*, and analyze the machination that connects mental "disorganization" in schizophrenia to the social organization of capitalism. The two texts investigate the historical production of cultural modes of creating social subjects, modes of subjectification. The first volume, *Anti-Oedipus* (1972), provides a theory of the critical subject with regard to psychoanalysis; a work that Deleuze claims is political through and through. It is the psychotic figure, a true anti-Oedipus, who leads the fight against Freudian interpretation. The second volume, *A Thousand Plateaus* (1980), develops a relational logic and a political theory of capitalism that passes through a critique of the social sciences and then requires the development of a semiotics that organizes ("assembles") discursive and nondiscursive signs with power relations.

This theory of assemblages provides a principled foundation for semiotics. This is because an assemblage provides a method of interaction while claiming to avoid internalist presuppositions regarding the notions of structure or system, which determine the value of their elements self-referentially through internal differences within a closed system. Deleuze and Guattari only conceive of systems as being open, connected, nonhomogeneous, and they call such a mechanistic system with transversal connections a "rhizome." The rhizome is modeled after the weed, where nomadic and blooming rootlets proliferate without the presence of a dominant root. The model of the rhizome as nonarborescent or acentric belief is borrowed from biology, which encourages the intersection of heterogeneous regimes, crossbreeding, and iteration without the presence of a given unity. In other words, signs do not preferentially form autonomous and closed linguistic systems, but every sign system, including linguistics, is open to other vital, political, signifying, or subjective semiotics. In *A Thousand Plateaus*, Deleuze and Guattari call these systems regimes of signs ["sign systems"], to avoid the closure of the sign system: a regime is an open rhizomatic system that functions through connections, enduring the pragmatic heterogeneity that arises when the system opens onto other semiotics. The sign is thus defined as a complex of necessarily hybrid forces, assembling disparate mental and social codes, as well as linguistic and pragmatic codes.

The concept of an assemblage causes semantics to bend into semiotics, and implies a critique of interpretation. It is not surprising that the Deleuze-Guattari duo produces a political theory of literature (*Kafka*, in 1975) during this period, a theory of impersonal writing as a collective assemblage—the same one that is put into use by their collective writing—that manifests semiotics. Thinking about painting or cinema, or exposing the effects of art beyond the literary effect, requires a theory of nondiscursive signs that separates the analysis of signs from the influence of discourse, and that critiques the primacy of the book as well as the traditional position of commentary (*Rhizome*, 1976). In other words, a theory of signs that develops a critique of interpretation is required.

This turning point intersects with the publication of *A Thousand Plateaus* in 1980, and the publications that follow speak for themselves. In 1981, Deleuze develops a theory of painting: *Francis Bacon, the Logic of Sensation*.[13] Even earlier, Deleuze had written a short text about painting in honor of Gérard Fromanger, "Cold and Heat," in the same vein as his book on Masoch, "Coldness and Cruelty." On each of the eleven pages, text and reproductions of paintings were printed across from one another, and images and concepts were placed face to face. Even the layout of the first edition of *Francis Bacon* split Deleuze's *The Logic of Sensation* and the reproduction of Bacon's paintings into two thin volumes. Painting and philosophy coexisted in this layout, and they were put into close proximity without disturbing the distinction between them. This first edition was an innovative example of an editorial format that attempted to revitalize the status of books written about painting. This work was followed by a masterful study of cinema, which appeared in the two volumes of *The Movement-Image* and *The Time-Image*, in 1983 and 1985. Two years later, Deleuze uses the artistic taste of a historic period to thematize the unity of the arts under one authoritative style, the peculiarity of a period in history, and the coexistence of the arts, sciences, and philosophy in his book *The Fold: Leibniz and the Baroque*, published in 1988. Deleuze pushes the question of the image to the forefront in all of these works, especially in the ones devoted to painting and cinema.

The encounter with Félix Guattari

This list of publications reveals the consistent alternation between art and philosophy in Deleuze's works. It also reveals an opening up of philosophy onto arts other than literature, and the affirmation of a semiotics that works just as well for literature as it does for the nondiscursive arts. From the analysis of a single novel (*Proust and Signs*) to the analysis of a collection of works (those of Kafka and Bacon), from a particular work to an entire genre, from the specificity of one art (cinema) to the art of a historic period (the Baroque), Deleuze never ceases to systematically expand the borders of the analysis of the arts. At the same time, he never stops alternating his writings on art with book studies written about authors and great literary works, or with concepts and problems that are not specifically artistic. This alternation continues, even if we have to wait until *Difference and Repetition* in 1968 for a text to appear that is not an explicitly monographic work of philosophy (Hume, Nietzsche, Kant, Bergson) or literature (Proust, Sacher-Masoch). Thus, a preliminary sketch is drawn: a clear trajectory from literature to the nondiscursive arts is formed, which underscores the status of the image and the importance of a critique of interpretation.

Thus, the first period is shaped by an experience with literature. The experience with signs builds upon the ground of literature before unfolding into semiotics. This does not mean that Deleuze discovers the importance of nondiscursive art later, but literature forms the first landscape where we witness art at work in his writing. Beginning with *Difference and Repetition*, Deleuze constantly refers to painting, and while he never devoted an entire book to it, music plays an equally important role in *A Thousand Plateaus* and *The Fold*. At first, Deleuze produces a philosophy of literature, which uses the literary form and the methods of modern literature as a theoretical meeting place between philosophy and thought. Thanks to literature philosophy is able to reformulate "the image of thought."[14] What forces one to think is the violent and involuntary intrusion of a sign, which is the object of an encounter that forces thought to create.[15] The physics of Proustian homosexuality that Deleuze analyses in his second edition of *Proust* in 1970 is a response to *Sacher-Masoch: An Interpretation* from 1967. Literature not only attempts to demonstrate the genesis of thought within thought (a methodology of the creation of thought) but also opens up a clinical critique. A clinical critique, or a Nietzschean symptomatology (developed in *Nietzsche*, in 1962), opens literature up to a diagnostic mechanism. Deleuze continues to follow Nietzsche's path, making the philosopher an artist and a doctor of civilization.

Nietzsche said it, the artist and the philosopher are doctors of civilization.[16]

This diagnostic function specifically characterizes a new plateau in the philosophy of art, which is transformed as it moves into unfamiliar spaces and expands through new social and political functions. The transformation in the philosophy of art can be attributed to the moment Deleuze met Guattari in 1969,[17] or better yet, the publication of *Anti-Oedipus* in 1972, which marked the first significant work written collectively by the two thinkers. *The Logic of Sense*, published in 1969, is interested in the constitution of sense, no doubt from the point of view of its external, nonsensical, unconscious, and corporeal limits, but always with respect to the internal borders of thought. This text examines thought in its formal dimension, while remaining in dialogue with Russell's mathematical logic, Husserl's transcendental logic, and Lacan's psychoanalysis. The watershed moment in Deleuze's philosophy can be said to revolve around the figure of Artaud. The intrusion of the schizophrenic "body without organs" in *The Logic of Sense* marks the entry point from the first to the second philosophy of art in Deleuze. With Artaud, we shift from an informal artistic experience, especially regarding literature, to a pragmatic ethology of modes of social subjugation.[18]

His encounter with Guattari is anything but anecdotal; it is decisive, and is decisive for Deleuze's philosophy as it is reorganized according to real empiricisms, political struggle, and therapeutic confrontations with psychosis and schizophrenia in the context of existing institutions. Deleuze developed a critique of the subject by using artistic and psychoanalytic methods, but on the grounds of pure philosophy. His encounter with Guattari results in a true submersion into empiricism, and coincides with an immersion into the realm of historical social struggle and militant engagement. This was the era of the GIP (the group for information about prisons) and the CERFI (the center for institutional study, research, and training),[19] and this change became known through the introduction of a political lexicon that did not exist prior to Deleuze's involvement. He espouses the effects of May 1968 in French society and responds to the political outrage seen in the militant anti-establishment demonstrations that turn intellectual life, and the French university, on its head. The events of May 1968 paved the way for the creation of the University of Paris at Vincennes, which Deleuze joined in 1969.[20]

From this perspective, his encounter with Guattari liberates and ignites something within Deleuze, which causes a shift in thought from the speculative toward real movements, political dynamics that shock the social body, and toward the practical field of madness within framework of the asylum. In a Foucaultian gesture, Deleuze sets out to establish a *clinical* critique from his very first texts. This move attests to Deleuze and Guattari's shared interest in the historicity and interpretation of the two poles of normalcy and pathology. Following Canguilhem, they pay attention to the "birth of the clinic" and demonstrate their admiration for the critical works of Bataille and Blanchot who evaluate the relationship between transgression and singularity in literature. Deleuze is interested in madness as the edge of reason, and in *Sacher-Masoch* and *The Logic of Sense* he sought to formulate a theory linking literary creativity with madness (Artaud, the schizophrenic) or perversion (the analysis of desire and the law in Masoch's work). With Guattari, Deleuze moves away from a formal definition of the unconscious toward a dimension that is simultaneously political and critical with respect to psychoanalysis.

Guattari described himself as being at the crossroads of what he considered three "discordant" theoretical and practical domains up until his encounter with Deleuze: the militant activism in different political, Marxist organizations; the clinical practice at La Borde with Jean Oury in the context of institutional psychotherapy; as well as analytic practice with psychotics within a Lacanian perspective. Lacan was his analyst and his seminars marked a decisive return to Freudian theory for Guattari and his entire generation.[21] It was during his analytic treatment of psychotics at the La Borde clinic with Jean Oury, which grew out of the institutional psychotherapy of Tosquelles,[22] that Guattari began to conceive of the unconscious as a social production, taken directly from the historical and political dimensions of the social. Guattari is the one who enables Deleuze to "restore historical perspectives to the unconscious," which implies "a reversal of psychoanalysis, and certainly, a rediscovery of psychosis beneath the tatters of neurosis."[23] Thus a double movement is formed by a critique of psychoanalysis and an interest in schizophrenia, characterizing Deleuze's work between *Anti-Oedipus* and *A Thousand Plateaus*.

This double movement unveils a critique of interpretation, because it rejects the supremacy and the very domination of the linguistic and psychic signifier. Guattari takes this critique from institutional psychotherapy, which is defined by its concern with the "institutional," instituted, political, and collective dimension of the psyche. The critique aims to close the gap between the private dimension of the Freudian unconscious and the sociopolitical constitution of subjects. Institutional psychotherapy plays a crucial role in the programmatic development of *Anti-Oedipus*, as it intends to shock contemporary institutions by reforming the structures of asylum. Its political dimension is simultaneously opposed to hospital psychiatry, institutional administration, juridical and medical administration of the abnormal within the social body, psychoanalysis, and the analysis of the constitutive processes of consciousness as emerging from unconscious flows.

> Guattari can thus reproach psychoanalysis for the way in which it systematically erases all of the sociopolitical content from the unconscious, which nevertheless determines the objects of desire in reality. Psychoanalysis, he says, comes from a kind of absolute narcissism (*Das Ding*) that hopes to reach an ideal of social adaptation while calling it a "cure"; but this approach always leaves a singular social constellation in the dark, which should be explored, rather than being sacrificed in the invention of an abstract symbolic unconscious.[24]

The political critique of interpretation

So, Guattari substitutes schizoanalysis for Freudian psychoanalysis. Psychoanalysis is dominated by the cliché of psychic normalcy, and schizoanalysis posits a Marxist inspired analysis of the unconscious that replaces the neurotic, individual-centric Oedipal model with an impersonal, political, non-Oedipal model of psychosis. Schizoanalysis attributes social production to the material realm of consciousness and historicizes the Freudian unconscious, whose instinctual economy is connected directly to social mechanics, rather than being considered a separate sphere, or an individual, familial, and private "empire within an empire." Schizoanalysis assigns practical, experimental value to madness, social maladjustment, and psychosis, and contains political dramatization and cultural value. Following Foucault and his examination of madness as the limit of reason, the artist becomes an agent responsible for changing aesthetic tastes, thus destabilizing norms. Art, as a critique of society, reveals its social criticism at the same time that it demonstrates new types of subjectification.

The critique of the subject is absorbed in this new social and political dimension, a critique of the communist and psychoanalytic movements that fuel the problematic in *Anti-Oedipus*.[25] Deleuze always credits Guattari for the following two eventualities: enabling him to *go beyond* psychoanalysis, and being given the chance to discover the concept's pragmatism.[26] At the same time, Guattari makes it possible for Deleuze to assign an essential political dimension to theoretical thought and artistic praxis, which leads to the development of the concept of an assemblage as an amicable opposition to the Foucaultian concept of a "*dispositif*."

The encounter with this practitioner of schizophrenia, this militant psychoanalyst, who became more and more critical of the "familial" dimension of psychoanalysis, managed to transform the Nietzschean symptomatology seen in Deleuze's previous studies into the realm of a political assemblage of signs. This reorganization is the guiding principle in Deleuze's expansion of the arts, setting off the transition from literature to semiotics while integrating a political dimension into the arts and thought, as both moments proceed from a critique of interpretation. In Deleuze's second philosophical period—collective philosophy—thought is no longer disassociated from its real assemblage *hic et nunc*. Art is no longer a matter of signification, but of function. Experimentation replaces interpretation once and for all. The sign as the affect and relation of forces supplants the signifier, be it linguistic or psychoanalytic.

An interest in social sciences emerges from this philosophical shift, particularly in terms of economics, history, ethnology, and the theory of civilization. Prior to this moment, Deleuze had not written any sustained analyses about these disciplines. Of course, he used the cleavage between active and reactive forces found in the Nietzschean schema to perform active critiques of civilization and nihilism, while also writing long analyses of Marx in *Difference and Repetition*, but now he was starting to think about the arts as "the actualization of a revolutionary potentiality."[27] The artist, like a doctor of civilization, is conferred a political role where the effect of art is determined within its two social dimensions, social production and revolutionary agency.

This opening of art onto the political landscape is inarguably a motif that can be specifically ascribed a date. In 1967 Deleuze makes art a higher end than the State or society, having found the means to avoid the combined dangers of the eternal and the historical in the untimely philosopher, Nietzsche.[28] It was out of the question to involve art in political and historical spheres, and if an allusion to Marxism is perceived in passing, it is in opposition to eternity. Eternity and history are like two similar and reciprocal positions that deny the very temporality of the work of art.

> What is clear to Nietzsche is that society cannot be a final moment. The final moment is creation, it is art; or rather, art represents the absence and impossibility of a final moment. From the very beginning of his works, Nietzsche

posits that there are ends that are "a little higher" than those of the State, than those of society. He erects his entire philosophy in a dimension that is not that of the historical, even dialectically conceived, nor that of the eternal. This new dimension which is both in time and acts against time, he calls *the untimely*. This is where life as interpretation finds its source.[29]

The untimely creates an escape from historical dialectics, as well as eternity. Even if Deleuze takes the time to mention that this position does not amount to a "certain aestheticism, a certain renunciation of politics, and a depoliticized individualism,"[30] this symptomology remains indifferent to political context, and the social body does not seem to be a constitutive dimension in art. At the very most, the "joy artist," the tragic humor and its *vis comica* imply a "liberation" whose political content remains pretty vague.[31]

> *The untimely*, which we spoke about earlier, is never reduced to an historical-political element. But sometimes it is the case that in great moments they coincide. [. . .] But when people fight for their liberation, there is always a coincidence between poetic acts and historic events or political actions [. . .] a joy artist who becomes associated with historical struggle.[32]

Starting with *Anti-Oedipus*, a book that is "political through and through,"[33] art and its effects are conceived rather as productions which are determined by social machines, and are understood within a context of critical analysis aimed at social, economic, juridical, and political processes. Art is no longer dissociated from its political dimension and effects, and it receives a messianic function. It is no longer the case that the joy artist occasionally coincides with historical struggle, but collides with the revolutionary political effect that determines the success of art.

> The literary machine is taken over by a revolutionary machine to come [. . .]. There is nothing great or revolutionary except the minor. To hate all literature of the masters.[34]

It is necessary to see that his new theory is first established in praxis which consists of inventing a multiple form of writing, a collective thought, and is developed in this form of philosophical writing while having split off from the sovereign isolation of thought; standing in the "middle" of this collective being is Deleuze *and* Guattari. The beginning of *Rhizome* sounds like a manifesto, an asubjective method of discourse. "We wrote *Anti-Oedipus* as a duo. Since each one of us was several, that already made quite a crowd." It is primarily writing that is assembled collectively. Philosophical discourse attributes the private aspect of thought to *one* subject. The relationship between thought and life, which Deleuze used to determine noetically, is now defined on an empirical plane of social becoming, pragmatic ethology, and the political constitution of subjects. There is not "one" author of thought but a becoming-social of the author function that corresponds to the liberating purpose of thought, and this becoming is functionally transformed by the dramatizations that permeate writing. This new way of doing philosophy profoundly transforms theory, and the status of the book changes as much as the author-function does.

> A book has neither object nor subject; it is made from variously formed matters, very different dates and speeds. As long as a subject is attributed to a book, this working of matters and the exteriority of their relations are overlooked [. . .].[35]

This is why the intense period of experimental, collective writing and collaboration with Guattari finds its culmination on a new plane, which can be considered an extension of the logic of multiplicities in the definitive cases of painting, cinema, and Baroque art. The publications that Deleuze returns to by himself are oriented toward a very detailed semiotics of the nondiscursive arts. The theory of art as a vital machine and assemblage of signs that is irreducible to language enables semiotics to become involved in the analysis of particular cases: Bacon, cinema in its entirety and the diversity of its periods, schools, and finally, the Baroque—which Deleuze capitalized.

Besides, Deleuze confirms this periodization.

> We tried to make a philosophy, Félix and I, in *Anti-Oedipus* and in *A Thousand Plateaus*, especially in *A Thousand Plateaus,* which is a huge book and offers a lot of concepts. We didn't collaborate; we made one book then another, not in the sense of a unity, but as an indefinite article. Each one of us had a past and previous works: he in psychiatry, politics, philosophy, already rich with concepts, and I with *Difference and Repetition* and *The Logic of Sense*. But we didn't collaborate as two people. We were more like two streams that met up to make "a" third that would have been us. [. . .] *One* philosophy, for me this was more like a second period that would have never started or finished without Félix.
>
> Afterwards, let's suppose that there is a third period when my concern was painting and cinema, apparently images. But those are philosophy books.[36]

Image, affect, and percept

Deleuze explores literature and then becomes interested in the nondiscursive arts, in painting, and in cinema, forming a trajectory that leads from language toward the matter of perception. Deleuze's definition of art as a capture of forces and then as an image corresponds to this movement. The capture of forces, which is first expressed in terms of literature, and then carried over into the analysis of painting in 1981 with *Francis Bacon: The Logic of Sensation*, instantly reveals the aesthetic identity that ties literature to the nondiscursive arts. Even better, the capture of forces reveals that the effect of art, including literature, is not reducible to its linguistic dimension, but requires a semiotics of the affect that is not reducible to the discursive, which is a true logic of sensation. It is this semiotics, this nonlinguistic philosophy of the sign that leads Deleuze to define art as the capture of forces in the 1980s with *Bacon*, and then he defines art in terms of the image in his two books dedicated to cinema, *The Movement-Image* and *The Time-Image*. After having relied on the experience of art in order to pressure philosophy into changing its image of thought, as we saw in 1964 with *Proust and Signs*, Deleuze immediately opens up a new path while he transforms the definition of the image. Following Bergson and being inspired by his analysis of *Matter and Memory*, the image as conceived by Deleuze is not a copy or a mental double, let alone a representation of the imagination, or a cliché formed by opinion. Rather, it is a mode of matter, real movement, and the effect of art must be understood from this strictly positive perspective. "An image does not represent an assumed reality, it is all of reality in itself."[37] Far from being a cultural fiction or anthropological criterion, for Deleuze, art robs consistency and innocence from an effect of subjectification, which causes affects to tremble within matter.

Art is real; it produces real effects on the plane of forces and not forms. The result is an extremely original shift within the fracture between the imaginary and the real. The imaginary ceases to be considered a mental fiction, and art is no longer considered a cultural distraction. Deleuze insists on the real aspects of the imaginary as long as the critique of interpretation, formulated in respect to literature, insists on the nonliterary dimension of the arts that do not first, or exclusively, pass through the medium of language. This shift happens in such a way whereby images must be considered from a nonsignifying, literal perspective, and this involves using extraction and not abstraction to reconstruct the thought that images produce. The imaginary is not unreal, mental, or subjective, but it offers a relative indiscernibility of the real and the unreal, an indiscernability that can be explicated through the notion of capture. All images are literal and must be taken literally in such a way that thought is inseparable from images, but is not signified by them as the abstract content that they might represent. Here we find a war cry for the nondiscursive arts, which are not subjected to the repetition or deconstruction of forms and do not fall under a signifying regime. All of that is not to say that they are deprived of intelligibility or thought, but they cannot be reduced to signification, much less discursive signification. The capture of forces and the image seek thought on the level of sensation. Art does not function in a private and mental, subjective dimension: it is not reducible to a symbolic system, or an appeal to the imaginary, the fantasy, or the dream, but actually produces images that give rise to thought. "There aren't any abstract thoughts that are indifferently actualized in such or such image, but concrete thoughts only exist through these images and their means." Here we find a definition for success in art: "an image is only as valuable as the thoughts that it creates."[38]

In 1981 Deleuze dives into the work of Francis Bacon and devotes an entire text to the nondiscursive arts. Even though he had previously dedicated numerous analyses and some articles to painting and music, this is the first time that he tackles an ensemble of pictorial work and analyzes it with a semiotics that was previously defined through literature. This was a matter of thinking about "the system of images and signs independently of language in general." This is the immense difficulty in analyzing painting, which cannot redouble the work while describing it, nor lapse into sentimental chatter and applied metaphysics.[39] Deleuze specifies that painting is nonsignifying and asyntactical since it does not put signifying words that follow a syntactical order into the work. Its material is not formed linguistically, but nonetheless, it does not lack the capacity to effect thought. Deleuze is invested in apprehending this plastic mass, examining the way in which it attracts our eye while raising "before us the reality of a body, lines and colors."[40] The image is not a statement, and requires a logic of sensation that is nondiscursive and not a logic of signification. "Therefore, we must create definitions, not by semiology but semiotics," as a system of images and signs independent from language in general.

This is where the difficulty in analyzing the nondiscursive arts arises, since it is a matter of bringing what is not revealed by discourse into discourse, and extracting thought from this nonlinguistic signaling material that is not at all amorphous, and is "pragmatically, aesthetically, and semiotically well formed."[41] This triple determination of the sign as being irreducible to language, being sensible, and producing an effect enables the logic of sensation that Deleuze envisions with Bacon, which corresponds to the move away from the logic of sense that he created in 1969. By moving from sense to sensation, one moves from the regime within a work whose focus is the signifying mental sphere toward a logic of sensation, which provides a true, programmatic definition of the aesthetic as a logic of the sensible. In this new and decisive sense, the image is not a representation or a double, but a composition of force relations, made by speeds and slownesses that also exhibit a difference in power, an affect. If the image is a reality and not a mental intention, then it is not a representation of consciousness (a psychological given), nor is it a representation of a thing (an object intention). Deleuze understands the image in a Bergsonian sense, as an apparition, a system of actions and reactions at the level of matter itself. This means that the image has no need to be perceived, but exists in itself as reverberation, vibration, and movement. Moving from thought to image in the coming chapters, we aim to reproduce a few of these paths along the way.

2

Critical and Clinical

Experimentation of Margins and Clinical Function

Experimentation allows us to enter into the clinical function of art. The critique is considered clinical from two perspectives: art becomes a clinical experimentation of vital positions, while a critique is considered a discourse on the work of art, diagnosing its vitality, its speed. Every artistic production engages this Nietzschean definition of *critique* in the evaluation of mores and is accomplished through an ethological reading of a complex of forces. Nietzschean symptomatology carries out this kind of reading of forces. It is not reduced to personal motives of individual history at all, but is developed into a physics of affects. Far from judging this kind of individual, diagnosis operates solely as a reading, or a mapping of its affects. It pertains to typology (it points out a kind of life) and turns symptomatology into an object of genealogical critique (a value critique of the precise type of life that is being implicated, from the point of view of forces). It is this symptomatology that realizes the creative innovation and success of art. For example, in Proust, the description of homosexuality is a matter of clinical examination. But this clinical position is critical from the outset, precisely because it arises from an ethological reading that is descriptive and nonnormative. Proust becomes a symptomatologist of genius because he evades the transcendent plane of judgment, and he is satisfied exposing the immanent plane of affects. This difference between the immanent plane of force relations and the transcendent plane of judgment is decisive in establishing the *critical* virtue of the clinical. Effectively, it is critical in the sense that it is not a critique or contestation that is initially intended, but rather, it is the clinical. The clinical evokes an affectology as well; it is the study of the powers to affect and be affected which characterize each work of art.

Deleuze takes "clinical" in a secondary Foucaultian sense of an epistemology of psychiatric and psychoanalytic medicine. While literature constitutes a privileged reference for Deleuze, Foucault is especially interested in literary creativity from 1960–5 and understands creativity as experimentation at the fringes of reason, which he connects to his work on the history of madness and the epistemology of the medical clinic.[1] With good reason, Pierre Macherey insists on the importance of literature in Foucault, and the fact that it "completely illuminates the history of our practices and our knowledge" to the degree that it "consists in the exploration of margins" while being marginal itself. It is through the model of "literary experience" that "other experiences" of exclusion, knowledge, punishment, and sexuality could be thought."[2] This description of the clinical and political role of literature is also meaningful for Deleuze, who admires Foucault, and expresses an enthusiasm for his book, *Raymond Roussel*, from the time of its publication in 1963, an enthusiasm that Deleuze never abandons. He himself published an article on Sacher-Masoch two years earlier which shaped his first contribution to the relationship between literature and psychological margins, including a critique of psychiatry and psychoanalysis.[3] This interest in the normal and the pathological comes to both of them from Canguilhem, and the attraction to the extreme border between madness and creativity comes from the *Collège de Sociologie*, from Blanchot, and also from Nietzsche, Hölderlin, and Artaud. Canguilhem's contribution turns out to be pivotal because it shows the relativity of the categories of what is considered normal and pathological from a Nietzschean perspective, which analyzes health from the point of view of sickness, and also suggests a dynamic distinction between abnormality and anomaly. The abnormal is a pejorative, normative term, which implies a reference to the value of what is "normal" and qualifies what is contrary to the norm. Meanwhile, anomalous, from the Greek *anomalia*, denotes "disparity and asperity," as opposed to smoothness, unity, and is a descriptive term that does not include the idea of disorder or irregularity, but only what is "strange and unconventional."[4] At bottom, the *abnormal* is treated as a deviation from the norm or standard, a hypostasized rule as a determinate rule (*major*), while the *anomal* (anomalous) only designates variation, difference, and a unique case that is given in the disengagement from the norm through variation (*minor*).

"Abnormal": a-normal, a Latin adjective without a noun, modifies that which is outside of the rule or what goes against the rule, while "an-omalie," a Greek noun that has lost its adjective, designates the unequal, the coarse, the rough, the point of deterritorialization. The abnormal can only be defined as a function of characteristics—whether specific or general—but the anomalous is a position or a collection of positions in relation to a multiplicity.[5]

Thus, deviation is not abnormal; it is normally *anomalous*. Illness and psychosis can appear as a source of creation, because they transgress the norm and provide a new point of view on health and normality, just as a deviant work of art produces a new point of view on its genre. Deleuze affirms this Nietzschean implication of the work of art as much as Canguilhem and Foucault do: Artaud and Masoch are creators because their extreme points of view push language to its limit.[6] As we see in Foucault's analyses of Roussel and Blanchot, and in Blanchot's own work, the function of literature is to illuminate the excess of language. Sade and Masoch use it within the restricted experience of sexuality. By taking up Bataille's analyses of Sade in *Masochism: Coldness and Cruelty*, Deleuze is clearly referencing Foucault's "A Preface to Transgression," from 1963. Foucault writes, "We have not liberated sexuality, but we have, to be exact, taken it to the limit: the limit of our consciousness [. . .], the limit of our language: it draws a line of foam with what can just barely be attained in speech on the sands of silence."

Yet, a few years later, the analysis of psychosis in Artaud pushes language to its agrammatical limit. He no longer confines the status of the limit to sexuality and also refuses to restrict the limit's potential to transgression. Deleuze continues to endow art with the power to explore margins, but the definition of what is marginal changes: it is no longer sexual, but sensorial and psychic. So does it follow that the artist must become mad or cultivate madness in order to create? The massive intrusion of psychic anomie witnessed in Klossowski's perversion, Proust's homosexuality, and, above all, Artaud's psychosis and schizophrenia, responds to this problematic by investigating the life of norms from the perspective of their external borders and margins. Along with marginalization and the minor, a theory of variation drives the philosophy of art, connecting culture and life. Meanwhile, Deleuze's interest in variation becomes completely unhinged from the scheme of transgression, which corresponds to the distinction between the "abnormal" and the "anomalous." Canguilhem specifically stated that "the experience of rules" entails "putting the regulatory function of rules to the test in a situation of irregularity."[7] Anomie does not consist of a transgression of the rule, but in a "normally" irregular functioning. This is demonstrated in the works of Geoffroy Saint-Hilaire, to whom Deleuze and Canguilhem refer. They refer to him since he founded the study of teratology, and he founded it as a positive variation, showing that the norm always varies in an immanent way: the monstrous is only an unusual variation that is more interesting than all other variations.

Sacher-Masoch and "The Masochistic Effect"

Symptomatology implies the proximity of art to life: the goal of art is to explore the intensities of life without being stuck in a moralistic attitude, but instead it captures the anomalous complexities of life and render them sensible. It is in this sense that writing brushes up against the border of social and psychic normality. Deleuze is interested in marginal figures because he assigns a clinical function to artistic creation, and his position is immediately clear and distinct. He introduces Sacher-Masoch as a writer, not a pervert, and this will be the case for all of the anomic creators. "What one must consider in Masoch are his contributions to the art of the novel," his "literary technique."[8] Deleuze goes even further: it is Sacher-Masoch's status as a writer that enables him to diagnose and "invent" a complex of forces that Deleuze interprets in the Nietzschean sense of vitality. Writing, as a positive experience, plays a role in exposing the human psyche, which is in direct competition with its medical etiology. It allows philosophy to depend upon it in order to reject psychiatric nosology and psychoanalytic theory. The writings devoted to Sacher-Masoch from 1961–93 open up a reading that follows from this primary function of art as a critical symptomatology of the clinical force of time, and it situates Deleuze within the relationship between literature and treatment.

Sacher-Masoch is the true inventor of the "masochistic effect," not Krafft-Ebing, the psychiatrist who provides the first clinical description of it and creates the neologism "masochism."[9] Sacher-Masoch explores the subjective effects of masochism, not because he is perverse, but because he is a novelist. Literature is not secondary, or an imaginary account of a real perversion. It actually contributes to the overall clinical picture of sexuality by use of its own means. As a result of being a writer Sacher-Masoch "invents" in the archeological sense; which is to say that he explores dynamisms, reveals positions and relationships that, without his intervention, would remain imperceptible. By this definition an artist is a symptomatologist. This Nietzschean perspective turns the artist into a physician of civilization who proceeds to diagnose vital forces at work, and Deleuze often stresses the fact that the artist is a physician, not the sufferer of the symptoms that he or she describes.[10] As a physician, he/she practices semiology, the concrete study and skilful understanding of signs. Even better than a physician, the artist is able to remain within the domain of real forces without being swept away by social structures. Deleuze distinguishes three different actions in medicine: symptomatology, or the search for signs; the search for causes, or etiology; and lastly, therapy, or the search for treatment. If the artist is a physician for Deleuze, it is neither because literature is therapeutic, nor because it rivals science on the grounds of etiology. One does not write to heal oneself, or to seek abstract causes. Deleuze subscribes to the Stoic critique of causes: etiology must be replaced by a sign system. Causes are abstract nouns that cover real processes of existing forces. A produced effect is isolated and its imaginary origin is sought. In reality, all causes are at the level of the signal; they arise from an encounter of bodies and involve perceptions that are individuated in real systems. Thus, the cause is a sign, and the sign is a real force, and not a signifier, but is an atom of sense. Therefore, literature is not etiological for the precise reason that causes remain abstract and illusory, which does not mean that they do not exist. They do not satisfy the description of the real, only the production of a social effect, which, more often than not, amounts to a power play. Both neutral and descriptive, literature makes intervention possible in medicine: it establishes itself at the foundation of signs in order to correct causes. Its symptomatological activity situates literature in positive space, an intersection that belongs "as much to art as to medicine," a "neutral point," Deleuze clarifies, which makes medical correction possible by opposing the usual etiology.[11]

Accordingly, the term masochism is not used because Masoch suffered from the perversion, but as a result of his comprehensive clinical portrayal of it. Furthermore, Krafft-Ebing highlights Masoch's clinical genius, and he creates the neologism "masochism" to pay homage to the finesse Sacher-Masoch's works use when identifying this symptom, and also to differentiate it from algolagnia, the desire for pain.[12] He uses the novelist's name to christen the disposition in tribute to his ability to discursively explicate the phenomenon, and not because the writer suffered from the condition: "not because he had an affliction of this sort," but "because in Sacher Masoch's works this sort of feeling in life is described in detail."[13] And Krafft-Ebing proclaims that masochism is irreducible to "algolagnia," since it is not pain that is essential to this condition but subservience with respect to the law. This reinforces Deleuze's idea that masochism presents a comprehensive clinical picture that is irreducible to sadism.

Against the sadomasochistic syndrome

Philosophy thus depends upon literature in order to denounce the collapsing of sadism and masochism into one clinical syndrome. Philosophy situates itself on a stylistic plane at a time when the concept of the clinic had yet to be developed, as evidenced in Deleuze's 1961 article on the subject.[14] Specialists confused the symptoms and had relied upon a false identity by identifying—and wrongly so, according to Deleuze—masochism with sadism, because they misunderstood the works of Sacher-Masoch. Blinded by a search for causes, clinicians did not pay attention to what Sacher-Masoch *said*.[15] This is an empirical argument that Deleuze often uses, which relies upon an explicit given, or an established fact: à *la lettre*, Masoch does not hold himself under the sway of Sade, but insists, on the contrary, on the unique clinical picture that he describes. In 1967, Deleuze becomes even more radical. The task is not only to object to psychiatry based on its failure to recognize the difference between sadism and masochism, but to use literature to rectify the psychiatric conception with respect to the law.

Why does Freud follow Krafft-Ebring's tendency to identify sadism with masochism, thus considering them to be inversely symmetrical within the same position? Because both of them put the law into play: they evaluate humiliation and pain, but according to completely different modalities that only results in a nominal identity of the two different tendencies. In fact, sadists and masochists differ on in all of these respects. Sadomasochism turns out to be one of "those poorly fabricated terms, an abstract, semiotic monster," which conflates clinically distinct symptoms with its generality. The only thing that sadism and masochism have in common is their position of anomie, their perverse features; in other words, their separation from the positive sense of the law. Echoing the lesson learnt from Foucault, Deleuze demonstrates that psychiatry acts as a force of social normalization when identifying sadism with masochism. It juxtaposes the two in an abstract nosological combination, which, in reality, is accomplished by an external imperative of exclusion. These distinct perversions are considered to be reversible because they arise from the same normative judiciary concept and a single moral condemnation.

That is why Krafft-Ebring's psychiatry and Freud's psychoanalysis have the tendency to unify sadism and masochism as two complementary attitudes. Sadists and masochists are supposed to show the active and passive sides of the same sexual perversion, where recto and verso they subordinate erotic pleasure to the painful experience of humiliation. On the contrary, Deleuze devotes himself to dissociating symptoms with use of a constant methodological process that is characteristic of his works, which emphasizes difference and rejects the contradiction or reversibility of symptoms. Deleuze denounces the logical plane that is said to move from one position to the other by way of dialectical inversion. Next, he devotes himself to detailing the clinical differences of symptoms. Finally, he shows that the unification of an abstract syndrome rests not only on a false postulation related to the reversibility of two positions (a logical error), but on the pragmatic principle of social exclusion (a normative trap). With reference to the law, Deleuze develops subtle differences beneath the general, abstract idea that prevents these differential relations from being reduced to the same figure, and he does so tangentially through stylistic analysis.

The sadist institution, with its demand for paternal transcendence and patriarchal authority, posits a separate, masculine, abstract law. On the other hand, the masochist multiplies contracts and privileges maternal figures. There is not a symmetrical inversion of positions, but a real and dissymmetrical difference that cannot be abstractly restored to unity by way of inversion. The sadist institution differs from the masochist contract, just as the identification of the sadist superego is distinct from masochist idealization. With its affinity for contracts and its fascination with feminine and animal figures, masochism proves to be "an act of resistance, inseparable from a minority sense of humor."[16] One can even abstractly see that sadism and masochism display certain similarities; a stylistic study of their works affirms the irreversibility of their positions: the masochist contract substitutes a maternal figure for the law of the Father, insists on animal encounters, and plays on the political and social experiences of minorities. Each point of nominal resemblance actually disguises a clinical divergence.

Without going too far afield in a debate with psychoanalysis, let us focus on method: in 1967, Deleuze advances on the frontlines of psychiatry and psychoanalysis armed solely with literary analysis. Deleuze employs a literary technique and reveals the clinical differences that enable him to affirm the irreducible specificity of the two symptoms. He then sketches a principle that proposes literary analysis as a methodological complement to the psychiatric clinic, since he considers literature to be descriptive and not normative. Most importantly, literature produces real, and not imaginary, effects. This speaks to just how much Deleuze advances the domain of medical sciences, as well as that of literary critique. The study of a stylistic process proves to be a sufficient and complete methodology. It is able to move beyond objective properties because it uses symptomatology to account for modes of subjectification; in other words, the way the subject is fabricated. It also becomes possible for Deleuze to take a stand against the foundations of psychiatry and psychoanalysis by employing a differential diagnosis that distinguishes the art of aesthetic suspense in Masoch—the master of fantasy with a Slavic soul approaching German romanticism—from the "apathetic and demonstrative" obscenity of Sade.[17] Masochistic pain is not the inverse of sadistic cruelty, but is bound to contracts, not to the institution of cruelty.

It rests in expectation, in suspense—"the fictional drive in its pure state"[18]—which makes Masoch's work a novel about taming and not development.[19]

Why, then, has Masoch been identified with Sade, while Sade's name becomes free and Masoch is forgotten? First of all, what unifies the sadist and masochist positions has nothing to do with their particular symptoms but has everything to do with the positive law that regulates moral customs. Thus, the only thing these two cases have in common is that they suffer the same social exclusion under the heading of sexual perversion, playing with pleasure and domination, "a twisted conception of the contract in Masoch, and the institution in Sade, as they relate to sexuality."[20] The nosological entity results from a grouping of theoretically fictitious symptoms, followed by a fallacious principle of generalization that, while real, corresponds to a concrete issue. But it is a social issue, and not a scientific one: the exclusion of sexual practices that are deemed to be abnormal. Therefore, the medical clinic does not seek to provide treatment, but to regulate moral customs. The medical clinic looks at things from the point of view of the judiciary with no regard for the therapeutic. The unity of symptoms only rests on the general sign of sexual perversion and the literary fecundity of agitations described by Sade and Masoch.

Next, "it is unjust to not read Masoch when Sade is the object of such profound studies that are inspired by literary critique and psychoanalytic interpretation at the same time, and which also contributes to the renewal of both."[21] Deleuze sets out to "rectify the injustice" that caused the works of Masoch to be cast into oblivion by relying heavily upon his generation's "knowledge of Sade." In other words, the posterity of Bataille and the pioneering work of the *Collège de Sociologie* in matters that explored the relationship between sexuality, the institution, and artistic creation. Bataille's *Eroticism* opens the discussion in 1957, followed a few years later by the remarkable studies conducted by Blanchot, Klossowski, Lacan, and Foucault.[22] The clinic in Deleuze is inscribed in this strong current of French thought that was inaugurated by Mauss and then taken up in the exploration of pathological norms in Canguilhem, whereby art intersects the exploration of variation in the normal with the pathological. Deleuze did not invent the literary clinic, and its origin is not exclusively Nietzschean.

Yet, Deleuze completely separates himself from his predecessors when it comes to transgression. This third issue explains why Deleuze takes such pains to distinguish Masoch from Sade. It is not at all a question of clearing Masoch's name for his own benefit in order to show that his advances would have already been in effect for Sade. Deleuze completely transforms the problem by modifying the relationship between desire and the law, and the relationship between writing and desire. By precluding the conflation of Masoch and Sade, *Coldness and Cruelty* implicitly contains a critique of transgression that calls for a radical reevaluation of psychoanalysis, and the role of the law and the Father. This critique that Deleuze formulates in 1977, in the chapter from *Dialogues* titled "On the Superiority of American Literature," humorously accuses Bataille of being the French pope of sad passions. It is the nature of perversion that changes: the treatment of homosexuality in Proust clearly demonstrates this, just like the study of voyeurism and exhibitionism in Klossowski in *The Logic of Sense*: "What one calls perverse is precisely this objective power of hesitation in the body."[23] Never does Deleuze consider perversion to be a transgression, and if he and Lawrence make fun of the "dirty little secret" that seminarian Bataille hides in his handkerchief, it is because he read and liked Spinoza. Transgressing the law does not make any sense, because the law does not exist as an external and transcendent moral imperative that would be possible for anyone to follow or transgress. If there is a law, it regulates real behaviors. An immanent and necessary law in Spinoza replaces the moral imperative in Bataille, and the possibility of transgression disappears with it. Perversion is totally different; it implies a real, anomic, and existent relationship, which is conceived as a corporeal differentiation that is prior to the principle of organization. This objective hesitation draws a zone of variation whose entire latitude will be provided by the concept of the body without organs, affirming itself as a polymorphism, a vital and joyous power of differentiation that is far from the "pious masturbation" of transgression along with its laudatory, constitutive relationship to the law.[24] This is why Lawrence makes fun of the "dirty little secret" that seems to traverse French literature. The famous secret turns out to be a superficial loop produced by the constitutive and transcendent relationship to the law, and not a principle of writing. There are no longer any secrets where the potential interiority of secrets joyously dissolves in a field of social forces. The very mechanism of transgression is invalidated, and Georges Bataille, the "very French" author, is no longer the epic hero at the frontiers of language whom Foucault admired. He is reduced to the dimension of a seminarian, blowing his little secret out of proportion and appealing to authorities (a pope for literature). Henceforth Deleuze has nothing but harsh words for French literature, its chapels and dogmas. Among the "movements" that he loathes, surrealism, with its pope (Breton) and its priest (Bataille), is particularly abhorrent to him.

> The little secret is generally reducible to a sad and pious, narcissistic masturbation: the phantasm! "Transgression" is too good a concept for seminarians under the

law of a pope or a priest, the tricksters. Georges Bataille is a very French author: he made the little secret the essence of literature, with the mother within, a priest below, and an eye above.[25]

From symptomatology to the capture of forces

Coldness and Cruelty opens up with a Sartrean question: "What uses are there for literature?" We must take it at its word. Literature is useful for something; it has positivity, an illuminating force—it produces something. In this text from 1967 Deleuze already takes a very strong position in favor of a functionalism of writing, which stringently rejects the principle of literature as autonomous, or an enclosure of the text. Art is not its ultimate goal, and it is useful for something, not itself, and not for nothing. Art produces a transitive effect. Thus, literature is useful for *something* here: to "designate two basic perversions, prodigious examples of literary efficacy."[26] A writer turns out to be a very "special" doctor, a more uncompromising symptomatologist than ordinary therapists.[27] This is because the writer is less susceptible to readymade social and disciplinary representations, and is not blinded by a search for causes, the fictitious representations of natural processes, and he/she is detached from the social and normative responsibilities of treatment.

The "neutral" approach that Deleuze quickly sets out to correct, as a philosopher concerned with the arts, medical nosology, turns out to be a different approach, a "literary approach." Since the clinical evaluation of a doctor "is full of prejudices," as Deleuze states, "one must begin with an approach outside the [medical] clinic, the *literary approach*, since perversions were first designated in literature."[28] Thus in 1967 Deleuze establishes the following relationship between the critical and the clinical: the perspicacity of the artist corrects what etiology carries over from the normative.[29] "Masoch is a great symptomatologist," not because he suffered from masochism, but because he "paints an original portrait of it."[30] The literary clinic is effective due to its ability to endure the variability of the minor, its anomaly, its "creative disorganization" that allows it to seize real and anomalous forces, and its endurance of minor expressions.[31] It is not pathology that makes the artist interesting, but the clinical nuance of her assessment. It is because Sacher-Masoch was a writer who knew how to show symptoms. He is the first to capture, outline, and render sensible forces that did not previously exist. Sade and Sacher-Masoch are not artists because they are perverted; they make complex drives sensible because they are artists. The forms they invent are distinct from the real forces that they perceive, and that are not representations in everyday culture.

The first appearance of art as a capture of forces is thus elaborated through this Nietzschean lens, as a symptomatology of processes of subjectification at work in society. The anomaly of the sadist or masochist symptom functions as an operator, and art's success consists in the ability to capture these imperceptible forces while producing new forms. An intensive and differential theory of form is sketched out in the Nietzschean symptomatology that Deleuze applies to Sacher-Masoch and Proust. It is now a matter of examining the constitution of this symptomatology, this capture of signs. What is a sign? A grouping of forces, an interpretation of forces, says Nietzsche; in other words, a mode of affection. A sign is a force as long as it is not interpreted, but it is felt in a living relation that allows the artist to be an experimenter, an operator of forces. This is where the invention of new forms takes place, which binds art to the exploration of margins about which it posits an intensive theory. The theory of art as minor that is developed in *Kafka* and the definition of art as a capture of real forces (*Bacon*) will expand this initial positing.

Sign as force: Spinoza and ethology

Continuing to affirm his interest in art and symptomatology, Deleuze appropriates the Spinozist critique of the sign and the imagination, which he could be seen to disregard or reject, since Spinoza opposes the sign, while Deleuze's entire philosophy, from *Proust and Signs* to his works on cinema, is a philosophy of signs. "Everything that I wrote was vitalist, at least, I hope, in constituting a theory of signs," he says in an interview from 1988.[32] For Spinoza, on the other hand, the sign does not have any positivity, being the inadequate idea of an effect that comes from the imagination, and not from reason, and which reveals a state of our body and not a real cause. Yet, Deleuze appropriates the study from the *Theological-Political Treatise*, and uses Spinoza to posit a totally new theory of the sign. Thanks to Spinoza, Deleuze is able to move from interpretation to ethology, from signification to the exposition of force relations.

Spinoza showed that art and prophecy are not independent from a social mechanism of domination. Signs serve power by appealing to our imagination, and they often make us "mistake a principle of obedience for a model of knowledge."[33] Additionally, "It's enough misunderstand an eternal truth, a composition of relations, in order to interpret it as an imperative." Such imperative signs "have no other meaning than to make us obey."[34] Deleuze completely agrees with this political critique, which applies less to the effective existence of signs than it does to the way they are used: their challenges and modes of social functioning. The regime of signs results from a critical analysis that drives Deleuze and Guattari in *A Thousand Plateaus*. But it is the critical, Spinozist perspective that is determinant. This perspective does not stop at the exegesis of an assumed signification; it only bears on the physical or real exposition of force relations by which these signs are affected and affect us. Spinoza's lesson, which Deleuze completely adopts, is the following: signs first call for a programmatic, the exposition of relations of domination within which they are inscribed and that they serve and often contribute to reinforcing.

If an immanent reading is applied to art and the sign, if the effective force relations that signs use to produce their effects are exposed, experimentation as a principle of explication for art replaces interpretation or hermeneutics.[35] This outcome is something that Deleuze always traces back to the genius of *The Ethics*, which completely changes the philosophy of art. Forces in Spinoza had already replaced the moral—the judgment "which always brings existence back to transcendent values"—with the ethical, "a typology of immanent modes of existence."[36] That is why symptomatology, which is ethical and not moral, is indifferent to social judgments. Creative literature is strongly ethical because it is situated on the plane of force relations and disregards stabilized social forms. As such, the ethical, or the ethology of force relations, replaces the moral. In the essay, "To Have Done with Judgment," from *Essays Critical and Clinical*, Deleuze offers a new look at the decisive role Spinoza plays with regard to Nietzsche, Lawrence, Kafka, and Artaud: one philosopher, three writers. To have done with judgment is not to opt for indifference, but to substitute the difference of modes in existence for transcendent values. To opt for the struggles of life and against transcendent judgments, "Perhaps that's the secret: to make something exist, and not to judge."[37]

By choosing modes of existence against abstract judgment, Deleuze does not intend to renounce the ability of combatting certain modes of existence. But their function will be excluded from encounters and forces that they allow to be captured, not as a function of "expert judgments" that are always "disgusting," especially in art. We begin to see at which point clinical critique reconstructs the habitual modes of critique by not judging through moral abstraction and transcendent imperatives, but by affinities and disparities, the acquiescence and increase of vital forces, and not by normative exclusion. Literature and art pose a medical, and not a moral, problem, and subjective perspectivalism does not return when posing a problem in terms of forces, since the problem of subjectivity is completely transformed.[38]

Deleuze always hails Spinoza as the thinker of immanence, but we must wait for *A Thousand Plateaus* and *Spinoza: Practical Philosophy* to clearly specify at which point this metaphysical discovery delivers art and literature from all signifying hermeneutics.[39] Whichever artworks served as a basis were no longer the object of moralizing interpretation relegating their material bodies to intellectual form, but are subjected to an ethical analysis, an ethology of effective forces. This program allows Deleuze to definitively distance himself from previous notions of sense and interpretation, the vocabulary of which he keeps when working on Nietzsche and Proust in the early 1960s. With help from Spinoza, Deleuze deploys a new conception of the sign as an affective force, and not a signification. The sign is no longer a feature of the human mind, nor an inadequate configuration of the imagination. It is an affect, the material of encounter and capture, and a composite of power relations and variations. This new ethology of the sign makes it possible for the philosophy of art to be a material sign system, and a semiotics. It is a matter of transforming the sign's status, and to turn an interpreted, imperative sign into an affect, a sign-image that is clinical and critical. The sign's status must be delivered from interpretation and thought of as a real encounter, a composite of relations: interpretation must be taken over by experimentation. That's how Spinoza contributes to Deleuze's aesthetic.

This powerful consequence was no doubt unanticipated by Spinoza, but is perfectly Deleuzean. Art transforms our powers to affect and to be affected, and this transformation only operates while exposing relations of real subjectification that are not sensed again. Deleuze can thus develop a new philosophy of art. This is what enables Deleuze to define clinical critique as an antidote to all systems of signification that are more or less enveloped by matter and figures in *The Logic of Sense*. He defines it in such a way that art is not only an agency of movements and affects, or a composite of signs forcing obedience, but it is also an experimentation of real modes of life, a "capture of forces" (*Bacon*, 1981). What we call art or literature consists of a symptomatology of real relations, a "capture of forces" that turns out to be a clinic. The relational clinic contains a critical power to elucidate modes of subjection that diminish our potential to act.

The clinic is critical because it forces us to feel, think, and laugh at the complex forces that compose our life. As such, Kafka, whose writing explores modes of collective social subjectification in bureaucracy, evokes joy and laughter through a playful and always joyful exploration of reality, and not through the atrocious complexes of forces that he expresses. Art only accomplishes its critical function of liberation by keeping itself strictly within the plane of composition of effective force relations. This is how symptomatology helps construct the first formulation of the theory in 1981: art is the capture of forces.

3

The Affect of Force

Semiotics and Ethics

In 1983, once he returns to the 1962 edition of *Nietzsche and Philosophy* when writing the preface to the English edition, Deleuze emphasizes that Nietzsche is often more influential for artists and writers than he is for theoreticians. That is not to say that he was a better poet than philosopher, but it makes sense that his thought radiates through practical and violent forms, which are more pragmatic than discursive, since his thought concerns forces. But force is always plural and is always given as force relations whose power can be evaluated symptomatologically. Deleuze proposes a shortcut with the intention of arranging Nietzsche's philosophy along two axes: one axis forms a general semiotics, while the other suggests an ethics and an ontology of power. This collective formulation affirms how Deleuze conceived of Nietzsche alongside Spinoza, and he could just as easily apply it to himself. He is frequently seen expressing phrases from authors he admires the most, such as Foucault, Nietzsche, and Spinoza, which summarize a particular feature of his own philosophy.

This coupling of sign and power suits a philosophy of force and the composition of speeds and slownesses that Deleuze develops through Spinoza under the heading of ethology in the 1980s, which he sometimes refers to as haecceity, paying tribute to Simondon.[1] To think force along the lines of semiology and ethics, sign and affect, is to define the vocation of art as a symptomatology, the capture of forces and image. These three distinctions correspond to three aspects of Deleuze's canon. All three state the relationship between art and forces: first, Nietzschean symptomatology and the medical art practiced by Proust, Klossowski, Sacher-Masoch, and Artaud; secondly, art as a capture of forces in Francis Bacon's painting and Pierre Boulez's music; thirdly, the image as action and reaction, coupling the force of the perception-image and the action-image with the power of the affection-image in cinema. Deleuze thinks of art as a composition of material force relations, or speed, and the latitude of power or affect. The ensemble of material elements belongs to a body where relations of movement and rest, speeds and slownesses, constitute longitude. The whole of intensive affects of which the body is capable, under a certain degree of power, constitutes latitude.[2] But this dual determination of speeds and affects defines the image by adopting the haecceity's split into longitude and latitude, with its compositions of speeds and slownesses, and its intensive variations in power. In other words, the split reveals the complementarity between the typology of signs and ethics.

Nietzsche's philosophy concerns forces above all, and then adds the evaluation of force relations to his consideration, including the determination of states of power that these forces address. All force relations fuel semiotics, and this one is a sign-system map of potentialities. According to this conception, "the mode of existence is the state of forces as it forms an expressible type through signs or symptoms."[3] Here, Deleuze commonly uses the term "symptom" when he is writing on Nietzsche in 1962, as well as on Sacher-Masoch in 1967, but which might be surprising in 1983 in terms of the masterful critique of psychoanalysis that Deleuze developed between 1972 and 1980 with Guattari, destroying the project of interpretation and every reduction of the symptom to a Freudian topic or Lacanian signifier. The presence of the term "symptom" indicates a very daring sort of arc that directly connects Nietzsche's symptomatology with Spinoza's ethology, while giving short shrift to Freudian interpretation. In effect, such a sign, or symptom of force relations, does not refer to a signifier at all, only to a state of power, or more precisely, a relation of forces (semiology) that corresponds to a certain affect (ontology and ethics). That allows us to show how, according to Deleuze, Nietzsche and Spinoza are related and both contribute to the production of this theory of forces that Deleuze puts to work in his philosophy of art, which connects to the problematic of the sign to that of the image. Like the sign, the image is also a force relation composed of speeds that is capable of affects, and this is what makes it possible for Deleuze to develop a semiotics as a typology of images and signs.

If everything refers to force relations, a composite of actions and reactions, speeds and slownesses, then the state of forces and the differential relation of forces in presence can be evaluated. This principle runs throughout all of Deleuze's works: stated with respect to Nietzsche in 1962, it is taken up almost literally in 1986 in *Foucault*. The concept of force is necessarily plural, since all of force is located "in the essential relationship with another force," so that there is no force that is not a *relation* of forces. A force is defined as "a force that relates to another force" (1962). Nietzsche's problem can thus be formulated as such (1983): "a thing being given, which state of exterior and interior forces presupposes it?" In 1986, "Foucault's general principle is: every force is a composite of force relations. As concerns given forces, one will first wonder with which outside forces they enter into relation, then from which form do they ensue."[4] This relationship between sign and image, forces and forms, draws a diagonal in Deleuze's works, which connects Nietzsche and Foucault by passing through Spinoza. Such a semiology of force determines a conception of form that completely revitalizes the philosophy of art at the same time that it expels the sign from the transcendent plane of sense in order to expose it on the material plane of forces. It is no longer a question of signifier or signified, nor form or matter, but forces and materials, in accordance with Simondon's principle of modulation. The only things that count in art are the materials capable of detecting forces that become more and more intense and affects that emit these configurations, "percepts" or "visions" of art. Since the affect designates this ethological mode of power that corresponds to such a state of forces, or images, we can define art as the affect of an image and suggest three trajectories that converge in this definition: Nietzsche and the will to power; Spinoza, haecceity, a new cartography of bodies; the material image in the process of subjectification, as seen in his fantastic analyses of cinema.

Nietzsche and symptomatology

Behind each "phenomenon," each state of force relations, Nietzsche detects affects and power and distinguishes its "active" or "reactive" mode. He diagnoses the ethological quality of force, or the valence of the will to power. This is why Nietzsche conceives of the philosopher and the artist as a physiologist and doctor. The philosopher and the artist "interpret" in the Nietzschean sense, entering into force relations without assigning them a "sense" or signification. Instead, they evaluate their "type" by materially constructing a new relationship with them, the affects of which can then be mapped. From this point of view, interpreting is developing force relations. From the first to the second version of *Proust*, Deleuze conserved the Nietzschean vocabulary of interpretation, but he treated it like a symptomatology and a typology of forces. In 1964 he writes, "To think is always to interpret, to explicate, develop, decode, and translate a sign," but in 1967 interpretation takes on a less and less philological perspective of translation in order to reconnect with a vital perspective of assimilation along the lines of oscillation found in Nietzsche.[5] Interpretation, like assimilation and nutrition, brings back a body-to-body relation of forces—a force, which captures and constructs a new, assignable relationship with other forces whose power can be evaluated. Thus, symptomatology rips interpretation out of a hermeneutic of hidden sense, and pushes toward a constitutive unveiling of forces in presence.

The philosophy of forces is split into a semiology and ethology of power: with certain signs being given, one wonders from which state of force they emerge, and which variation of power they put into play. All force relations— phenomenon, organism, society, consciousness, mind, every state of an existing thing—becomes traceable to a question of power, which releases a typology, a critical examination of types of life that are put into play. The will to power designates "the differential relation of forces in presence," and expresses itself through these dynamisms of an affirmative or negative type, which leads Nietzsche to devise a typology of active and reactive forces.[6] Semiology (the certain state of a thing), like a symptom, corresponds to a certain state of forces and implies an ontology of power: the sign constructs a certain force relation that knows its own variation of power. Nietzsche can thus distinguish between different modalities of force and sketch socio-historic types according to the active, acted, or reactive forces that are at work. Accordingly, a Nietzschean symptomatology implies a sociological and a political theory, a pragmatic of signs that evaluates actions and social productions according to the types of life that they promote. This is why Deleuze borrows this symptomalogical function of art from Nietzsche, replacing the interpretation of signification with an experimentation of force. Demanding that art engage in experimentation does not result in another rejection of the surrealist imperative, which has become a tired cliché after a century of discussion about the avant-garde. Deleuze literally understands literature to be a physician: Sacher-Masoch for masochism, Proust for homosexuality, Klossowski for perversion, Artaud for schizophrenia, and Kafka for bureaucracy. Their writing renders a seismograph of forces sensible, a threshold that would not be crossed without it having been made sensible. This is why art combines the logic of sensation with a medical, symptomatological function. If art's virtue consists in locating signs, capturing them, and making them sensible, then the philosophy of art provides the corresponding typology, an inventory of signs and images on an open and variable list that forms an intensive map.

The philosophy of art entails a semiotic scheme that must be understood on the plane of forces and signs. In 1964 Deleuze writes, "We only ask that we agree that the problem with Proust is one of signs in general, and that signs constitute different worlds, empty worldly signs, deceptive signs of love, material sensible signs, and finally, the essential signs of art (which transform all the others)."[7] It is thus a question of signs, and not of forces, but Deleuze specifies that signs coexist in different worlds that are not all homogeneous. Worldly signs, signs of love and jealousy, sensible signs, signs of art: this necessary system, or regime, of signs is not reducible to one linguistic or signifying mode. For signs, as is the case with rhymes, one can neither "seek the explication on the side of a superior form that unifies them," nor put them back in the regular or irregular "sequence" that would constitute them.[8] The signs of art conserve their prospective disparity, their fragmentary irregularity. Art thus becomes a "symptomatology of worlds" and Deleuze describes the distinct and enveloped sign-systems of worldly signs, signs of love, encounters of the sensible, and signs of art.[9] If in 1962 Deleuze uses the notion of essence to make these disparate worlds communicate around a neo-platonic trajectory that leads from ordinary experience toward art (the only way to "transform" all the other signs), then the later versions from 1970, and again in 1976, insist on the nontotalizing feature of the fragment, the heterogeneity that constitutes signs by conserving their distinct plurality and their irreducible singularity. The work of art operates through impersonal experimentation, and by demarcating types of signs and captures while distinguishing between forces.

It is not enough to merely show that the sign system is medical, or that the diagnosis of signs is equivalent to a clinic; it is necessary to explain how this clinic develops an ethology of power that is ethical and ontological. Art is located beyond the morality of good and evil, and emerges from an ethics, or an ethology, of force relations. This capture of forces simultaneously makes a semiotics, a symptomatology, and an ethics possible.[10]

Haecceity and art: The capture of forces

In order to support this movement from the morality of interpretation to the ethology of power, Deleuze uses Spinoza's conception of the individual and the microphysics of the *Ethics* II, 13. How does Spinoza define an individual, as body or soul? He does not define it by form, organ, function, or as substance or a subject, but as a mode; that is, a complex relation of speeds and slownesses, and a power to affect or be affected. With this double, modal determination that constitutes Spinoza's ethology, Deleuze revitalizes the relationship between the sign, force, and power. Developed in *A Thousand Plateaus* and *Spinoza: Practical*

Philosophy, the concept of haecceity posits a new philosophy of the subject, changing the status of form while also establishing a doctrine of the sign and the image.

The concept of haecceity helps to posit a modal, nonsubstantial philosophy of individuation: each individual is composed of infinite, extensive parts that belong to it within *one* particular relationship. The uniqueness of this relationship establishes an individuality with corporeal complexity, a state of forces, and "movement and rest," as Spinoza says, or "speeds and slownesses," since rest is not the absence of movement but slowness relative to a particular speed. This existent, kinetic relationship that composes an individual also expresses a degree of power. Since an individual, a certain multiplicity, not only implies a kinetic composition of force relations but also a dynamic capacity to affect and be affected. After reading Spinoza, Deleuze takes away the distinction between two "very different" modes of individuation: existence, as the divisible totality of *extensive* parts (longitude); and essence, as the *intensive* part (latitude).[11] An individual differs according to its material composition and the intensive mode of power that it puts into play. A particular body exists by forming a relation of relations, which must be understood materially as a fluctuating totality of material particles that belong to it within a particular relationship (longitude). This relationship contains a certain fluctuation, a particular "latitude," in the way it expresses degrees of power that is not always constant, but which fluctuates between birth and death. Thus, longitude concerns the state of forces and their relationships in terms of speeds and slownesses, while latitude is the intensity or variation of their power. Longitude is extensive, extrinsic, and kinetic, and latitude is intensive and dynamic: it evaluates the movement from one degree of power to another; it lines the kinetic state of forces with a temporal vector that demarcates intensive variations, the fluctuations of power within a certain threshold of temporary individuation. Latitude expresses the threshold of power's intensive variation, which results in extrinsic modifications, or encounters that create the body (thus, the theory of evil as a bad relationship, according to Spinoza).

This distinction between longitude and latitude brings about the elaboration of this fantastic theory of haecceities from 1977 (*Dialogues*) to *A Thousand Plateaus*, which pays homage to the philosophers of modal intensity: Duns Scotus, Simondon, and Geoffroy Saint-Hilaire, the naturalist Spinozist hero of modal variations of the body. Thus we have the theoretical axis around which Deleuze posits this new cartography of the body. Each individual is defined by its longitude and latitude, by the force relations that it forms and by the affects that qualify its capacity for power.

> You are going to define an animal or a man, not by its form, organs or function, and not as a subject either; you are going to define it by the affects of which it is capable. The affective capacity, with a maximal threshold and a minimal threshold, is a common notion in Spinoza.[12]

The division between longitudes and latitudes explains the distinction between a semiotics of forces and an ethics of power. Longitude corresponds to the map of signs, and latitude corresponds to the ethics of affects. This fact simultaneously transforms individuation, subjectification, and the image. This is because Deleuze uses the concept of haecceity in order to advise us to think about a mode of individuation that is "very different" from what we generally consider a form or subject. A haecceity does not cut out a class of beings, but captures becomings in action. The geographic cartography of modes replaces the historic genesis of individuals. This new cartography of modes of individuation rejects the transcendent position of the substantial subject, and does not call for the imposition of form over matter. As such, subjective entities do not cause Deleuze's worries to disappear, but they become the object of a transformed, modal, nonsubstantial theory. The concept of haecceity is less about being opposed to subjects, bodies, or constituted forms than it is about changing thought: it is not concerned with constructing a different individuality, subjectivity, or corporeality, but with a different theory of the individual, the subject, the body, or form.

> There is a certain kind of individuation that is not reducible to a subject (Ego), not even to the combination of form and matter. A landscape, an event, an hour of the day, a life or a fragment of life . . . proceeds in another way.[13]

Subjects are affects of force, modes of force that are affected themselves: this is the outcome that Deleuze derives from the concept of haecceity. For a mode is a "concrete" composition of speeds and slownesses, comprising these two axes of semiology and the ontology of power. A mode is a composition of speeds and slownesses on the plane of force (longitude), which determines the material condition of forces that Deleuze calls the movement image, the action and reaction of matter in *Cinema I: The Movement-Image*, and what he calls a percept in *What Is Philosophy?* On the plane of power variation (latitude, or affect) "is a power to affect or to be affected."[14] Art thus consists of making imperceptible forces perceptible by allowing us to capture these "longitudes." Sacher-Masoch renders complexes of forces and becomings perceptible, which qualifies masochism as "the forces exerted on the body," as we see with Bacon.

This is why Deleuze specifies that art does not entail reproducing, or even of inventing "forms," but in "capturing forces." [15] This is rigorously explained: form, as we saw, is an intensive and fluctuating composite of force relations, a haecceity. Art is carried out on a real and material plane of forces, not on a secondary plane derived from forms that one can deduce, abstract, or extract from these forces, and which never make up anything but compilations or indexes. Thus, Deleuze develops a modal and intensive conception of form, the criteria of which we can pick out from his work. First, form is immanent and variable. It is not given as substance, as it is never any more than the effective variation of force relations that make it up. Secondly, given these conditions, it is useless to oppose form and matter: both are composites of force, and only an abstraction of a theory that institutes the cleavage of a transcendent and separated form from devalued matter can avoid seeing that all forms are "haecceities" in reality, "relations of movement and rest between molecules or particles, being capable of affecting and being affected." Finally, form is characterized by its intensive mobility: it is modal, and not substantial, and accommodates all types of variation. This is why Deleuze rigorously correlates the composition of the body in Spinoza with modulation as a relation between forces and materials in Simondon, and the intensive variation of bodies in Geoffroy Saint-Hilaire. And that provides art with its symptomatological function: art draws a map of affects.

Deleuze elaborates this intensive conception of form that comes to Spinoza via the life sciences with Geoffroy Saint-Hilaire and Simondon, who contribute to a theory of the "body without organs" and intensive matter. This intensive determination of unformed and kinetic matter is employed in the philosophy of art. Form can be defined as the modal variation of force relations in such a way as to renew our interest in the forms of art on the condition that they are determined to be the outcome of a variable agency of materials. As such, the image's material sign-system can provide the space for a typology, bringing a semiology and ethology of power along with it. What counts is intensive variation. In literature, for example, the deformation that style imposes on language (syntactic material) allows it to capture previously unknown modes of existence. Kafka's stylistic invention allows him to explore modes of bureaucratic subjectification, just as Masoch's style allows him to explore masochist formations. It is less a matter of repudiating forms than proposing a new conception, a material and sensible form that is both intensive and variable, and not a given, abstract form. Form is a composite of force relations; rigorously speaking, there are only forces, and forms are a becoming of forces. Thus there is a good use of form in Deleuze, which emerges from artistic creation. Force makes the difference: is it a question of secondary presentation, *representation* of a form, or a capture of forces? Form is a question of forces when it relates to sensation, while it remains a clichéd reproduction when it sticks to imitation or the constitution of pictorial formulations of the past. The force of sensation allows Deleuze to develop the concept of the Figure in Bacon, which he opposes to banal figuration or the reproduction of clichés. The Figure is a form that becomes an event, because it directly relates to sensation, without passing through the cliché of a representation whose object is supposed to be intellectually valued. The direct and intrusive mode of force allows form to concretely affect sensation and to create a shock to thought, which is the mark of a masterpiece. He is the one who allows us to define "the community of arts": capturing forces, trapping new imperceptible forces in new materials, and this definition can be applied just as well to literature, painting, cinema, or music.

> The task of painting is defined as the attempt to render forces that are not visible, visible. Likewise, music attempts to render forces that are not sonorous, sonorous.[16]

As soon as this modal cartography of the haecceity is applied to individuation, everything changes. Art and philosophy become capable of treating individuality as an event, not as a thing. It is thus also possible to be interested in these perfect individualities that are well formed no matter the singularities, which the theory of substantial subjects could not accomplish. A season, a winter, "5 o'clock in the evening," are such haecceities, or modal individualities that consist of relations of speeds and slownesses, capable of affecting or of being affected.[17] A quality of whiteness, the vibration of an hour, the squatting of a stone, and an afternoon in the steppe form these modes of individuation that are more fragile, less anthropomorphic, and not necessarily more unstable or evanescent, but much more interesting than human individuals, or rather, the divisions we are used to, which borrow some aspect of substance (*a* thing, *an* animal, *a* man).[18] Instead of holding itself to clichés of form, art captures and renders such imperceptible forces perceptible. This is how art is defined as creator: whatever its medium of expression happens to be, art captures forces or constructs new haecceities from consolidated spaces and times which contain the new within them, because they create the event and render forces that were imperceptible beforehand perceptible.

The novelty of a work of art is attached to these divisions or new categories, which are sensible modes of impersonal, pre-individual individuations. "It's not a matter of telling a story in a determined space or time; rhythms, lights, space-times must themselves become true characters."[19] These new entities affect us with an irresistible power because they cause the force of the percept to vibrate within the image's affect. Whatever art captures is never suitable as long as it acts like a force in an implacable and sensible mode of an intensity that is perceived for the first time. Art does not need anything other than this physical description. Have imperceptible forces been rendered perceptible?

Accordingly, in Bergson, the cartography of the body enables the trembling of sensation to render the fall and deformation of the body perceptible with the use of color. But on the other hand, the theory of images accomplishes this capture of forces. Art is not confined to the capturing of longitudes, but allows them to be expressed as latitude. It is not simply a matter of rendering imperceptible forces perceptible by exposing their longitude, but of rendering their latitude subjective and delightful by introducing the intensity of power, which doubles their force relations. Thus we enter the percept and affect "like autonomous and sufficient beings."[20] This second moment of evaluation is inexorably correlated with the previous moment. This is where semiology necessarily implies an ethics: the sign, force, and image are developed into an affect, an ethology of power.

The image, longitude, and latitude

From this point on, everything is defined as an assemblage of movements and affective vibrations, which Deleuze calls an "image" in reference to Bergson. Defined as such, the image recalls Simondon's haecceity and Spinoza's ethology: a relationship of sensible forces emitted from an affect, the individuation of which is perfectly accomplished without being bound to substance. As such, force is not only power, but it is an image.

With the movement image, the opposition between movement, physical reality, and image, psychic reality, is overcome, abandoning the duality of image and movement, which implies a separation between consciousness and the thing. Instead, art is considered a real operation, not just a mental figuration, or a subjective representation.[21] Deleuze relies on Bergson's definition of the image in *Matter and Memory* when he develops the haecceity into the materiology of effects with regard to cinema. The image is no more an image-of-an-object than it is an image-for-consciousness. It is not a representation of consciousness (a psychological given), nor a representation of the thing (an object's intention). It is understood in the Bergsonian sense as an apparition, a system of actions and reactions at the level of matter itself, such that the image has no need to be seen, but exists in itself as a trembling, vibration, or movement.

> Let's call the Image the ensemble of what appears. We cannot even say that an image acts or reacts on another image. There is not a moving body that is distinguished from the executed movement; there is not something moved that is distinguished from the perceived movement.

The image is not a support, but a force relation, of actions and reactions, and like force, it is necessarily plural. An isolated image has no sense since it is a relation of forces. There is always a plurality, or rather, a multiplicity of images. Thusly defined, the image possesses two characteristics.

First, it is a being, a thing, and not a copy, or a representation in the psychological or psychic sense. The image is not inside the brain. It is not "in the head; on the contrary, the brain is an image among other images."[22] There is a *realism* of the image, as Bergson reiterates in the first pages of *Matter and Memory*. Movement is inflated into an image. Along with Bergson, Deleuze says that we find ourselves before an "exposition of a world where Image = movement." This realism of the image means that the image is movement and matter, a force relation, a vibration of movement from matter. Defined as such, the image is no longer relegated to the plane of representation, but takes on a physical existence. It defines a new hyletics, a philosophy of matter, and it is in this context that cinema attracts Deleuze's interest. But it must be insisted that the image, in both volumes, does not only indicate an operation proper to cinema, but is qualified as matter itself, as a movement image. The image has a physical range prior to producing its aesthetic effects, and the titles "movement image" and "time image" denote a real exposition of force relations before forming categories to classify and conceive of cinematographic productions. Cinema is not "an art of the image" in the ordinary sense (from clichéd reproduction), but art responds to the movement image as a physical state. Cinema is especially interesting, but it does not hold a privileged position with regard to the image, and is by no means limited to the visual, for it concerns all sensible appearances. There are also sonorous images, or tactile images (*opsigns, sonsigns, tactisigns*). "From one art to another, the nature of images varies and is inseparable from techniques: colors and lines for painting, sounds for music, verbal descriptions for the novel, movement images for cinema."[23]

A movement is thus an image, an atom is an image that goes just as far as its actions and reactions go; the brain, the subjective center of indetermination, is an image, and this is why it does not "contain" images like a psychic representation that differs in nature from exterior movements. It cannot contain images because it is itself an image.[24] Strictly speaking, it is only movements that are diffused into images. Deleuze thus defines a hyletic by material flows. Matter is energy; there is a matter-light equivalence whose scientific correlate is the condition of possibility for the invention of cinema. And this luminous, shining, and illuminated capacity of the movement material explains that the image is given in-itself, as reality, or force relations. The movement image is not a static body, but a bloc of vibrating space-time, an "image in-itself."[25] The identity of the movement image corresponds to the identity of matter-light: cinema is the mechanism that corresponds to our time, which corresponds to "the machinic assemblage of movement images."[26]

The cinematographic image and affect

How the cinematographic image differs from other images remains to be explained. This involves the second characteristic of the image. The image is a reality. But, under certain special conditions it can become withdrawn and equipped with an inside. This is a new property of the image, which endows it with the beginnings of subjectification on the material plane. This subjectification does not mean that the image refers to a subject, or that it relies on a subject that experiences it. On the contrary, under certain conditions of life, the image can produce a difference between action and reaction, a difference that stabilizes the image with density and capability that doubles its effective production of affects (subjective). Images thus have an "inside" in the sense that they produce their interiority (this is where Deleuze calls on Simondon's theory of the membrane, and this twisting of matter within the image and the affect foretells the fold).[27]

> But images also have an *inside* or certain images have an inside and are experienced from inside. These are subjects [. . .]. Indeed, there is a *gap* between the action undergone by these images and the executed reaction. It's this gap that gives them the power to store other images, that is, to perceive. But what they store is only that which interests them in other images: to perceive is to subtract what does not interest us from the image . . .[28]

Thus, the "subject" effect is produced while the gap between action and reaction of the movement-image is sufficient to make room for perception, meaning a subtractive light on other images. Perception—the argument is Bergsonian here, too—results from the constitution of a center of *indetermination* (or of subjectification) that distances the series of actions and reactions. The subject-image is produced within this gap, does not have existence outside of this gap, so that the subjectivity of images is no more than this interstice, this relaxing, this gap between action and reaction. Deleuze systematically returns to the first chapter of *Matter and Memory*, which allows subjectivity to be defined with astonishing economy, without being given a substantial, fully formed subject, but by carrying out its constitution genetically. As such, the subject is no more than a gap, a delay, a small pocket that strains and separates actions from reactions. Thus the subject is defined as a cut, as a temporal delay.

These "special" images, which "frame" other images, are haecceities. In this universe, where all reacts against all, the image, in the ordinary sense of a perceived image, is an image in the second degree, an *interval*, an image torn by the operation of framing, a perception-image: this is the living image, which is inscribed between action and reaction, an "instrument of analysis," as Bergson says, "with respect to the collected movement," the undertaken action, and the "instrument of selection with respect to the executed movement," or the motor reaction. It is within this interstice that subjective-images and captive forces are released, which also applies to active framing, as we see.[29] Cinematographic images are this type of subjective image. Hence, we have the bold definition of subjectivity by two material properties or operations: subtraction and action. Subjectivity, the living image that perceives other images and frames them, is first subtractive, because it deducts and neglects the interaction and variation of all the movement-images that do not interest it. This is the perception-image. This subtractive and realist definition of perception is also found again in Bergson. In reality, perception is not an image of another nature from the movement that it perceives, but a simplification, a selection, a framing. For Deleuze, as for Bergson, photography is already within things, "lines and points that we retain of the thing as a function of our receptive facet."[30]

The movement-image fills the perception-image as soon as the delay between action and reaction is increased, in such a way that subjectivity can even be considered a center; this is a center of indetermination, a gap delaying reaction by doubling the action that it subtracts from a sensory facet. But the image resolves its perception in motility so that we move "imperceptibly from perception to action," in a sensory motor mode that is slow enough that the motor response becomes endowed with a subjective percept (perception-image) and affect (affection-image)—an "inside." The subject is thus dilated between subtractive perception and action bending the world around it, so that "perception is only one side of the gap, where the action is the other side."[31] So subjectivity is not only subtractive, it is also active and capable of curving the world around the perceptive center that it establishes by elimination or subtraction.

> The operation considered is no longer elimination, selection or framing, but the curving of the universe, therefore resulting in the virtual action of things on us and our possible action on things at the same time. This is the second material aspect of subjectivity.[32]

The same gap is expressed in terms of time in action and space in perception. Instead of instantaneously releasing undertaken action into motor reaction, these living images, perception-images, subject images, provide "the black screen" that allows the influential image, the undertaken action, to be disclosed, and to capture force relations by framing it perceptibly (perception-image), and by experiencing it (affection-image), before acting upon it in reaction (action-image). Cinematographic images are such images that frame and stabilize a perception in the series of actions and reactions; that is to say, a special image that is mechanical and vital, endowed with a nonorganic vitality and subjectivity, and not because it should be attributed to the vision of a filmmaker or introduce a projection resembling forms of nature, but because it materially fills the subjective image on the screen that a spectator can frame as he/she likes. The cinematographic image offers its perceptions like a camera, its affects like lights, colors, and sounds, so that there is a screen for cinema and the brain. Since it frames other images, it functions as a living image, possessing its own life, with a nonorganic vitality. What makes cinematographic technique so interesting is the problematizing of the framing and editing that characterizes classical cinema (which movements and which times are compressed in which framing and which montage?), as well as the way that the movement-image is resolved in the time-image (modern cinema), which explores the double system of the movement-image in an exacting way: the image in-itself, which is related to all other images to which it reacts immediately, or the special image, which frames other images and only retains a partial action, to which it only reacts in a mediated way (motor reaction).

The movement-image thus serves to frame a free and mobile classification of cinema, according to types of montage and modes of actualization of movement-images. The perception-image of cinema, like the living image, doubles from a perceptible membrane of the action it undergoes: instead of being dissipated suddenly into action, it develops an affective zone between its perceptible facet (perception-image) and its motor facet (action-image). As such, a perception-image, an action-image, and an affection-image intrude between action and reaction and form the three main kinds of images.

> All things considered, movement-images divide into three types of images when they are related to a center of indetermination as a special image: perception-images, action-images, and affection-images.[33]

And "each one of us, special image or potential center, we are none other than an assemblage of these three images, a consolidation of perception-images, action-images, and affection-images."[34] This analysis requires the classification of *The Movement-Image*: if all films mix the three varieties of the movement-image, styles and works of art can be differentiated by occasionally relating them to the perception-image, above all, accentuating the establishing shots and wide shots (Anthony Mann's westerns), then to the medium shot and quick jump cuts of the action-image (Hawks' film noir), and then to the close-up of the affection-image (Dreyer, Ozu).

Typology of signs and ethology of power

The plane of interiority of force is housed in this interstice between action and reaction, which ensures the theoretical articulation between the concept of the image and that of the fold. Since the subjective image—this image that is endowed with an inside—is none other than force that is folded and affected itself—longitude that gets experienced as latitude. Interiority can be strictly defined from force and exteriority, and "the inside is constituted by the folding of the outside."[35] The movement-image, the subjectified image of vital and cinematographic individuations is a stretched image, curved on itself, having expanded within itself, under the guise of a center of indetermination, the affect of force. This completely new and stimulating theory of the subject remains on the plane of images, or that of forces: a subject is an image that is "experienced" *from inside*.[36] The image, defined as material existence, knows this mutation that distances action from reaction and curves, twists the image on itself until releasing this space of indetermination, this provisional and subtractive center of subjectivity. The passage from the matter of force toward the form of subjectivity operates according to these two properties, which suffice to define all subjectivity: subtraction and action. The subjective image is nothing more than an image that "frames" by subtractive action, by ignoring everything that does not concern its action in all other images. With this framing the image expands between action and reaction, subjecting the interstice to a perceptive response, an affective doubling, and a motor response. Such a subject-image corresponds well to a haecceity. It is defined by its longitude—a composite of speeds and slownesses, force relations, and a material complex of action–reaction. But this longitude vibrates in a slower, more hesitant and complex way, the arc vacillating from a variation in power, and a capacity to be affected itself. The subjective image is none other than a longitude that is itself affected, and that is subjectified by indetermination.

Like the living image, the perception-image of cinema develops an affective zone between its sensory side (perception-image) and its motor side (action-image), through which it displays and deepens its subjective receptivity by experiencing itself, by destroying the circuit from perception to action and by bringing movement back to quality as a lived state (affection-image), rather than actions (action-image) or bodies (perception-image). That is all Deleuze needs in order to define his "cinematographic concepts" and to establish a classification of types of images that form cinema, and the signs that correspond to each of these types.[37] Cinema offers a physical semiotics and an ethics of power, so that its value consists in a wonderfully groundbreaking development of a unique sign system.

Thus, Deleuze posits a very free semiotics as a function of numerous cuts that aim to seize the irruptive and disturbing violence of cinema in accordance with the quality of the images themselves and which distinguishes modes of subjectification and cinematographic types of signs by way of natural history. This is a "mobile classification," he says, "that can be changed, and that is only worth what it makes visible."[38] The example from cinema helps demonstrate that the sign-system of images results from ethology, not from morality, and that this kind of semiotics does not depend on a signifying interpretation, but on an ethology of power. We can now see how Nietzsche revolutionized the theory of interpretation: to interpret is to construct force relations according to a vital mode of evaluation. Such an embrace of force does not imply any moral judgment by means of transcendent values, but only the vital effectuation of an encounter that Deleuze calls a "combat." In such a combat, a "powerful nonorganic vitality [...] supplements force with force, and enriches whatever it takes hold of."[39] Here also, Deleuze avoids placing himself at the level of subjects and forms, functions, and constituted organs, but considers the combat a constituted intensity. To evaluate comes back to appreciating what art made us become, the experience of new relations into which we enter by materially drawing up a cartography of affects, by rebuilding a new haecceity and determining if it turns out to be favorable or harmful. This is where we rediscover the theory of evil in Spinoza: an existing mode is defined by its power to be affected, and this is called "good" while it forms a new relationship that augments its perfection and its power to act, or "bad" if it destroys it.[40] Critical evaluation consists of drawing up such affective maps.

Judgment used to presuppose preexistent and transcendent values, while clinical critique does not call for any other ingredients except the vital mode of the encounter, which forms a "category," according to Deleuze. These categories are not abstract but concrete and extracted from effective force relations; they are not functions of judgment, or classes of noetic or grammatical attributions, but arrangements of semiotic relations that engage vital classifications. Thus, they meet up with common notions in Spinoza, which do not consist of a general idea that is "common to all minds," but in "something common in bodies," a common relation of all bodies, like size, movement, and rest, or only to certain ones—at the minimum it consists in the relation that connects my body to another body.[41] Under these conditions we understand why semiotics forms a relation of forces that return to a vital evaluation: signs disclose an ethics. The well-founded category must be traced back to the symptom, because a classification always expresses a symptomatology.[42] Thus, the semiology or classification of images and signs consists of an evaluation of power in itself. The category is an embracing of force, whose list necessarily remains open and in flux, since it corresponds to the relations into which our bodies enter, or the intensive map of its affects. Longitude, the haecceity of encounters, expresses the advantage or disadvantage of this formation, depending on what is shown to be beneficial (or not) to the body that it causes to "become," or that enters into this new combination. The table of categories is moveable and transformable and is capable of new redistributions, new determinations, and it even functions like an editing table.[43] It slices and cuts into the flux of images and inserts a vibrating interval between them: the interstice of a subjective affect. The table of signs thus discloses a map of powers.

4

The Body without Organs

Artaud and the Critique of the Organism

The function of experimentation in literature arises with the concept of the body without organs, which Deleuze borrows from the poetic works of Antonin Artaud. If the expression of the "body without organs" seems obscure, its definition is clear, and its trajectory in the system is revelatory. It is a question of thinking of the body without reducing it to organic form along the lines of the logic of force and the modal conception of individuation that we saw in the examinations of the masterpiece and haecceity. For Deleuze, the organ is the opposite of life, and life must be understood as *nonorganic*. The concept of the body without organs has two functions: to treat modes of corporeal individuation prior to their centered organization, by saving hypostasis from an organizing center—and for that, Deleuze appeals to the poetic experience of Antonin Artaud and the painting of Francis Bacon; he pursues his examination on the epistemological plane of the life sciences by studying Geoffroy Saint-Hilaire and embryogenesis, which he opposes to organology. On the other hand, the body without organs involves thinking about the junction between art and the body, and it is in this regard that Deleuze takes the concept from the works of Antonin Artaud for *The Logic of Sense*. The first determination of the body without organs takes place in the extreme climate of thought that reaches its radical limit through the artistic experiment and into the "incapacity of thought." Like Blanchot, Deleuze grants the greatest importance to this "impossibility of thought that is thought," which signals the success of Antonin Artaud.[1] But with Artaud it is also schizophrenia that causes this appearance and qualifies this incapacity. The relationship between art and madness establishes itself around the schizophrenic figure of Artaud and sheds light on the difference that Deleuze continues to establish between clinical pathology and clinical poetics.

The concept is constructed through these two tendencies. Along with Blanchot, Deleuze determines creation to be an impossibility, an athleticism of the limit, and this incapacity is the condition for the creation of thought and its capacity to create the new. Confronted at its limit, thought is summoned to create: there is a constituent exteriority of thought regarding itself. Deleuze causes thought to be born at the disjunctive encounter of a perceptible shock, which marks the end of its power, its encounter with exteriority—the injunction which forces it to discover its lack of preexisting content—and this is its creative vitality. The shock designates a heterogeneous, violent encounter with the body where thought is shown to be passive, but the shock also makes it possible for thought to take place as an outcome, an operation, or a disjunctive synthesis. This incapacity also opens up the door to psychosis. Deleuze says as much in *Difference and Repetition* when he stresses that it is not about opposing two images of thought, one borrowed from dogmatic thought, and the other from schizophrenia, but remembering that schizophrenia "is a possibility for thought."[2] Artaud pursues "the terrible revelation" of a thought that is not innate, but genital. "I am an innate genital," writes Artaud to Rivière:

> There are imbeciles who believe themselves to be beings, beings by innateness. *I am the one who must whip his innateness in order to exist* [. . .].
> Because thought is a matron who has not always existed.[3]

The body without organs later concerns the intensive definition of the body and arises from the life sciences, from Simondon to Canguilhem, and from Geoffroy Saint-Hilaire to Dalcq.[4] It is only with respect to a third tendency that the concept of the schizophrenic receives a more defined, (psychiatric) clinical meaning in *Anti-Oedipus*, which occurs at the same time that the body without organs and the Figure of Artaud become the *anti-Oedipal* critical forces fighting against the psychiatric and psychoanalytic definition of the unconscious, as well as psychic and somatic normalcy. The body without organs turns out to be an essential piece to the critique of interpretation, and the reconstructed conception of the body passes through a political critique involving the notions of organism and organization, which combats the model of centralized, unitary, and sovereign power upon which they actually depend.

"November 18, 1947—How Do You Make Yourself a Body without Organs?"

The concept of the "body without organs" is constructed from a theory of literature that, in its proximity with madness, is capable of causing an image of the body to emerge prior to individuation. Access to this intensive, pre-individual, material corporeality is given by literature. The body without organs is useful when thinking about the corporeality and morphogenesis of bodies without tying them to an external unifying principle, such as the soul, form, or the unity of organism, but by being located at the level of matter that is not yet informed and is on the plane of forces. Artaud releases it on the immanent level of matter itself by avoiding all principles of external unity, and he expresses this corporeality without organs through syntax without articulation. This is where Deleuze sees a reconception of the body that is not blinded by a presupposed, transcendent, final, or abstract unity said to reduce the body to a constituted organism or a hierarchy of differentiated organs.

After all, an organ suggests a unitary and hierarchical model of the auto-centered body. Whether it is embryogenesis or phylogenesis, organology has been the theoretical seat of a conception of evolution and the morphogenesis of living things since Antiquity, and it has been decisive for the status of forms and corporeality.[5] Through much logical articulation of wholes and parts, and by the biological constitution of corporeal identity, in its own way, the organ reproduces problems that are posed by unity, individuality, and the organization of bodies. Organology is a challenge for Deleuze, who, in accordance with Simondon, conceives of the unity of the body as the individuation of intensive difference on a pre-individual field of singularities. Neither organic form nor the unity of the subject can be postulated as preconditions for the process of individuation. The subject, as well as the body, is formed in reality by multiple force relations in becoming and cannot be conceived as individuals preformed by a transcendent principle, which is represented by the soul, consciousness, a transcendental subject, or an organic form.

The body, then, must be said to be without organs, and the organ is considered a derivative or product of the process of organic differentiation, like the species is to the individual, or the individual to its process of individuation. Hence, the concept of the body without organs is established from the studies that Deleuze devotes to biology, and embryogenesis, in particular, which holds an important place in the philosophy of life. Deleuze studies embryology in *Difference and*

Repetition while being interested in the epistemology of the natural sciences and Étienne Geoffroy Saint-Hilaire, specifically. But the fact that the first mention of the "body without organs" appears in the context of the relationship between thought and corporeality, and literature and madness, in *The Logic of Sense* shows the key role the philosophy of art, and the entanglement of art and life, plays in an intensive philosophy.

That which is beyond the organism, but also at the limit of the lived body, is what Artaud discovered and named the body without organs.[6] On November 28, 1947, Artaud declares a war on the organs: *To Have Done Away with the Judgement of God*, "and bind me if you like, but there is nothing more useless than an organ."[7]

In the poem, *To Have Done Away with the Judgement of God*, Artaud writes:

> The body is the body / It is alone / It has no need of organs / The body is never an organism / Organisms are enemies of the body.[8]

"Organisms" are enemies of the body, not in the sense that it would be advised to do without them, but in the sense that they convey an image of the organic body that Artaud contests: the assemblage ruled by constituent organs, subjugated to a principle of corporeal unity. It is thus not a matter of tossing these organs out the window, but of ceasing to rely on them as a form of pyramidal hierarchy where the major organ, the brain, regulates and controls the rest of the body.

> No mouth/ No tongue/ No teeth/ No larynx/ No stomach/ No anus/ I will reconstruct the man that I am.[9]

The body without organs is not a body deprived of organs, but a body below the level of organic determination, a body of indeterminate organs, a body in the process of differentiation. To go back to the categories used in *Difference and Repetition*, it is the virtual plane of forces that are not yet actualized in a determinate form. Deleuze thus thinks of the organism as a form that imprisons the body in a definite, corporeal organization, in an organic determination that traps life and imprisons it. The body without organs designates *nonorganic* life and is a power of individuation that is not yet actualized in the form of an organism. In Bergsonian terms, the organism is the determined capture of the *élan vital*, which implies delimitation as well as limitation, and art goes to the beginning of the process of individuation: it captures nonorganic forces and, seizes the processes of intensity prior to stabilized forms. So the organ is instead "what life opposes in order to limit itself," life being all the more powerful for being nonorganic.[10] This nonorganic life animates the body as force relations, the intense power of differentiation, and is not yet individualized in a given form.

The virtual and the actual

Thus, the body without organs and nonorganic life sets in motion the modal conception of the individual and the primacy of force over form that we encountered in the theory of haecceity and the image. During the time of *Difference and Repetition*, Deleuze determines the relation between force and form to be two moments, or two vectors of difference, and he explicates it through Bergson and Simondon. In Simondon, the individuation of a crystal, for example, is physically formed by the resolution of a difference in potential, which levels out what Simondon calls a "problematic field of pre-individual singularities": individuation is a resolution of a difference in intensity. In Bergson, matter, and thus the form of the organism, is an effect of intensive duration. Deleuze translates this ontological difference, this entropic arrow between tension and individuated matter, in terms of oscillation or simultaneous vibration, which is nonsuccessive, between the actual and the virtual.

The virtual and the actual present two modes of difference: a whole can be differen*t*iated (with a *t*) when it is virtual, well singularized, and completely real, without being stabilized by an actual individual. Such is the case with the body without organs, which is on the side of virtual and intensive corporeality. When this virtual differentiation is actualized, it individuates itself and moves from the virtual to the actual, resolving its difference in initial potential in order to differen*c*iate itself (with a *c*). These two regimes of difference express the energy axis of an intensity, which is individuated by resolving its difference in potential: a differen*t*iated (with a *t*) body on the virtual plane differen*c*iates (with a *c*) itself by individuating itself. The organ results from such an individuation, from a differen*c*iation (with a *c*), while the body without organs approaches individuation by considering unformed difference with the power of intensive differen*t*iation (with a *t*). Thus, the two moments of difference take up the axis of virtual forces (differen*t*iation with a *t*) and actual forms (differen*c*iation with a *c*). But, contrary to Bergson, and even if he values the intensive axis, as the entire theory of the body without organs indicates, Deleuze is less opposed to the organ, or the formed individual, so he does not critique the organic conception that reduces the corporeal to a hierarchy of individuals. It is the organic conception of the body that is in question, more than the existence of the organ, so Deleuze can critique those who reduce the body to the organ and affirm that the organism "is necessary" in order to continue to live. The body without organs is not set against organs, only "this organization of organs that is called organism."[11]

This is because the actual and the virtual coexist. Instead of the Bergsonian split between duration and matter, or the distinction between the milieu of pre-individual singularities and individuation that Simondon posits, Deleuze transposes the arrow of intensity and its successive resolution of modal coexistence in the virtual and the actual. Each is as real as the other, but the actual concerns the formed individual, the material crystal, while the virtual designates the problematic, pre-individual field, or nonactualized intensive differentiation. Except, the virtual does not disappear once individuation is achieved: for Deleuze, form is not an exhausted force, but a provisional relation of forces, however slow. Thus, the body without organs designates the virtual side of a body that has an organic actuality at the same time. But, with respect to intensive corporeality, Artaud shows himself to be capable of rendering the virtual perceptible within the actual. The organ is an actual, formed individual that presupposes the body without organs and the intensive force relations. The body without organs thus corresponds to virtual differen*t*iation (with a *t*) of nonindividuated singularities, while the organ presents the state of actual organization. The body without organs is an intensive body, a body in the process of differenciation. This is why Deleuze always uses the model of an egg to explain the nonorganic vitality of this web that is not yet stabilized in the form of an organ, and is still capable of multiple transformations: "The body without organs is thus defined by an indeterminate organ, while the organism is defined by determinate organs."[12] It is not about going without organs, but of replacing the formed, adult organ with a polymorphic and juvenile conception that is metamorphic, an organ in the process of differenciation. Deleuze positions himself at the level of constituent and unstable intensive forces, and not at the level of constituted organic form, and as regards the same existent body, he values the virtual axis of unformed forces to the detriment of the vector of forms in the process of organization.

Deleuze assigns art the task of providing access to this corporeality below the level of organization and of capturing life before it stabilizes in differenciated organs. It even seems that art goes from origin to process of differenciation before the vital flux is set in an organic form. The power of literature and its pictorial effect grasps this active capacity of *involution*, which causes life to emerge as nonorganic force in organic form. Artaud brings a limit experience to expression, to the limit of consciousness, which escapes the simple image so that consciousness is given over to the body. It is not an accident that the body is considered in light of poetry and schizophrenia. Poetic invention, appropriated by Deleuze in terms of creative inspiration, is shown to be indifferent to named individuations and is sensitive to the power of individuation that works below the organic body. The body without organs clears the way for a material not yet formed, a nonrepresented body, and a language pushed to its nonsignifying limit. Here, Deleuze opposes constituted individuals (articulated language, organized bodies) and processes of individuation, and he considers madness an intensive experience that enables nonorganic life to be captured. The opposition of an organized form creates a shift toward the material, toward the unformed mix of forces and materials and the intensive, nonorganic life of materials, which clears the way for "singularities that do not have forms and are neither visible bodies, nor speaking people."[13]

Furthermore, organization is not only a matter of form that individuates itself, but it also arises from a faulty conception of form from the perspective of representation, and the critique of organic organization infers a critique of representation's dominant position, which is then applied in *Anti-Oedipus*. This questioning of organic articulation is conveyed at the formal level by the disarticulation of prose, which seems to be the condition for access to the nonorganic plane. Artaud is a poet because he knew how to push articulated language and the organized body to their breaking points: madness seems to be the operator that ensures a superior vital power for art. By siding with the vehement, psychotic utterance of Antonin Artaud, Deleuze definitely leaves the domain that is marked out by sense and signification. Artaud the schizoid dismantles Lewis Carroll's mannerisms and language games, and in 1969 *The Logic of Sense* splits apart to leave room for this intensive definition of art that Deleuze develops in 1981 with respect to corporeal becomings painted by Francis Bacon. The concept of the body without organs develops its circuit between these two works. Appearing with *The Logic of Sense*, the concept disappears after the Figure is posited in *The Logic of Sensation*.

Antonin Artaud and Lewis Carroll

With *The Logic of Sense*, psychosis and the body cause an irruption in language. Deleuze continues his studies of psychopathology, but he no longer confines himself to the connection of desire to the law, or perversion, as he did in *Sacher-Masoch*. At the same time, he abandons the connections between paradox and literature that he had been adopting since the beginning of *The Logic of Sense*, which he said was "an attempt at a logical and psychoanalytic novel," and was written about Lewis Carroll. Logic and psychoanalysis find themselves disavowed along with Carroll himself, whose book celebrated "the marriage of language and the unconscious" by way of playful paradox. This is the point of inflexion of a *Logic of Sense* that was centered on the discursive and the articulation of sense up until that point: Artaud's poem, without punctuation, is situated at the limit of articulated language. Deleuze stresses Artaud's howl-breaths that open up a path for corporeal language that is direct and nonmediated by consciousness, yet is vertiginous at the same time.[14] This corporeality without organization is manifested by syntax without articulation on the plane of style, and through the dimension of sense it reveals the insistence of a corporeality that has up to this point been resistant to literary or philosophical language. Deleuze calls it a glorious body, and it signals the first appearance of the body without organs: "the superior body or Antonin Artaud's body without organs."[15]

> A glorious body as a new dimension of the schizophrenic body, an organism
> without parts that operates entirely by insufflation, inspiration, evaporation, fluid
> transmission (the superior body or Antonin Artaud's body without organs).[16]

This discovery is effectuated on the poetic plane, and it is a poetry fueled by psychosis. Writing, the limit experience of discourse, encounters schizophrenia here, the limit experience of the lived body. Beneath the organic body, the schizophrenic body grants access to a glorious body, which implies the proximity of poetic and schizophrenic success: the collapse of syntax accompanies the corporeal intensity of a life that is irreducible to consciousness. The body without organs thus designates the way in which the schizophrenic poet pushes language to its maximal point of material elasticity, and this experience concerns the intensive becoming of syntax and the transformation of the image of the body at the same time. Deleuze does not waver on this point: in the impressive opening chapter of *Essays Critical and Clinical*, "Literature and Life", he defines the *delirium* that causes language to "come off of its hinges," which Artaud uses to cause language to vibrate at its asyntactic limit: letters fall in the disorganization of maternal syntax, but there is also a creation of syntax and a recovery of letters in new nouns, and finally, there are "breath-words" that push language to its oral and pneumatic limit. And yet, it is important to avoid confusing this invention with a pathology in language: "among those who write books with literary intentions, even among the mad, very few can be called writers."[17]

Deleuze always refrains from confusing poetry and psychosis. At the heart of psychotic experience, he distinguishes the schizoid position of great health that is capable of putting biological and social organizations into question, on one hand, from psychotic collapse, on the other, which is driven toward silence and suffering. Indeed, if Deleuze always cleanly separates poetry and psychosis, the stylistic criteria of the "language of schizophrenia" turns out to be psychopathological. The translation that Artaud gives to the *Jabberwocky* by Lewis Carroll marks this shift, a "central collapse" that is situated in "another world and in a completely other language."[18] To wit, see the example of the translation of the third verse:

> Until rourghe is to rouargue has rangmbde and rangmde has rouarghambde.[19]

A kind of bodily hum of the oropharynx, a poetic drum beats in the schizo portmanteau and distinguishes it from the Lewis Carroll's portmanteau. Deleuze uses a clinical approach to differentiate between the two authors and states that Artaud's style is more profound than Carroll's, a depth that is recognized "without any problem" whatsoever from the terror of schizophrenic language. Artaud uses the same criticism when reproaching Carroll for holding fast to his "happy leisure" and "successes of the intellect," without descending into the "terror of the anus."[20] Deleuze sides with Artaud and presents Carroll as an affected and artificial little girl who is incapable of enduring the loss of homogeneity and the autonomy of sense in the schizophrenic experience, where the surface is reduced to fragments.

"The first evidence of schizophrenia is that the surface is cracked." With this declaration Deleuze leaves the surface of sense that is elaborated in the first part of the book: "The consequence of this is that the entire body is nothing but depth."[21] Without a doubt, the surface-depth opposition can make it seem like the intensive body serves as an origin, a prior principle, or a hidden essence. But Deleuze forcefully declares his hostility toward the division of essence and appearance that would be reestablished in the resignation of surface, the movement from an order of language and conscious logic to a rougher semiotics that is irreducible to lived, impersonal, and pre-individual experience.

This is how Deleuze characterizes the virtual in Simondonian terms during the time he wrote *The Logic of Sense*: the task is to escape from "undifferentiated groundlessness and imprisoned singularities."[22] In other words, the unformed is not personal or individual, without necessarily being confused with an undifferentiated abyss, because it is singular, and in this way, perfectly real and defined. Singularities are not prisoners of the alternative, *whether* that means indistinct chaos *or* the prison of form; there is a mode of well-defined, though nonindividuated, reality that comes back to the virtual, which is not actualized but differentiated (with a *t*). This is what Deleuze calls a real transcendental field made of nomadic, impersonal, pre-individuated singularities.[23] Organs are these types of imprisoned singularities of individuated form, whereas the body without organs exposes their intensive subversion. Poetic experience is able to seize this subversion by pushing language into a physics of affects.

Here we find the first formulation of the agrammatical as the determination of style in a modified form of "language without articulation."[24] In order to reach the body without organs, language must get rid of its organized form. The psychopathological definition of Antonin Artaud's poetic system is borrowed from agrammatism (*akataphasie*, or syntactic aphasia), and its description is troubled by a morphology that includes the impossibility of grammatically constructing words or arranging them in statements that conform to syntax.[25] These clinical symptoms become Deleuze's stylistic criteria for schizophrenic language. On one hand, the word loses its designating power, exits the signifier-signified articulation system, and is cashed out at its physical, excremental value: a noisy element that the body expels. This is Artaud's scream: "All writing is bullshit" which entails the anal function of expression.[26] But the psychotic utterance largely exceeds the signifying framework of psychoanalysis, including the anal framework. Writing is produced as an operation of the body, of the senses; it is an excremental element emitted by the voice and deposited by the hand, and is nothing more than an expelled, physical fragment. Its dimension of ideality is inoperative, converted into a material effect, and this is where *The Logic of Sense* reaches its corporeal limit. Essentially, schizophrenia exhausts the corporeal dimension of language by releasing it from the plane of conscious signification: articulated language intensively dissolves into cries, vocal noise, voiced and oral corporeality, just as articulated corporeality was driven to its material plane of pre-individual flux by the body without organs.

Secondly, as this passion of sense becomes an element expelled by the body, a tonic action responds to phonetic material. The alimentary excrement of the word explodes into phonetic pieces in Artaud's translation of Lewis Carroll. In Carroll, the portmanteau essentially remained an invention of vocabulary and welded two active significations together in a teratologic fold, tying sense and nonsense together with a paradoxical ribbon. A game of scholarly variation stretches the signifieds and puts a series of anamorphoses into play, which is less about an invention of syntax than it is a knowledgeable modulation of nouns, a kind of cry Babel. The linguistic *chaosmos* of Joyce in *Finnegans Wake* stages this type of semantic compression. In Artaud there is nothing of the sort. Schizophrenic utterance attacks syntax and grammar. Artaud does not play in the same realm as Lewis Carroll, because his lexical invention does not stabilize on syntactical and semantic planes. It moves from the series of sense to the association of tonic and consonantal elements, to sound effects, and to the phonetic action of words that are valued for their physical and sonorous phonic modulation, not their signification. In other words, the noted, ideal virtues of sense—semantics, syntax, and even syllabic articulation—are tied together in a flood of "exclusively tonic values" that are postural and not so much bound by accent or vocalization than by bodily tone. This is where Deleuze looks for a definition of intensive linguistics, which remains negatively defined in his text. The work on schizophrenia in *Anti-Oedipus*, and especially in the linguistic analyses in *Kafka*, *Rhizome*, and *A Thousand Plateaus*, will give this intensive linguistics a more defined shape. Just as the body without organs opens thought onto the nonorganic vitality of the body, a body without organs of language is attained, with its power contained in its nonsignifying and asubjective expression.

Louis Wolfson

A duality at the heart of the schizoid position allows Deleuze to distinguish between literature and madness, and his explicit statements about this are unwavering. It is not madness that makes Antonin Artaud a poet. However, it is preferable that this understanding of poetic expression be more precisely defined, even if Artaud is always characterized by the schizoid nature of his speech, producing the creative syntax that Deleuze assimilates into syntactical disorganization. What makes Artaud distinct from Carroll is the capacity to invent a syntax that closely resembles disarticulation, a disintegration of language, which is difficult to distinguish from psychotic collapse. This is where Deleuze's work on the strange works of schizophrenic writer, Louis Wolfson, is important, as he never grants him the designation of a poet.[27] Wolfson is important for drawing the line between the clinical and the artistic without going so far as to separate illness from life. He is the counter-example of a schizophrenic who is talented but remains imprisoned by his illness. The state of his writings is revelatory for locating the border between schizophrenia and poetry.

Deleuze tackles Louis Wolfson's works in *The Logic of Sense*, and in 1970 he writes a preface titled "Schizology" for the publication of Wolfson's book, *The Schizo and Languages*. He focuses his preface on indexing and analyzing the procedures that Wolfson uses, borrowing the term "procedure" that Foucault employed when describing Raymond Roussel's poetic innovation. Like Roussel, or even Jean-Claude Brisset, another great innovator of procedures, Wolfson deserves attention. Yet, he does not accomplish the works of art that his predecessors do, remaining in the grips of clinical pathology.[28]

Wolfson uses a complex procedure of substitution in his native English language—a language he found intolerable—transposing it as quickly as possible into every other language he knew of that was capable of adequate phonetic and semantic conversion. He accomplishes an impressive and extraordinary feat of linguistic gymnastics: in order to neutralize the English language he had to dress it up in at least one other real language, dedicating all of his efforts to becoming a "student of languages"—this is what he calls himself in the narrative of his adventures written in French.[29] Thus "where" can be radically altered to fit a German equivalent by slightly changing the adverb "*woher*," ("from where"), which provides a phonetic affinity, and such is the case for all of the Anglophone offenses he suffers and seeks to neutralize by pilfering French, German, Russian, and Hebrew lexicons.

> What ideas he had! In his naiveté he thought to do what no one had thought to do before, to change the English *where* to the German *woher* so the monosyllable would be "scientifically," methodologically, immediately, and completely destroyed, and he did this mentally and habitually every time he was confronted with the aforementioned monosyllable.[30]

Thus, not all schizophrenics are poets. Deleuze opposes Artaud's literary genius to Wolfson's schizophrenic account, whose "beauty and density remains clinical."[31] His works, as intriguing and interesting as they are, do not rise to the level of literature, but remain clinically imprisoned, which involves pathology in this context. "Wolfson's book is not a work of literature, and does not claim to be a poem."[32] Thus, at the heart of psychosis, Deleuze distinguishes between the pathogenic protocol that remains imprisoned by the psychotic procedure, and the creative process, just as we saw when he wrote *Sacher-Masoch*, where he pointed out the pathogenic "source" or symptomatological "object" of the work. Deleuze does not abandon his initial position regarding Sacher-Masoch, and he continues to affirm that the psychotic Artaud is a doctor of civilization, but Wolfson is not.

How is a protocol distinguished from the Procedure? In 1970, Wolfson's combat is "not without relation to Artaud, Artaud's combat," but it is not in the same realm as his, remaining "clinical" without crossing over into the "critical" threshold of art, because Wolfson's linguistic transformations remain subordinated to the real accident of the intolerable features of the English language. He stays trapped in a procedure that hardens into a pathogenic protocol without breaking through with truly creative work.[33] In *Essays Critical and Clinical*, from 1993, Deleuze clarifies this distinction between a pathogenic accident and a creative event.

The Procedure attacks language in its living structure, transforming it, causing it to become: a protocol, which is meticulous and palliative, only looks for a procedure to render language more noxious, without transforming the regime. Instead of feeding this shocking dislocation of form with the nonsignifying vitality of language, the Procedure hardens into mere protocol.

Wolfson intends to hold onto his language and push away everything its uses could do for creativity, and he is not the least bit interested in the world of new effects that could be pulled from it, which is what distinguishes him from Raymond Roussel or Brisset, the other virtuosos of language transmutation whom Foucault praised as true creators. This is not the case with Wolfson who sticks to his automatic and passive protocol of annihilating his native English. A prisoner of the established definitions of loathsome English words, his protocol of substitution keeps a condition of homophony and semantic resistance with the language source in disguise. He does not wish to transform the syntax, nor produce new expressions, and does not care what the new effects of his protocol could lead to. Even though his psychosis is inseparable from a linguistic procedure, its effects lie fallow, subjugated to phonetic and lexical forms of organization, and subjected to complex alliterative equations that do not correspond to a body without organs within language.[34]

Wolfson's combat can seem to be of the same nature as Artaud's, but psychotic transmutation alone does not have poetic virtue within it. Artaud's genius rests in his ability to pull words and bodily affects from the schizophrenic body, which puts syntax in check and opens up new poetic territory, while Wolfson remains caught within conditions of resemblance in a sense that keeps him from moving from clinical psychology to art. With Wolfson, procedure remains within protocol because he "idles and does not reach a vital process capable of producing a vision."[35] He stops himself at the ironic simulacra of poetry and linguistics. In Deleuze, irony is always opposed to joyous and naive humor, and it pejoratively designates a reflexive, representative, and reverential movement by which a given reality is academically doubled. Wolfson does not end up creating art because he is shown to be incapable of settling into a level of literature or a playful and nonformal science, so his protocol remains a private condition that does not stretch into the vital resources of language.

Thus, Artaud is not a poet when he is schizophrenic, but he is schizophrenic because he lets himself catch up to the experimentation that he poetically expresses. He is also more of a doctor than a patient. As opposed to Wolfson, he is able to extract a symptom from the vital situation that he brings to art, while Wolfson remains the witness of a subjected protocol. Artaud releases the event trapped within the symptom, and Wolfson enforces the symptom, using it in his literary works.[36] This is the difference between accidental actualization in bodies and the creative counter-actualization of the incorporeal event as thematized in *The Logic of Sense*. The body without organs is a capturing of intensities, not psychotic disorganization, and Deleuze does not have harsh enough words for "the grotesque trinity of the child, the poet, and the madman."[37]

Simondon and the modulation of forces and materials

The body without organs makes it possible to demonstrate a physics of the body, and for Deleuze to develop this work by borrowing Gilbert Simondon's intensive physics and semiotics of force.[38] If the body without organs concerns both the determination of the body for the life sciences and creative thought in art, it is because it puts force relations and matter into play. Simondon's analysis of modulation is rediscovered here, which simultaneously attests to the importance of the arts for philosophy. For the analysis of art requires a new status of the object and reconceives the status of subjectivity at the same time that it transforms the relations between form and matter. In 1978, Deleuze affirms: "we are led, I believe, in every sense, to no longer think in terms of form-matter."[39] It is a literal repetition of the critique of hylomorphic schema proposed by Gilbert Simondon. In order to explain individuation in the case of molding, which opposes inert matter with active form, it is necessary to substitute a process of modulation that conceives of form as a coupling of forces and materials. Deleuze takes this wonderful analysis that allowed Simondon to develop a metaphysics and epistemology of intensity, and transposes it in the domain of art.

Modulation is able to establish itself at the level of matter itself so that it can be considered a carrier of singularities and features of expression. The static opposition of form and matter is bypassed in a zone of intermediary dimension that is energetic and molecular, which endows thought with an "energetic materiality in movement, carrying *singularities or haecceities*, which are already like implicit forms [...] which are combined with the processes of deformation."[40] It is a completely new definition of art, where the power of deformation, active in material, explains the effect that the work has on thought.

All of the arts capture forces, regardless of their media: this exhilarating and positive definition of the arts profoundly transforms their status. It is no longer permissible to trace the arts back to an abstract unity, but they respond to the commonality of a problem: the capture of intense forces in new materials.

> From another point of view, the question of the separation of the arts, of their respective autonomy, and of their inevitable hierarchy loses all importance. There is a community among the arts, a common problem. In art, in painting as in music, it is not a question of reproducing or inventing forms, but of capturing forces.[41]

A problem has types of solutions that are very diverse in respect to what is given, so this definition does not at all compromise the singularity of the arts or the difference among works of art. The problem concerns forces, not forms. Deleuze dismisses two positions that are often considered antagonistic, which have regulated the question of the arts and are subordinated to, or issued from, the imitation of nature and figurative representation. The modest capture of immanent forces replaces the invention or reproduction of forms: it is not a matter of reproducing existing forms, or inventing new ones, but of being limited to the capture of real existent forces, which turn art into an operator on the terrain of a symptomatology of forces, or a strictly immanent ethology.

The fact that passive capture operates at the level of forces and not forms implies that it has a polemical dimension even in its passivity. Just as the clinic is critical, the capture of forces performs a critique that is more radical than a revolution of form or a transformation of form would be. Art does not consist in subjecting passive matter to a form, nor of producing a subjective effect on sensibility, but only in "following the flux of matter."[42] In other words, it sets itself up on the haecceities of material, taking advantage of material features of expression in a heterogeneous synthesis, a disparate synthesis that explains the subversive capacity of sensation.

Thus, the capture incorporates sensation in material and consolidates the expressive forces of material and affect in the work of art. "The *form-matter* couple is replaced with *force-material*."[43]

> It is not a question of imposing form on matter, but of developing a richer and richer, more and more substantial, material that is henceforth capable of capturing forces that are more and more intense.[44]

Art, like modulation, can be defined as a captor of forces: that is the "community of the arts," their "common problem." We move from the opposition of form and matter to the constitution of a material that is expressive at the level of the work itself, and it benefits aesthetic analysis, which is pushed toward a true analysis of material. The logic of sensation rests on this kind of analysis that counts its "haecceities" or singularities, and uses them to address the relationship between the work of art and the spectator in terms of affects and sensations, which must also be understood as modulation. This transforms the analysis of painting just as it does music. That is why Deleuze replaces the form-matter couple with a coupling of more developed material and imperceptible forces that only become perceptible through this material: this formula, which is valid for the arts, is equally consistent with the intensive definition of the body without organs.

Becoming versus resemblance

The title of this section is the reason why color is defined in *Francis Bacon: The Logic of Sensation* as "a variable, continuous, temporal mold, whose only suitable name is *modulation*, strictly speaking."[45] Modulation creates an escape from resemblance and the ability to think about the heterogeneous relationship between the material of art and the sensation that it produces, which is temporalized. This heterogeneous relationship, which is theorized as a capture of forces—becoming and not imitation, the indiscernible, heterogeneous forces that are put into presence—forms a bloc of becoming. The difference between the photographic image and the cinematographic image arises out of the same principle. Cinema replaces the static equilibrium of the immobile cut with a mobile cut, or modulation "that does not cease to modify the mold, to constitute a variable, continuous, temporal mold"; in other words, of passing from static form to the intensive conception of form as a becoming of forces.[46]

The distinction between abstract forms (mold) and intensive forces or sensible forms (modulation) in this new intensive conception of form in continuous variation provides a relation between art and expression that offers an alternative to taking refuge in imaginary resemblance or structural analogy, as if art should copy a sensible model or seize an intelligible structure. Starting from his collective work with Guattari, Deleuze replaces imaginary resemblance and structural analogy with a theory of becoming, becoming-animal, and becoming-minor that opens up the space for thinking of expression in art without abandoning its mimetic factors, but while moving from imitation focused on resemblance to a kind of vital symbiosis, a co-evolution, or becoming aparallel, demonstrated in the capture of the wasp and the orchid,[47] which turns art into a vital operator. With the notion of capture, Deleuze means to disabuse art, as well as the social sciences, from the theory of imaginary semblance or structural homology: "[imaginary] resemblance and the [symbolic structural] code have at least in common to be *molds*, one by sensible form, the other by intelligible structure." Here, "Mold" is taken in the sense of hylomorphic representation and the abstract of form. At the same moment, Deleuze dismisses the imaginary (and along with it, the entire psychoanalytic theory that reduces the work of art to the interpretation of its creator or receiver) and structure (and along with it, the entire formalist theory that reduces art's effects to its internal structure). The capture of forces opens up a new path for the philosophy of art. Against hermeneutics, which pins the work of art onto the subject, and against structural or sociological interpretation, which locates the effectiveness of objective structures in the work of art, the capture of forces allows the force-material relation to replace the form-matter relation. By putting heterogeneous forces that produce previously unknown captures into contact with one another, the work of art combines the creator and the receiver into a real becoming that realizes a mutation of cultures.

This is why Deleuze says that modulation is "the operation of the Real" and allows art to be defined as the operation that "renders forces that are imperceptible perceptible":[48] a philosophy of the arts is in solidarity with a theory of sensation, materially understood as a force that is exerted on the body through modulation, rendering heterogeneous forces that it captures in previously unheard of material perceptible. Modulation makes it possible to combine the indiscernibility of forces in presence with their heterogeneity. It is no longer a question of figurative resemblance or structural identity, but of a becoming—a becoming of the work of art and its referent at the same time—as well as the becoming of reception and its public, along with the artist and her milieu. Every type of sign thus engages the modulation of the object itself,[49] the differenciation that allows a material sign, a nonlinguistic material capable of producing effects on sensibility and is variable in accordance with the arts, to include "all kinds of features of modulation."[50]

5

The Critique of Interpretation and the Machine

Literature is created through an exploration of margins, a clinical sympto-matology. Starting in 1967, but in a more explicit manner from 1970 onward, Deleuze moves from the conception of literature as an operator of a critique of representation to the notion of literature as symptomatology, and assigns art, not just literature anymore, the function of impersonal experimentation. From *Coldness and Cruelty* in 1967 to *Kafka: Toward a Minor Literature* in 1975, literature remains the privileged ground for the philosophy of art, but the theoretical challenges of the analyses have nothing specifically literary about them and apply to other artistic practices, and above all, call for the abandonment of the implicit primacy of the linguistic sphere, and this goes for literature, as well.

The move from the philosophy of literature to a philosophy of art in this second period takes place on a main point of fracture: the abandonment, pure and simple, of the interpretive position, which is present in the first edition of *Proust* and maintained in some senses in the second edition, offers a different inflexion and an unexpected development of themes that are already present in the work. By dismissing interpretation as a discourse that is secondary to the creation of a new pragmatics of reading, Deleuze moves toward a general semiotics that subverts the relationship between philosophy and the arts. This move from interpretation to "machinic functioning" continues with a critique of hermeneutics, but condemns the structural position in the same way, which appeared again in *Difference and Repetition*, and especially in *The Logic of Sense*, as a possible alternative to exegesis, by substituting a functioning, immanent textuality for the transcendence of sense.

At least two consequences can be taken from a radical refusal of interpretation. The first concerns the political turning point of the critique that corresponds to

Deleuze's encounter with Guattari in 1969, and the repercussions of May 1968 for contemporary thought—the same inflexion can be seen in Foucault's work. The concept of experimentation, which we already encountered regarding Sacher-Masoch, Nietzsche, and Artaud, takes on a decisively political inflexion that was absent in previous readings, all the while conserving its positive ties that are amplified by the theory of the sign as effect. The sign remains a physical event but is produced in a social system that it acts upon in return. The Nietzschean reading of art as symptomatology, which fleshed out the notion of experimentation, also receives a political function: the artist, "the doctor of civilization," is not only the expert who diagnoses the pathologies of civilization. He/she becomes the agent that causes new constellations of force and symptoms of types of life that culture is able to make appear; she critiques actual conditions and is an agent for transformation. The work of art, in its aesthetic function (the kind of sensation that it reveals), takes on an immediate critical value, because it transforms taste, but above all because it is directly inscribed into customs and modulates a real relation between the work and the social body, which simultaneously transforms the space of its reception and contributes to changing the status and position of the artist. In accordance with Simondonian modulation, the relations between the creator and her work, between the work and the public, and between the artist and the social body, must be understood as fields of individuation that produce individuals. The work of art and the artist, as well, are such individuals. The critical value of art no longer restricts writing to thought, or work to intention. Art is opened onto impersonal life, the intensive potential of pre-individual singularities that traverse the social, metastable field of individuation that serves as a milieu for its crystallization. The author becomes a social figure who is impersonal and collective. The opening of art onto its social and political dimensions is a direct consequence of the analyses of Nietzsche, but Deleuze, with the help of Guattari, draws conclusions from these analyses that were not possible in 1962. This connection to politics turns the political philosophy of culture into the touchstone of art; it transforms Deleuze's vitalism and focuses it squarely on social critique.

Secondly, the fight against interpretation, the status of art as experimentation, and symptomatology as a modulation of social forces push Deleuze to systematize the relationship between art, the unconscious, and vital norms, which is already implied by the term "doctor of civilization." Deleuze investigates the life of norms in culture, in their normal aspects, but especially in their pathological aspects, in accordance with the Nietzschean reading of sickness and health that was proposed by Canguilhem. The massive intrusion of "madness"—perversion, but especially psychosis and schizophrenia—applies to this examination of the life of norms, which are evaluated with respect to their external borders and margins: within marginality and the minor is a theory of variation that shapes the philosophy of art and formulates the life of culture. This interest, which was already present in his works, but that is connected to a critique of interpretation, leads Deleuze, with the help of Guattari, to get free of the operating framework of psychoanalysis that strongly influenced his previous works: the principle of Freudian pleasure, Kleinian partial objects, and the Lacanian signifier, and object = x of the unconscious and symbolic "outside," which played an important role in the passive syntheses from *Difference and Repetition* and *The Logic of Sense*. The critique of psychoanalysis as a technique and doctrine, and the rejection of the signifier, were related to the critique of interpretation and logically tied it to the rejection of formal symbolism in structural systems. This critique of psychoanalysis that is maintained from the first collaborative works with Guattari, slowly develop from 1970 to 1975 until a definitive position is established with the publication of *Kafka*. From this text onward, the status of interpretation, the signifier, and psychoanalysis is settled: it again becomes the object of radical critique in 1980 with *A Thousand Plateaus*, and then disappears as a theoretical concern. These four factors—the critique of interpretation, experimentation, symptomatology, and the critique of the signifier—contribute to the designation of a semiotics that is no longer linguistic. With the matter of semiotics settled, Deleuze no longer needs these controversial topics to support his analysis.

Guattari and the critique of psychoanalysis

Deleuze says this often: it is Guattari, who was a therapist, who was faithful to his psychotherapeutic engagement with schizophrenics at the La Borde clinic his entire life, who made it possible for Deleuze to distance himself from psychoanalysis.[1] It is important that we not become mistaken about his departure from psychoanalysis; this break implies a reevaluation of the relationship between thought and its pragmatic dimension. The relationship between thought and life that Deleuze, via Nietzsche, had always considered to be essential takes on a social dimension: life is not just nonorganic power, but creates political reality that is endowed with empirical history. This new tendency transforms the status of philosophy and art, which is marked by the appearance of a theme involving desire and power. Guattari's materialist psychiatry completely reorients Deleuze's clinical criticism and injects a problematic concerning the politics of domination into the heart of the theory; he does so at a point where theory and practice are forced to communicate, and where the question of art is further elaborated. Deleuze soberly recounts the situation in July of 1972 at the "Nietzsche Today?" symposium. When an interviewer asks Deleuze how he reconciles his contributions to Nietzschean thought with *The Logic of Sense*, which are fraught with new concepts that arise out of his meeting Guattari, he responds, "I changed. The opposition of surface-depth no longer concerns me. What interests me now are the relations between a full body, a body without organs, and the running flows."[2]

With Guattari's influence, the signifier and structure, the system of psychoanalytic interpretation, and the personal unconscious continue to be the objects of a critique that run through *Anti-Oedipus* and *A Thousand Plateaus*. The machine replaces the signifier, and experimentation replaces interpretation. From *Kafka* onward, the status of the signifier and that of psychoanalysis as an interpretive technique are considered together: interpretation is definitively cast aside since it replaces manifest sense with latent sense and aims to replace sense. Psychoanalysis serves as an object of radical critique in *A Thousand Plateaus* in 1980, and then it disappears as a theoretical concern.

We can systematize the phases of Deleuze's connection to psychoanalysis: up until the second edition of *Proust* in 1970 psychoanalysis is present and reinforces Deleuze's plans to articulate thought as a pre-individual, impersonal power that is irreducible to a subject or personality. From *Difference and Repetition* to *The Logic of Sense* there are great analyses devoted to the Freudian unconscious, a critique of the subject in Lacan, and Melanie Klein's theory of partial objects that is used in the development of the body without organs. In 1967, when asked to reflect on the question, "What Is Called Structuralism?," Deleuze analyzes the Lacanian signifier, which attests to the proximity of Lacan's thought to his own, where the signifier is defined in a serial mode as a differenciator allowing the introduction of an impersonal singularity, a transcendental without a subject. *Coldness and Cruelty* confronts psychoanalysis with a conciliatory and corrective stance, which confirms psychoanalysis' position as a provocative interlocutor for Deleuze. Up until the second edition of *Proust* in 1970 Deleuze uses psychoanalytic categories in order to revise his theory of subjective syntheses. Psychoanalysis, as an unmistakable reference for thought, loses its influence as soon as Deleuze becomes interested in social life alongside Guattari.

A second period of active critique gets under way when Deleuze levels a charge against psychoanalysis and develops a theory of productive desire once he meets Guattari. Deleuze engages psychoanalysis only when it is a minor discourse in culture. As soon as it attains a major position, as is the case after May 1968, its status changes. The rejection of interpretive practice and the signifier becomes a theoretical position of ultimate importance. This happens with the partial liberation of moral customs after 1968, and above all, with its acquisition of the hegemonic position within a discourse that designated it as the dominant theory. Thus from *Anti-Oedipus* to *Dialogues*, from 1972 to 1977, psychoanalysis serves as a theoretical adversary and is still treated as an interlocutor.

But after the publication of *A Thousand Plateaus*, the interest in psychoanalysis plummets and the relevance of desire and sexuality fall along with it. Once the theoretical plan for *A Thousand Plateaus* is set out, and once it perfects its attack on the structural methods of the social sciences, psychoanalysis becomes no more than an outmoded, dogmatic, and localized position. Deleuze decides that he is finished with it. At the same time that he loses interest in psychoanalysis, he also loses interest in sexuality, which, in its own way, is too dependent on a personal theory of the subject, so he turns away from the study of desire in favor of a physics of affects. When Arnaud Villani asks Deleuze in 1980 if thought is related to sexuality, he replies, "This would be true up to *The Logic of Sense*, where there is still a notable relation between sexuality and metaphysics. Afterward, it seemed to look more like a poorly founded abstraction to me." A little later he states, "Our last text on psychoanalysis (with Guattari) is about the Wolf Man in *A Thousand Plateaus*."[3] We can draw a parallel between this trajectory and that of Foucault, who is also invested in demonstrating that sexuality and social repression are poorly grounded abstractions in *The History of Sexuality*.

From interpretation to transversality

Between the first (1964) and second (1970) phases of his study on *Proust*, Deleuze systematically develops a critique of interpretation and attains his definitive stance with *Kafka*. The second edition of *Proust* introduces an intermediary step: Deleuze keeps the term "interpretation" here and there, but transforms the doctrine by dressing the new theory of machinic functioning in semantic clothes (interpretation), which he tears apart. The analysis in the first edition of *Proust* is always situated on the plane of systematized ideas, on a plane of pure deduction, with an internal logic. It is clear that Deleuze maintains what he said in 1964: "what forces thought is the sign," the necessity of which is guaranteed by the contingent, empirical encounter at the same time that it realizes "the genesis of the act of thinking within thought itself," but this genesis was defined as interpretation and the development of the sign. Deleuze completely rethinks this relationship between art and thought within the medium of pure thought in light of Simondon's theory of modulation, using the clinical analysis of relations between thought and corporeality initiated by the body without organs in *The Logic of Sense*. The first important break concerns the status of interpretation, which Deleuze accepted as a term, though not a principle, in his first works on Nietzsche and Proust, and which he violently opposes as a term and method from 1972 onward. In 1964 he wrote,

> To think is always to interpret—to explain, to develop, to decode, to translate a sign.

In 1970, he replies,

> To interpret has no unity other than the transversal.[4]

This is the first occurrence of the transversality that Guattari had been developing on his own since 1965, and which Deleuze welcomes in 1970: "Previously, we saw the importance of a *transversal dimension* in the most diverse directions within Proust's work: transversality," and he explains by noting: "In connection to his psychoanalytic research, Félix Guattari formed the very rich concept of 'transversality' to account for the communications and relations of the unconscious."[5] The appearance of this transversal dimension subverts the status of analytic theory first, but then Deleuze uses it liberally to elucidate what he calls "the formal structure of the work of art," putting literary critique and institutional psychotherapy into conversation at the intersection of critique and clinical psychology, which becomes a familiar technique from then on.[6] Nonetheless, in the 1970 text, he claims that interpretation is "transversal."

In 1975, Deleuze goes even further in *Kafka* in his collaboration with Guattari. The book opens up with a stated rejection of interpretation and a new principle, "the principle of multiple entries," which develops the previous "transversal unity," and is charged with a direct polemical task: it is destined to "prevent [. . .] attempts to interpret a work that is only open to experimentation."[7] In this case, experimentation not only replaces interpretation, it eradicates it.

Transversality means substituting the vertical model of pyramidal hierarchy with its horizontal corollary of ordinate connections, a new kind of acentered system, which marks the first formulation of the notion of the rhizome. We see at what point a convergence is established between the body without organs and transversality. In both cases an intensive model that resists ordered integration according to external means or internal principles affirms the priority of relations over structures, and becomings over identities. For Guattari, transversality connects the critique of the ego in psychoanalysis to the political rejection of authoritative group practices in terms of the sociology of power. At base, transversality is a militant concept that is hostile to the reification of power relations within leftist groups. By opposing groups that are centralized, thirsty for domination, and who privilege vertical relations and horizontal organization to small acentered groups that function according to a rhizomatic model of transversality, Guattari sets up a model that already contains the opposition between stratified organization and the body without organs. The political concept of transversality in Guattari serves to distinguish two modalities of the group: "subject-groups" that ward off hierarchies and look for a creative way to produce an apersonal subjectivity, and "subjected-groups" that are characterized by their pyramidal organization and their centralized structure.[8] This distinction operates in the critique of political organizations and in the psychotherapeutic examination of social structures.

In the second edition of *Proust*, Deleuze applies transversality to a totally new domain: literary critique. Here, Deleuze does not bother to explain how a critique of power and organization can apply to the literary conception of the work in its totality, or on what grounds the rejection of centralized and unifying power that produces hierarchical organization can show itself to be fecund in matters of literary critique, as will be the case with the concept of minor literature. Nonetheless, we see how he methodologically transfers transversality to literary critique. Literature becomes the field of political, social, and psychotherapeutic plights. If the artist is a doctor of culture, then elements within a political critique of the psychopathology of the social are applicable to literary works. The challenge posed by institutional psychotherapy consists in placing the unconscious in the political, in associating therapy of the ego with critiques of social conditions, which are considered triggers for individual psychopathologies. Initially, transferring the political dimension to literary critique allows pyramidal hierarchy to be confronted by a complex of trajectories and wandering lines *à la* Deligny, an acentered network that does not match up with a predetermined structure of the work and ceases to return to an organic totality. Transversality thus determines linguistics and pragmatic literary critique.

> The new linguistic convention, the formal structure of the work, is thus transversality.[9]

The theoretical benefits of transversality can be seen in *Kafka*. The initial critique is not indifferent or arbitrary to sense, but is aleatory and remarkable for the reading experience. Transversality goes further than simply putting the structural hierarchy of a work into question. An entire pragmatic theory of reading is implied in this movement from the beautiful totality to the disjointed fragment, and Deleuze and Guattari provide a demonstration of this on the first page before making a theoretical statement about it in *Rhizome*. The entry into the book is fragmentary: it necessarily takes up an arbitrary spot in the book, a nondetermined point of *entry*. "We will thus enter at any point [. . .] no entrance has privilege," since there is no longer a totality hierarchizing the directions of the book, nor is there a predetermined ordering of its sections. At best, the entry will be shown to be, "we can hope, in connection with other things to come."[10] The organic beginning and hierarchical totality of the work is replaced with a kinetic entry that takes account of the reading, and is materially understood as an action that carves a path in a burrow that opens up a unique gallery. Not all readings are valuable, or have the same circulatory density, but each one transforms the work.

> We will only look at which other points are connected to our entry point, what crossroads and galleries we pass through in order to connect two points, what the map of the rhizome is, and how it would immediately be modified if we were to enter at another point.[11]

By demanding an entrance, the work produces an effect; in this sense it "walks," its function belongs to its material instead of being confined to the metadiscursive plane of commentary. Such an entrance is necessarily fragmentary, since it calls for the act of reading as an effective introduction, which is a real intrusion. The act of reading clears a path, which conveys contingency less than it does its operational action. This is shown in the first few sentences of *Kafka*, which describe the work as a burrow or rhizome: "How do we enter into Kafka's work? It's a rhizome, a burrow." The work creates a residential area that constructs a space for circulation, as well as a reservation (a burrow), and a nourishing network (a rhizome, which stretches its roots in predefined directions, through iterations). The critical application furnishes the burrow with circulation, an entrance into the rhizome—a kind of wandering that allows the work to function. The connections within the work depend on a survey of real territories: this is where we find the cartography that defines the rhizome and enables critical activity to be outlined.

> What a strange twist the line took in 1968, the line with a thousand aberrations! From this we get the triple definition of writing: to write is to fight, to resist; to write is to become; to write is to draw maps, "I am a cartographer!"[12]

It does not matter where the entrance is; it modulates with the path of writing. Reading differs from an interpretation that seeks to find the latent or available sense, because it is a real act of intrusion ("entering into the burrow") that affirms the living character of the work and the nurturing, residential network; reciprocally, it affirms the necessity of putting the text to use. As a theory of reading, the rhizome takes the act of reading into account and turns reception into a productive act, a veritable transformation that captures the work.

Movement on the grounds of life, with the concepts of the rhizome and of capture, demarcates the relationship between transversality and ethology, allowing us to expose the triple ramification of transversality: starting with Guattari's critique of power as it applies to the therapeutic institution, it crosses over into theory—a theory about the connection of theoretical and practical fragments (Foucault and Guattari), that Deleuze names the theory-practice of multiplicities. This theory-practice launches into an ethology of vital movements, which Deleuze finds in Proust, with the transversal theory of homosexuality that he connects to the theory of haecceities, speeds, and slownesses, which then crosses over into a philosophy of art and the capture of forces.

Critique discloses the vital cartography that is inscribed in ethology in the ordinary sense of an *ethos* of animal habitation. The status of the complex and "alloplastic" habitation—an excorporeal production—of the molded burrow outside the body, which is nutritive and endoplastic for the circulatory rhizome, will be determined in *Rhizome*.[13] Its polemical value is made tacitly clear. Just as he did in 1970, in 1975 Deleuze opens up the possibility of a transversal interpretation of a fragmentary, incomplete work. The fragmentary ontology of the work employs a method that is able to account for the plurality of the work, as well as the pragmatics of reading it. The principle of multiple entries, which is loaded with polemical force, now seeks to preclude any interpretation that "blocks" paths within the work.

> The principle of multiple entries prevents the entry of the enemy alone, the Signifier, and the attempts to interpret a work that is only open to experimentation.[14]

Experimentation, which replaces interpretation, concerns the plural cartography of paths as much as it concerns the forces that the work or art extracts from the social field, or symptomatology. This transversal, then, rejects the typical separation of art from life, or the work of art from its interpretation. From this point on, Deleuze rejects the word "interpretation," rejecting the name of the signifier (he will not waver on this point). This is one of the clearest positions that distinguishes *Difference and Repetition* from *Kafka*, and it highlights his encounter with Guattari and their critique of psychoanalysis. The second edition of *Proust* introduces the literary machine as a mode of textual operation, which is evidenced when he uses this fashionable new critique on the works of Joyce and Lowry.[15] His new critique is shown to be a bit vague with respect to the precise consistency of this machine, this undetermined *thing*.[16] Each reading contributes to the functioning of the work, and there are as many possible readings as there are paths, and each reading contributes to the function of cartography and recognition inside the territory. From here we get the principles of reading that serve as the introduction of *A Thousand Plateaus*, and the systematization of the rhizomatic theory that is so hostile to interpretation.

From transversal machine to literary machine

Deleuze goes outside the psychoanalytic framework by transforming the unconscious and by critiquing the signifier: in accordance with Guattari's theory of the machine, he distributes the unconscious throughout the social field. There is a critical and offbeat renewal of Freudo-Marxism, which is sensed in the coupling of an analysis of desire and the plight of emancipation, but since it goes along with an official critique of psychoanalysis, it is the political aspect of desire that prevails. So, interpretation is rejected in favor of a theory of reading that emphasizes the political purpose of art. *Kafka* forcefully determines this new theoretical program. Art becomes political and experimental when it ceases to emerge from an interpretation that refers aesthetics to the psychological dimension, which involves phantasm (the imaginary) or discursion (the symbolic). Art refers to the transpersonal and the social body. The machine is in solidarity with politics and experimentation; a real art process chases away its imaginary or symbolic effect, whether phantasmal or structural.

The program of substituting experimentation for interpretation in art can be explained as follows: writing is not autotelic and does not refer to the individual writer; art, as a productive activity, fills the social body with an experimental process that produces (that "machinates") political effects. Neither the individual psychological dimension of the imaginary phantasm open to interpretation, nor the structural dimension of the signifying, symbolic dispositif are capable of producing the effects that only art can produce: we started with the subjective effect of aesthetics and later arrived at a critique that turns art into a procedure enacted upon social customs.

Guattari develops the concept of the machine as a methodological complement to the concept of structure that is put to work in *Difference and Repetition* and *The Logic of Sense*, which gives it a pragmatic effectiveness that is politically oriented and in accordance with his militant activity.[17] Deleuze ascribes particular importance to this text, where "the same principle of a *machine* that frees itself from the structural hypothesis and is detached from structural ties" in order to point out the flaw of the concept of structure: its abstract formalism. Guattari combines the symbolic articulation of structure with a historical type of machine that is at once social and political, which he borrows from the history of techniques. But he immediately reorients this history in the sense of a social machine—an assemblage accumulating a technological state of the instrument of production and Marxist relations of production, understood as a pragmatic assemblage of production that a given society uses to mold its subjects. Guattari's machine thus recasts discursive formations as nondiscursive formations, and the technological segments are connected to types of social subjectification (relations of production and working conditions).

Both a Marxist and a therapist, Guattari is interested in the relations of production that introduce certain kinds of unconscious subjectification. The unconscious is thus thought according to the model of the machine of social production, and not the model of ideal symbolic structure. In this case, there is an objective confluence between Guattari's machine and Foucault's concept of a "dispositif" from *Discipline and Punish*, published in 1975: a dispositif, like a prison, is "machinic," social and technical at the same time, and a machine is always social before becoming technical. That which is machinic reveals that relations of production, whose technological form is always determined by a certain social state of forces of production, the relations of production and bodies of knowledge, produce effects on the subjects that are subjected to them. Marx did not say anything to the contrary, but Guattari goes further: a social machine produces all kinds of unconscious subjectifications, and what it produces above all are subjects who are determined, first, by the collective and productive unconscious. He aligns with Foucault on this point, for whom the social dispositif also produces subjects, but Guattari breaks away from him in pursuit of a Marxist analysis combined with a Freudian reading that is closer to Lacan than it is to Reich. When Deleuze embraces the concept of the machine for the first time, he remains unfazed by its social context and applies it to Proust, transforming it into a concept of literary critique: the literary Machine in the second edition of *Proust* describes an artistic production that is, without a doubt, socio-historically determined (the *modern* work), but Deleuze does not spend much time on this aspect, and when he concretely describes the kind of function that Proust puts into practice, Deleuze uses psychoanalysis to embody different kinds of literary machines.

> [. . .] The search is a machine. The modern work of art is anything we want it to be [. . .] from the moment it works: the modern work of art is a machine and functions as such [. . .] To the *logos*, organ and organon whose sense must be discovered within the totality to which it belongs, is opposed an anti-logos, machine and machinery whose sense (whatever you would like) depends on its functioning, which is the functioning of its separate parts. The modern work of art does not have a problem of sense; it only has a problem of use.[18]

In this formulation, where sense becomes the object = x and the missing placeholder ("whatever you would like"), it is necessary to retain the pragmatic principle that it works! The theory of the machine takes over from the famous search for truth in 1964. A functionalist theory of the work that is reduced to its mode of operation and its immanent textual function takes the place of the interpretation of essence. Deleuze often goes back to the importance of Proust when discussing his functional theory that characterizes modern literature; namely, in his conversation with Foucault, "Intellectuals and Power."

> It is strange that this author, Proust, passes as a pure intellectual, who had clearly stated: treat my book like a pair of glasses directed to the outside, and if they don't work for you put on another pair, find your own instrument that is necessarily an instrument for combat. A theory is not totalizing; it is multiplied and multiplies.[19]

Indeed, Proust posits an analysis of style's aesthetic power (an operating mode of language) as a technical instrument, a kind of elevator, train, or airplane, as a means of phenomeno-technical communication in Bachelard's sense of the word, creating realities that would remain imperceptible without him, and that are consistent with the capture of forces.[20]

The desiring machine

The desiring machine results from a Lacanian analysis of the unconscious constitution of the subject, rethought through Marx. Guattari fully retains the positive status of psychosis from Lacan's teachings, not only its independence from neurotic repression, but also its superior ability to teach us about the unconscious syntheses in the constitution of the subject. Ever since his doctoral thesis in psychiatric medicine, Lacan demonstrates his interest in the group of psychoses, a limited, pathogenic phenomenon that illuminates the constitution of the subject. In 1953, Blanchot perfectly locates the innovative nature of his analysis: "Jacques Lacan, in his book on paranoia, does not see a defective phenomenon anywhere in psychosis."[21] Guattari combines a social critique with his Lacanian reevaluation of psychosis and his theory of the constitution of the subject via unconscious coding. His social critique is influenced by Marx and oriented toward a communist practice that allows him to connect real schizophrenia as the object of social repression. His professional engagement as a psychotherapist at the La Borde clinic forces him to think about the epistemology of clinical nosology while also considering the mode of social production regarding the madman. Guattari constantly describes schizophrenia as a process that is hostile to the Oedipal social model (capitalism) and psychotic collapse, the patient's reaction to the social dispositif that constrains her. Beginning in 1965, he applies a Marxian analysis to his clinical theory and his institutional practice of care. The critiques of the institutional clinic and the social status of the madman are inexorably linked to the process of social normalization that drives the medical clinic without its realizing it.

This prolonged engagement with Marx explains the convergence between Foucault and Guattari, which takes pretty different approaches: Foucault assumes an epistemology of reason that comes from Canguilhem, in *Madness and Civilization* and *The Birth of the Clinic*; Guattari's critique concerns existing insane asylums, arising from his therapeutic practice. Scientific order cannot be dissociated from a strategy of social domination, and thus a theory can only conquer its positivity by returning to its material and social conditions of production (something that psychiatry and psychoanalysis refrain from doing, according to Guattari). Intellectual plights are added to revolutionary plights, which is something that Guattari inherits from *La Voie communiste*: it is not enough to interpret but one must transform existing structures. This double motif of therapy and politics transforms the status of schizophrenia. Just like Lacan, psychosis is more important than neurosis for Guattari. But this is because mental alienation becomes an acute manifestation of social alienation, and schizophrenia is resistant to the established order. Therapy affirms its political nature with institutional psychotherapy, and desire becomes a machine or social production that is impersonal, asubjective, and is not private energy.

Guattari also retains Lacan's idea that the subject is never given but always produced as a result of coding operations and division. Guattari substitutes the machine and its real, collective, social functioning for the coding signifier, as well as the introduction of a signifier that cuts the imaginary relationship between the mother and child in order to introduce the signifier as the subject in the symbolic order. Desire is thus always relative to the social, and it does not arise out of a private, personal, or individual dimension. It cannot be relegated to a mental register or unconscious representations, nor can it be conceived as libidinal energy that diffuses social stratifications. If desire exists, it belongs to a regime of production, on the material plane of actual relations of social production. For Guattari, desire is not hyletic flux itself, but in accordance with Lacan's theses, it is the assemblage of this flux, through coding and division: desire is a social production, and the produced subject is a remainder of this operation. Desire is thus constructed secondarily, and is a product. Far from injecting an angelic desire into the historical process (like Marcuse did), inversely, the social collective produces a desire that is never natural. There is no spontaneity, then, but a constructivism of desire, which is indicated in the very title "desiring machine": desire is not given, but constructed, assembled, and "machined" by a double operation of coding and division.

Instead of understanding coding as symbolic and division as signifying, as Lacan does, with the introduction of the major signifier, the symbolic Phallus, Guattari turns coding into machinic jargon that is unconscious and pragmatic, modeling it on Markov's codes, or genetic code, and he understands division as an effective operation, not a signifying act. The desiring machine thus receives the typical Lacanian function of the "operation of detachment of a signifier as differentiator," the division by which coding is produced.[22] Instead of understanding this coding as symbolic structure inscribed by the signifier, he uses Marx to think about it as social production. The machine that divides and codes is closer to a factory than a theatre. This coding takes on a historical thickness at the same time that it loses rationality, becoming a semi-aleatory and nonsignifying code, instead of being held to the Lacanian ideality of a symbolic structure. But what the machine loses in ideality, it gains in pragmatic efficacy: the desiring machine exposes the mode by which a social body produces a subject through coding and unconscious division, having been seized by a "Lacano-Marxist" development of a theory of "machinic assemblage," or a machinic production of subjectification.

The machine refutes any conception of the unconscious as being purely mental and private. We must avoid conceiving of the machine as a totality, and hypostasize its function of division. It is always connected, dependent on heterogeneous elements that it divides and its own temporality. By definition, it opens onto external elements that it connects and that it divides. Endowed with historicity, and susceptible to being taken by flows for a new machine in a disjunctive synthesis, it acts as a divider for whatever it is connected to, and as a flow for the force relations into which it is taken. Machine and flow are relative to the acts of division and coding. "Every machine is a machine of a machine."[23] The machine receives three main functions that allow it to be applied to desire: it is a divider of flows, it is a nonsignifying machinic coding, and it is social. It is not individual or subjective in the sense of personal subjectivity, but is collective, and in this sense, immediately political.

Guattari was ready to welcome the body without organs—which he willingly abbreviates in a Lacanian way as BwO—and intensive individuation since it continued the same process of de-subjectification on Marxist and Lacanian grounds.[24] He employs a double movement: he opposes the machine of real production to symbolic structure, and within social realities he distinguishes between productive realities (machines) and produced realities (structures). Next, he qualifies structures as oppressive and an "anti-productive" value to their resulting products. The libidinal reality of desire is classified among productive forces, whereas the family—a social form historically tied to property that is not simply considered an anti-productive outcome, but is still a structure of oppression—is not content with conditioning desire, but subjugating it with a form of social domination. Guattari, thus, transforms Lacanian psychoanalysis through Marx, and loads the body without organs with this new perspective. At the same time, he levels a critique of law and the signifier against Lacan: the signifier takes on an inscription that is historically determined and emerges out of despotic formations. It is the signifier's role as a marker of power—a consideration that is completely missing in Lacan's works—that will polarize every critique from that point on, serving as the driving force behind the critical works on psychoanalysis from *Anti-Oedipus* to *A Thousand Plateaus*.

The schizo versus Oedipus

The body without organs moves around the terrain of unconscious syntheses that occur alongside the dissolution of the subject that began in psychoanalysis, and then it serves as a critique of psychoanalysis. For the position of the unconscious remains blind with respect to its own sociopolitical constitution, and the Oedipal triangle marks the origins of the idealist turning point in psychoanalysis. Instead of opening the unconscious onto flows of desire put into place by determined, singular, social institutions, psychoanalysis imposes a coding of a historically determined society on the unconscious: the Vienna turning point of the century is erected as the natural position of the unconscious. Incapable of decoding social conditions that inform the production of the Viennese unconscious, psychoanalysis acts as if it were a matter of an ahistorical nature of the psyche, and provides an erudite representation of it with the well-informed support of Sophocles' plays. The argument is Marxian: the unconscious necessarily has a specific, atemporal nature in psychoanalysis because it was developed with a complete misunderstanding of its real conditions of production. The entire venture of *Anti-Oedipus* culminates in this critique of the Freudian unconscious, and schizophrenia, inspired by Artaud, becomes the *anti*-Oedipal combatant, the central polemical part of a book directed against the Oedipus complex as theorized by Freud, and against the status of the unconscious and interpretation in psychoanalysis.

The critique in *Anti-Oedipus* can be summarized in two theses: the unconscious does not function as a theatrical representation, where the parental figures are staged in a private manner, but is like a factory that really (not just in a phantasmal sense) produces social subjectifications. Delirium is not familial but historico-worldly: we become delirious politically and historically, not in a subjective, private way. "*Anti-Oedipus* is a break that is made all alone, according to two themes: the unconscious is not a theatre, but a factory, a production machine; the unconscious does not become delirious through daddy-mommy, it always becomes delirious through a social field."[25]

Artaud said it here:

> I don't believe in father
> or mother
> I have no
> papa-mama.[26]

The substitution of a factory for the theatre implies a turning point from representation toward production. Instead of a phantasmal scheme where the actors of a bourgeois play are shown as representations in front of a passive public in an unreal manner that is delineated by a fiction bordered by the footlights of the stage, the unconscious takes the form of a factory where desire is produced and formed, transforming nonformed flows into objects of consumption. By substituting real production for imaginary representation, the regime of the unconscious is transformed, which ceases to be expressive or representative of productive becoming and is put into the totality of the social field, rather than the family members. By diluting the representational forms of the family drama, desire extends into all of the historical diversity on the social field: this is what is implied by the term "desiring machine."

Foucault was right to emphasize the innovative and radical character of this critique of psychoanalysis: instead of proceeding in the name of a traditional conception of the sovereign subject, as was still the case with Sartre, Deleuze and Guattari radicalize the unconscious and dissolve the subject in the name of political protest aimed at analysis. Oedipus becomes the consequence of social repression, the form which psychoanalysis "interprets," taking down the productions of the unconscious through predefined social codes. Thus, as Foucault remarks,

> Oedipus would not be a truth of nature, but an instrument of limitation and constraint that psychoanalysts since Freud use to contain desire and forcing it into a familial structure that is defined by our society at a determinate moment. In other words, Oedipus, according to Deleuze and Guattari, is not the secret content of our unconscious, but the form of constraint that psychoanalysis tries to impose on our desire and our unconscious in the course of treatment. Oedipus is an instrument of power.[27]

This is why psychotic delirium bears on the names in history and not on the personal history of the subject, her familial whim, or the theatre of Oedipus. If the unconscious ceases to be a private theatre, a personal affliction of social coding, then delirium no longer finds its depth in an individual origin, but flees instead, like a liquid pouring, seeping, and spilling into the entire social field. Starting with *Psychoanalysis and Transversality*, Guattari affirms that the subject is historical, political, and machinic, and he reproaches analysis for "systematically erasing" the sociopolitical contents of the unconscious. Delirium does not bear on the name of the father, which is a complex of the Freudian Oedipus and the major signifier in Lacan, but it bears on "all the names in history."[28] The expression echoes the declaration that Nietzsche made when writing to Burckhardt at the time of his collapse: "What is unpleasant and impedes my modesty, is that at base all the names in history are me."[29] We would be sorely mistaken, says Klossowski, if we were to reckon that the Nietzsche-ego that is expressed in these letters, the former professor of philology in Basil, had gone mad. Nietzsche carries out the real experience of the dissolution of the self, and if he takes himself for Jesus Christ or Caesar, the antichrist or Borgia, it does not mean that he is inaccurately identifying himself with these other people, but he is actually running through the zones of intensity that he lifts from history.

In reality, Nietzsche does not usurp these foreign identities, but he experiences that an identity is always fortuitous and collective, and corresponds to a social zone of intensity, not a defined personality. "The subject spreads out across the perimeter of the circle where the ego has left the center." Deprived of a fictive center of the Nietzsche-ego, the impersonal, dislocated Nietzschean subject spills out into known history and passes through a series of states circulating around it.[30]

These two theses of the real factory-unconscious production, and the historico-worldly, nonprivate delirium are enough to destroy Oedipus. It is not true that the unconscious naturally produces members of the family, and if the familial triangulation is definitely operative within families, it is a result of a social desiring machine coding the unconscious in a determined way, that of the European bourgeoisie. Oedipus is not an essence of the unconscious, but a social coding that sets out "to domesticate the genealogical matter and form that escape it from all sides."[31]

The machine versus the signifier

With *Kafka*, a new technique for reading, the use of literary texts, and the practice of collaborative writing, Deleuze and Guattari take a strong position with regard to literary critique. Minor literature defines text as a machine, and this polemical concept results in the joyous affirmation of a new use for art.

> We only believe in a Kafka *politics*, which is neither imaginary nor symbolic. We only believe in one or more Kafka *machines*, which have neither structure nor phantasm. We only believe in Kafka *experimentation*, without interpretation or significance, but only processes of experience.[32]

The machine replaces models of symbolic structure or imaginary phantasm and dismisses structural models, and the formal style that is inspired by linguistics and psychoanalytic interpretation—the models that dominated literary critique during the 1970s. The machine replaces interpretation with a principle of experimentation and connection that has immediate political ramifications that are neither imaginary, private, and individual, nor symbolically ideal and formal. Ever since 1969, Guattari demonstrated that the machine, which is connected, open, and productive of real effects, should replace structure in studies of unconscious productions.[33] The machine takes over the function of the symbolic signifier in Lacan and produces the subject as a remainder of its operation, but this production must be conceived in Marxian terms that are historical and social, rather than signifying and private.

The concept of the machine that appears in *Anti-Oedipus*, *Kafka*, and *A Thousand Plateaus* owes a lot to Guattari, who developed the concept as an antidote to structure, starting in 1965. The machine posits its vital, mechanistic, and concrete features against structure: it is not signifying and self-regulated but historical and open to the outside. It is not ideal, but pragmatic, producing real effects; it should not be confused with a kind of mechanism that would reduce it to a technical machine, because a technical machine is always integrated into a social machine, a dispositif of power, and is an assemblage of training, research, and commercialization. Hence, the machine is not mechanical, but is operative and functionalist, and is determined by its Lacanian properties of coding and division. A machine can be understood as an operation acting upon flux: the machine codes flux by dividing it, and divides it by coding it. These two functions of coding and dividing, which are completely reversible, are effective properties that ensure the distinction between machine and flow: the machine is flux put into a form, and every machine is seen as flux for another machine.

This enables Deleuze and Guattari to define a machine as social and productive of social subjects, replacing psychoanalysis, which is too focused on the individual subject and a family model that was determined by a specific social condition—Freud's capitalist and bourgeois Vienna. Instead, we have a functionalist model of production of sense that is not attributable to a subject, and is immediately political in nature. This determination of the machine is applied to the literary machine.

A principle of external functioning replaces the internal signification of the text: "a book only exists from the outside and on the outside."[34] We must stop attributing a book to an author, to a personal subject, and consider it a textual machine, a material dispositif that correlates linguistic signs with other sign systems, which are discursive and nondiscursive, with social states, regimes of power, and of varying speeds. This new status of the book as a "machinic assemblage" requires that other heterogeneous discourses be used in connection to literature, namely, philosophy, as well as other heterogeneous sign systems. This is why Deleuze and Guattari refuse to allow the text to be closed, autotelic, and autonomous to literature. Literary expression opens onto social exteriority, so that the goal of literature "is the movement of life within language."[35] Writing turns into becoming that amounts to a true transformation and metamorphosis. It is not redundant, and it does not return to a self that has no existence: "to write is to become, but this is not at all becoming a writer": "writing isn't its own end, precisely because life is not something personal."[36]

In reading, just as in writing, experimentation replaces interpretation. A book does not have an inside, an internal signifying structure, but functions through external processes and connections in a machinic way. Looking to Bachelard's epistemology, and not his poetics of imagination, Deleuze adopts the idea that theoretical facts must be materialized through a phenomenological method, and he applies this idea to literature by replacing phenomena, which are too subjective, with Nietzschean complexes of forces and materials that are diffused throughout the entire social body, taking on the consistency of determined processes in whatever work they inform.

Consequently, literature is defined by its external functioning, and this machinic functioning is not reducible to the imaginary—namely, the phantasm of the author that is conjured by the reader's private unconscious—nor is it reducible to the symbolic, which is an unconscious collective structure that rigidly imposes a formal transcendent code onto the text. Deleuze wants to hold fast to what is suggested by Foucault's innovative method in *The Archaeology of Knowledge*: the real function of the text produces a singular machine through its mode of operation where it is only a question of locating the effects. Literature renders sensible previously unknown, unmarked, invisible forces that work on societies and produce effects of subjectification (the desiring machines from *Anti-Oedipus*). But this critical function arises out of a clinical sensibility of real forces, such that art must be defined as a capture of forces.

The practice of capture specifically helps define the function of two-handed writing, which Deleuze and Guattari invent and whose method is formalized in *Rhizome* (1976), where they also explain their use of literature. The practice of capture comes from Proust and his analysis of homosexuality, which draws an analogy to the mimetic symbiosis of wasps and orchids and conveys a vital plane of reproduction without filiation, opening up the possibility for a general theory of art and life as becoming, not imitation. This theory of capture works both to describe what happens between Deleuze and Guattari and to define the literary effect as a movement of life. It sets up a neighborhood without imitation or resemblance, but as a collision of two deterritorialized, heterogeneous series that are pulled into a becoming that transforms them without assimilating them to one another.

> Becoming is not about attaining a form (identification, imitation, Mimesis), but finding a zone of proximity, indiscernibility, or indifferenciation such that we

can no longer be distinguished from *a* woman, *an* animal, or *a* molecule [. . .].
We can establish a zone of proximity with whatever we want, provided that it is
created by literary means [. . .].[37]

Literature, then, creates methods to explore a complex of forces, endowing it with
clinical role, which Deleuze illuminated in his previous texts. With Proust and
homosexuality, Sacher-Masoch and masochism, and Klossowski and perversion,
literature is established as an auxiliary for medicine and symptomatology,
creating diagnoses in terms of forces and social subjectification. The effects of
clinical marginalization, which is the first feature of the minor, turn literature into
an exploration of margins. From the artist-clinician (Proust, Sacher-Masoch)
to the schizophrenic artist (Artaud), then to the animal explorer (Kafka),
Deleuze moves away from modes of subjectification that are still connected
to psychology—normativity and sexual anomaly that is still focused on the
subject marked by psychoanalysis—to modes of impersonal subjectification that
capture social affects, as we see with Artaud and capitalism, as well as Kafka and
bureaucracy. Literature is experimental in the sense that it captures clinical force
relations and employs its critical function by rendering them sensible. The three
traits of the critical, the clinical, and impersonal becoming are necessarily in
solidarity with one another. They are the ones that engage the literary machine,
making it immediately political.

Minor Art

The concept of the minor is no longer understood as art that is said to be minor, marginal, popular, or industrial, as opposed to exceptional art that enjoys extraordinary success, but is an exercise in minority and minoration (even amputation, as we see in *Carmelo Bene*) that destabilizes the major norms of society. With Guattari, Deleuze develops the theory with regard to the works of Kafka in a book whose title also includes *Toward a Minor Literature*. Art is defined here by three relations of minoration, which concern the medium, the social body, and the subject-producer. The relation between medium, expressive material, and literary language determines a linguistic criterion for minority; the relation between the social body, the transmitter of assemblages that brings visibilities to the work and its receiver, defines a political criterion; and finally, the relation of the author, who must be forced into an exercise of depersonalization that is far removed from a transcendent subject or omniscient narrator, determines an asubjective criterion. These three linguistic, political, and asubjective criteria are delineated along an axis of intensive variation whose stake is immediately political, even if it is not activated in a dimension of actual social struggles. The politics of art is a politics of the work and not personal action.

> The three features of minor literature are the deterritorialization of language, the individual's connection to political immediacy, and the collective assemblage of enunciation.[1]

Minor literature is defined, at first, by its minor use of its medium, language, and is less concerned with the state of language than its use: "a minor literature is not from a minor language, but from a minority that literature makes within a major language." A correlation between political and asubjective criteria spills out of this minor treatment of signifying material: "everything is political," "everything takes on a collective value."[2] The three criteria are systematically linked and converge at the determination of art's political value.

With Guattari, Deleuze defines a "literary machine" that coheres stylistically and politically. In the aftermath of May 1968, "the literary machine takes over as a revolutionary machine," and the successful style arises out of its powerful protest against established social and literary structures.

Only minor literature is great—to hate all literature of masters.[3]

To think that the minor undermines or overthrows the major, even if this protest operates in the name of the oppressed and claims a literature for minorities, would still be a negative definition, which only inverts the hierarchy of major and minor art. The minor does not aspire to attain a major position, and the outcome of a subversion of codes or the minor's relative position would not be sufficient for creativity. It is positively defined as a variation of language and a transformation of the author-function, which allows a new definition of enunciation and style. "This is to say that the minor does not apply to specific works of literature, but the revolutionary conditions of all literature at that heart of what we consider to be great."[4] The minor is supported by the existence of the major just as the body without organs requires an organism, but as a kind of tensor that describes the effects of protesting major norms, whether linguistic, stylistic, or social. The minor and major are obviously not states or essences, but variations that initiate a becoming that causes a norm to meet up with an anomic variation, or an intensive transformation. As such, defining literature as a minor practice anticipates the concept of continuous variation that Deleuze continues to employ in his analysis of art as a capture of forces in *A Thousand Plateaus*.

Minor language and the line of flight

At first, minority refers to a situation in language. For Kafka, it corresponds to a real impasse evidenced by the speaking subject in Prague at the beginning of the twentieth century, which was the capital of the Bohemian monarchy, inserted into the Austro-Hungarian Empire, marking an impasse that determines a kind of blockage. But in accordance with Spinoza's theory of evil, the apparent privation is actually a positive determination. This blockage is not a lack, but a configuration that produces a line of flight, opening up another path and inventing a new resource. For Kafka it is, above all, a matter of triple impossibility: the impossibility of not writing, connected to the impossibility of writing in

German, and the impossibility of writing any other way. "They lived between three impossibilities (that I will arbitrarily call language impossibilities for the sake of simplicity, because I could call them something else): the impossibility of not writing, the impossibility of writing in German, and the impossibility of writing any other way, to which I'm tempted to add a fourth impossibility, the impossibility of writing," Kafka writes to Max Brod.[5] These impossibilities correspond to the speaker's situation, to her representation of the literary field and diagram of forces where he/she is situated and which determine a line of flight that is relative to the real pressures to which he/she is subjected. This line of flight becomes a stylistic criterion, detailing the political situation (Kafka is the author who experiments with the bureaucratic machine in which he participates) and the linguistic situation (his position as a speaker requires Kafka to use German like a foreign language).

The German language in Prague involves a pragmatic situation characterized by deterritorialization: it must simply be understood as an expansion of a national idiom outside its territorial borders. The German language is exported to the East as a process of subjection that is as much political as it is cultural, and Prague lacks a major language. Czech is an available language for speaking, but not for literature in the sense that Kafka and his Germanophile background understand it. The deterritorialized German in Bohemia is minor, at the same time that Czech is in a minority position vis-à-vis the dominant German language. Minority is less about the political subjection of Bohemia with respect to the empire than it is the reciprocal foreignness of the German citizen as much as the Czech citizen, and then put into a situation of political contiguity that renders them indiscernible in Bohemia.

We will pick up on the distinctions that Henri Gobard makes between the *vernacular* language of the Pragueans (a native language that is private, spoken, and familial) and Czech, which is mixed with Yiddish, even though Kafka is a German-speaker. Deleuze is interested in these distinctions because they offer a multifunctional analysis of language.[6] His father is Judeo-Czech but raises the children in the language of his social aspirations, German, which he speaks with difficulty. Kafka evokes "this German that we learned from our non-German mothers."[7] The *vehicular* language of commerce and exchange in the Austro-Hungarian Empire, which the adult Kafka uses in his professional interactions, is bureaucratic German. The *referential* language, the national and cultural reference of the Austro-Hungarian Empire, pertaining to literature and its symbolic production, is the German of Goethe, classical German, *Hochdeutch*;

to which Kafka adds yet another language, *mystical* language, which refers to the moment of Zionism and the birth of a spiritual earth, Hebrew.

So, if Kafka lacks a fitting language for his literary project and ignores the typical literary norm for the Czech literature of his time, it is because his pragmatic situation as a speaking subject includes too many languages: the apparent lack corresponds to an uncomfortable multilingualism, caused not by privation, but an accumulation of codes that are too disparate to accommodate one true major use that can break free from the rest. This impossibility is not a lack in the sense of an absence, but is a blockage that establishes a constraint, pushing the subject Franz Kafka to unleash a line of flight, which is related to his literary creation, but concerns the linguistic situation of Czech speakers just as much, for it creates a variation within major German. A stylistic line of flight is made possible by a linguistic line of flight.

The minor situation, then, connects creation to innovation, but connects innovation to creation through a blockage that renders a given situation strictly intolerable. Innovation is not attained by negating, misunderstanding, or escaping these particular sociopolitical conditions, because the line of flight is actually produced by the blockage. Paying attention to the historical conditions of the creation provides an entry point once and for all regarding Deleuze's works. The previous analyses of Proust, Sacher-Masoch, or Artaud were established on a plane of systematic unity for the work, without taking the relationship between the work and its real conditions of actuality into account. Minority forces us to leave the domain of pure thought and connect thought to its social conditions in practice, establishing this "connection of the individual to political immediacy," which opens the author-function onto a collective assemblage, and charges its practice of enunciation with a responsibility of active resistance, understood as an active critique.

Indeed, the theory of the line of flight precludes pinning political implications onto a representation of social conflicts. The line of flight substitutes an ethology of dynamic forces for Foucaultian resistance, which is conceived as a secondary response, and it also replaces a Marxian contradiction of force relations. An ethology of forces includes a vector of disorganization at the heart of the diagram of organized forces. According to Deleuze, the line of flight is immanent to other forces on the social field and is truly present in every determined assemblage: it does not arrive later and it is not produced by a subjective reaction to determined forces, but is truly given as a becoming that is actualizable or nonactualizable. In it virtual reality is active. The function of art consists in detecting and enhancing these lines of immanent force on the social field, not in representing them in a mode of the imagination, nor in being substituted by real struggles that affect it, but in literally making them function.

Creation is truly determined by the diagram of real forces, and not in a weak sense where literature would perceive and conform to lines of flight as its mission, as if lines of flight were already broken up as a revolutionary network in the real. This view involves a naive determinism that attempts to transform the flight into a future resolution out of contradictions in the present. The revolutionary mission of literature and cinema does not involve diagnosing preexistent lines, or imaginarily arranging them in an inoffensive space of fiction. These lines, which are truly immanent on the social field, only become revolutionary when literature actualizes them and causes them to function by decoding their movements. In itself, literature is this action that causes the social body to flee. But it rescues the body from impossibilities, not from outcomes, if there is an outcome, which comes from the actualization of a blockage, not its avoidance. Creation is thus produced through impossibility. "Creation must be talked about as running its course between impossibilities . . . it is Kafka who explained: the impossibility for a Jewish writer to speak German, the impossibility of speaking Czech, and the impossibility of not speaking at all."[8] Or yet again: "Creation takes place in bottlenecks." The creator is the one who is "strangled by a set of impossibilities."[9] One must mistrust a determinist approach that seems to fix the paradoxical condition of impossibility onto creation—which comes back again to a process of attributing the necessary space of creation to the causal fabric of the social, even if it is created in a void. Impossibility is created, and the blockage is the creator, not its effectuation.

> A creator is someone who creates her own impossibilities, and who creates from the possible at the same time.[10]

The creator is thus not the subject who identifies the outcome that is determined by the diagram of forces, but she who claims this diagram of forces and enacts, through this same process of claiming, a line of flight that exceeds the determined conditions of the blockage. In herself, the creator operates a differenciation. As concerns animal behavior, Ruyer distinguished the "right" line of an action regulated by a determinist causality that came closer and closer, along with the "geodesic" that was inflected by nonpreexistent tensors, as a function of the opposition he set up between physical causality and vital differentiation. The "geodesic animal," when the animal is removed from danger, is not causally determined, but creates a differentiation that is, according to Ruyer, a veritable creation.[11] The line of flight corresponds to this positive action, which consists less in resisting confrontation (taking flight) than in carrying it elsewhere, literally to "go on a tangent" and not just change one's position with respect to the diagram, but changing the diagram itself by actualizing virtual lines of flight that behave positively: "making the world flee, like we do when we drill a hole into a pipe."[12] Borrowing from the discipline of ethology doubles the socio-historical analysis of a new component, which makes the line of flight seem like a condition of creation, a nonconditioned becoming that operates through social causality. The relationship between social causality and creation undergoes a mutation. Art is endowed with the mission to make the social "flee." Breaking down the wall of signifier comes back to dismantling the regime of interpretation, bypassing organized multiplicities of major formations and moving toward their movements of actualization and their minor intensities.

The line of flight is not preexistent, but is produced as an intensive virtuality that actualizes the work of art's affect, so that minor literature expresses the assemblage while actualizing it, renders it visible, employing a function of exposition for the social, which always entails a struggle and a real complicity with power and money. The situation in literature is not different from that in architecture, or cinema, the art of the masses, or in industrial arts, which must first be created through social powers. The creative position causes the blockage to appear at the same time as its line of flight. Whatever is creative is an effectuation of a blockage, whose impossibility is not constituted by a privation or lacuna, but a positive excision that releases active modifications that are either linguistic or literary. In a very cautious way, Deleuze explains the relationship between art, lines of flight, and the social body.

> It is only possible to write, one might say, in an essential relation with lines of flight.[13]

In any case, art is not the keeper of a specific circuit of lines of flight in the sense that it would open up tracks for autonomous circulation that arise out of auxiliary detours or openings within the social body.

Minor linguistics

Minor literature is first defined by a minor use of language and is less concerned about the state of the language than the use that it makes of it.[14] Minority concerns the transformation that is imposed upon the major German language, the deterritorialized *Hochdeutsch* in Bohemia, which is pushed to a point of excellence by a Jewish Czech writer, is characterized by Deleuze and Guattari as a point of intense sobriety. This intense sobriety signals the situation where German is deported to Bohemia, or rather, the relationship between them, since it is necessary to be careful not to hypostasize one of the terms only to consider the reciprocal tension between a dominant, major use of the language, emphasized in normal use, and its intensive, minor variation. The deterritorialization of the language is applied to the situation of the German in Bohemia, which sounds Yiddish, Kafka says, who cannot even write the shortest sentence without the syllables running into one another and clattering under the pen, rendering Goethe's language unrecognizable. This linguistic situation of colonial mixing, conceived here on the grounds of political domination, enacts an epistemological reconstruction of linguistics and an intensive definition of style at the same time.

Deleuze and Guattari thus posit that language is made by minor variations, and there is not a stereotypical speaker actualizing the major, grammatical invariant, except to methodologically erect, in principle, a face of domination that is first a mark of social power (a social standard for proper use). They reject Chomsky's postulate by which "language could only be scientifically studied under the conditions of a major or standard language,"[15] because there are no "constants or universals of language" that would allow the language to be defined as a homogeneous system.[16] Just as Labov demonstrates when studying black-English idiolects in New York, even as they are circumscribed to a group of speakers at one site and one determined moment in time, the variations are too numerous to permit reintegration into a unitary system. Reducing these inconsistencies to an explanation given by other nonidentified systems is "a desperate expedient that eventually reduces the concept of system to an inconvenient fiction."[17] As soon as linguistics becomes sociolinguistics and is interested in the status of minor languages in various regional and social forms, languages worked on by complex social and political fractures—and they all are—the notion of system must be transformed, turning its constitutive dimension into variation. Deleuze thus shows that the internal postulate does not work for the analysis of language in specific situations. Linguistics can misrecognize these pragmatic and social conditions of existence. The deterritorialization of the minor creates the conditions for a definition of language as variation.

Now, every major definition of language depends upon a strong notion involving a consistency of grammar, without any variation. For Chomsky, for example, grammar and structure are equivalent, and grammar crosses his scientific threshold: the laws that it establishes must be capable of being validated by empirical observation, and it is endowed with a supplemental, axiomatic property so that the predictions of the body can be rigorously connected to the theory.[18] From here we get a very ambitious conception of grammar, which is conceived as a homogeneous or standard system that is described as a condition of abstraction and idealization that makes a scientific study possible.[19] In order to mar grammatical consequences so they become agrammatical, it is necessary to maintain a consistent standard that is a core matrix for correct performance. Chomsky's theory rests on an ambition to push grammar toward the formal purity of a generative structure, which requires an epistemology of invariance, and also claims that we can cleanly extract a consistent core of rules from real performances.

Under these conditions, grammar is never satisfied by being descriptive, posterior, or empirical, but instead becomes generative, capable of generating an indefinite number of grammatical statements that are correct and derived from syntactical structures. The invariant in structure is not opposed to change since the transformational rules are involved in predicting the variation of statements, but they are supposed to link the transform with its derived structure in a way that is fixed and constant. Variation is reduced to a homologous relation that is fixed and static.[20] The same is left, and variation marks a gap with respect to the invariant structure. This allows the postulates of linguistics to be isolated with extreme chemical purity, which Deleuze and Guattari attack in the fourth of *A Thousand Plateaus*.

This kind of linguistics is only capable of scientifically studying variation by stabilizing it in a homologous, constant subsystem. There would have to be a postulate that says, "there would be constants or universals of language that would allow this one to be defined as a homogeneous system" (postulate III).[21] Deleuze contests the presupposition of this doctrine—the real character of the mother tongue—by observing that it is never just a part of language in variation (a subsystem) that linguistics lifts out of the flux of language and fixes in its atemporal matrix, without being able to decide what justifies the selection of a particular section. Placing the subsystem at the same level as variations, Deleuze refuses to give Chomsky the essential, the postulate according to which "language could only be scientifically studied under the conditions of a major or standard language" (postulate IV).[22] Grammars do not rely on mental competence of a determined type that is otherwise absolutely invariant (since we know very well that languages change), at least invariable in a way that is necessary for a given competence. If Chomsky pushes linguistics toward an algebraic theory of languages, which is a very noble effort toward scientificity, it is because he wants to be able to show that generative grammar is empirically justified as an "innate mental structure that makes language acquisition possible."[23] What is in question is the very existence of major grammaticality that is transcendental and invariant, whatever the differences may be that affect empirical languages.

The notion of a major grammaticality depends on a structural invariant, which depends on a mental structure of the subject. This is a position that Chomksy clearly assumes by claiming a filiation with Descartes. Yet, generative grammar, which bets on the development of artificial intelligence, encounters a fundamental difficulty: acceptability resists description in mathematical terms. Grammaticality cannot be reduced to the empirically observed utterance, because a large number of correct sentences do not necessarily appear in a corpus, and above all, because a theory of proper use would be needed that links the correct practice to a determined class of speakers. For each state of a considered language, grammaticality is content with making an intuitive criterion for it: there is not a determinable theoretical test of grammaticality outside of the consensus of speakers. Resenting its imposing formal components, grammaticality is reduced to this truism: the correct state of language must be proven by "the subjective consciousness that apprehends its principle (that of the linguistic herself)."[24] What the authorized speaker says is major, is major.

Linguistics and semiotics

Deleuze and Guattari's critique of grammaticality, through the lens of the major and the minor, integrates linguistics into the heart of other social sign systems. The critique of major grammaticality rests on a semiotics that rigidly rejects the thought that a system of language can be isolated from other systems that determine the concrete social arrangement of language. Not only is there not an origin of language, but language is also not a closed system. It "is given all at once, or not at all" as an open and pragmatic system that Deleuze and Guattari call a social "assemblage of enunciation."[25] The critique of the subject done through psychoanalysis, and then against it, is applied to linguistics: language cannot be started with individuated people, whether physical, spiritual, or linguistic (shifters presuppose the preeminence of the "I speak," which Deleuze and Guattari incessantly oppose with an impersonal "we speak," as seen in Foucault and Blanchot). But when it comes to a critique of the subject, which is a consequence of the critique of the signifier and phenomenology: language no longer depends on the logical, mental, structural, and internal signifier, which functions like a major and transcendent organization (the "it speaks" as a closed system) and not as an originary, ante-predicative experience that shows the birth of sense in things within the work. The signifier is not, however, a fiction, but is given as an indicator of social power in language, just as it is in psychoanalysis.

By drawing from their pragmatic theory of an assemblage of enunciation in order to critique the four postulates of internal linguistics, Deleuze and Guattari offer alternative, positive principles for a semiotics that rejects the artificial extraction that removes linguistic signs from other sign systems.

Thus, we cannot accept that signification could be intelligible, while not social or contextual, as is claimed in the first postulate: "I. Language is informational and communicational."[26] Neither informational, nor communicational, language is pragmatic: it "insigns," teaches by ordering words, and not by signification, and so it prescribes.[27] Deleuze offers two arguments as a complete objection to linguistics—one that takes account of the social nature of language, and the second, which accounts for the epistemological system of the invariant. It is useless to fix certain laws within pragmatics if it will be inserted into a syntactical and phonological machine, namely, a purely linguistic structure. In itself, linguistics is never separable from a pragmatics that demands that nonlinguistic factors be taken into account. Signification is contextual, and it is not delivered as an essence that follows a predetermined structure, because sense does not preexist its effectuation in some invariant way, but it depends on the contextual assemblage of enunciation.

As such, structural linguistics, or all internal linguistics that base sense on the abstraction of the signifier, or on the enunciation of a person, is not abstract "enough." Such a linguistic system remains "linear" and two-dimensional, solely taking place on the plane of statements, without attaining the real complexity of an assemblage that weaves the linguistic system into other social semiotic systems. Its level of abstraction takes place in the second postulate, which establishes an abstract closure for linguistics: "II. There is an abstract machine of language that does not appeal to any 'extrinsic' factors."[28] In other words, this mediocre process of abstraction is happy to employ an "isolationist" conception of language through selection that is capable of signifying on its own. In fact, the linguistic selection abstracts and separates linguistic features from nonlinguistic features, then treats the former as valuable constants independent of all empirical contextualization. This definition of the field is not attained with the help of pseudo-constants and produces nothing more than a synchronic, fixed, fictitious portrait of language.

This brings us to the third postulate: "III. There are constants or universals of language that enable us to define it as a homogeneous system,"[29] which shows contempt for real variation that affects languages diachronically as well as synchronically. This third postulate of linguistics concerning the nature of language necessarily imposes the fourth epistemological postulate that definitively founds the existence of language on the necessary imperative of science, at the cost of falling into the following circular argument: since science requires constants, it is necessary that language introduce them so that it can be studied scientifically.

"IV. Language can only be scientifically studied under the conditions of a standard or major language."[30] Internal and major linguistics, even when it exhibits a formal claim with incredible rigor, is always accused of not pushing analysis far enough for Deleuze, and of lacking abstraction, because it remains unaware of its own pragmatics and misunderstands the political stakes of its constitution. What was found to be valid for psychoanalysis is henceforth applied to all other epistemological systems, and this misunderstanding of political stakes and domination does not result from an abuse of the theory, but from incomplete theorization. Linguistics does not account for the entire assemblage from which is taken and constituted.

Just as tools have no real existence outside of the social assemblages that ensure their technical efficiency, by the same token, linguistic signs do not enjoy any sort of autonomy. Since language is not productive by itself, it only becomes so under the collective or semiotic condition of a socially determined assemblage. There are not more words than there are tools that exist, and the linguistic sign does not only refer to a system of signs that would constitute it, but to a plurality of social signs, of which it only forms one, no doubt decisive, dimension that is not remotely isolated.

As such, linguistic elements are not arranged in a separate sphere. They depend on assemblages of enunciation that are not just syntactical, semantic, and phonological, but are social, political, material, and concrete.

An assemblage does not actualize a "structure," but what Deleuze and Guattari call an "abstract machine" of language—a virtual diagram is never exclusively signifying, like was the case with Lacan's structure, but is always heterogeneous as defined by the semiotic rhizome, which arranges segments of disparate codes that are taken in their empirical functioning, and this precludes its consideration outside its social context.

It is language that depends on the abstract machine, not the reverse.[31]

The minor and the major

The discussion opposing Chomsky, a proponent of systematic grammaticality, to Labov, an advocate for sociolinguistic variation, is pivotal for situating the concepts of the major and the minor, and for the determination of continuous variation, as well. Labov demonstrates that as soon as one becomes interested in language variation, the notion of system becomes obsolete. He maintains that not only do the idiolects in New York City not form a homogeneous system, but they also show the idea of a homogeneous system of linguistics to be inconsistent. It is on the subject of variation and the treatment of variables that Chomksy and Labov differ. Both obviously agree on the factual existence of variables, but Chomsky reduces them to the system but disagrees with Labov by saying that dialects, minor languages like black English can only be studied "by applying them to the same rules of study" as standard English, precisely because dialectical variation cannot be reduced to a "sum of faults and infractions," and for this reason, must be designated a homogeneous system.[32]

Consequently, every minor language is major as soon as it is studied in practice, which grants it consistency and a "homogeneity that makes a locally major language capable of forcing official recognition." Chomsky enhances the claims for the minor in the context of an opposition between a homogeneous major and a minor variation. What Labov had in mind was something very different. When Chomsky argues that a language, even a dialectical language or ghetto language, can be studied outside the conditions that enable the release from its invariant grammatical state, Labov retorts by claiming that a language, even a major language, cannot be studied without taking account of the variations that operate within it.

What is at stake is how to deal with the variable and not the minor or major character of the corpus in question. Labov treats language as a continuous variable, while Chomsky reduces change to a transformation that is regulated by using fixed positions. The two authors not only diverge about the nature of systems (homogeneous or heterogeneous, static or dynamic), but they also differ with respect to the epistemological status of variation. For Chomsky, the variable is treated as that which enables extraction from constants. Labov shows that variations are not mixed or extrinsic, and he connects the same variables back to the state of continuous language variation instead of extracting them from constants.

Either variables are treated in a way that extracts them from constants and constant relations, or in a way that puts them into a state of continuous variation.[33]

For Chomsky, variations are regulated transformations. On the contrary, Labov values their lines of inherent variation and rejects their reduction to either external variants, or a mix between two or more homogeneous systems. He rejects the alternative where internal linguistics closes itself off: either variants are attributed to different systems, or they have to be considered from outside structural linguistics. Thus, Labov proposes a systematic variation, or a system in the process of variation. Variation becomes "a *de jure* component that affects each system from within" and is, in principle, forbidden from fixing it and "homogenizing it."[34]

> Thus, must we not agree that every system is in variation and is defined not by its constants and homogeneity, but on the contrary, by a variability whose traits are immanent, continuous, and regulated in a very specific mode (*variable* and *optional* rules)?[35]

This concept of an open system corresponds to the definition of a rhizome. It is not a question of repudiating the more or less distinct rules and zones of grammaticality that attach to this or that use, but of considering these grammatical sections to be demarcated areas that inhibit neither the blurrier areas, nor inherent variations.

Languages are thus less like "porridge," as Deleuze claimed in 1975 and 1976, which could lead one to believe that a mixture would dissolve the rules, but they are more like a disparate fabric with discordant rules in variation.[36] In 1978, he corrects the expression of porridge of floating and mixed rules with packs of diverse lines.

> A minor language only consists of a minimal amount of constants and structural homogeneity. Yet, it is not porridge, a patois mixture, since it finds its *rules* in the construction of a continuum.[37]

Accordingly, it is not a question of contesting the existence of rules, but of defining an intrinsic variability that affects all systems and necessarily opens them. The line of variation that will not be confused with the line of flight, expresses this real capacity. As such, the line of variation must be continuous because it is inseparable from language, but it does not affect the relative constancy by the fact that it is freed from local uses. Simply put, modifications work less by discontinuous leaps than by a continuous coexistence of use and different frequencies.

The continuous variation of language draws a line of virtual variation that does not at all inhibit the existence of arborescent systems, the constant nodes that are defined as a function of their pragmatic capacity to assume the function of a center "at certain points in time."[38] Thus, there is an orthopedics and orthodoxy of language, which takes on the political function of ensuring forms of organization. These organizing centers play the role of constants well, but the constant is not a primitive given. It is the pragmatic outcome of a certain state of language consolidation, which is always provisional and always in a process of becoming. The constant is thus not opposed to the variable, and the existence of constants is not contested at all by Deleuze: it is their status that is transformed. The constant, which is eventually posited as an extract of variables, is not at all elementary, but derived and secondary. Here, we rediscover the ramifications of the analysis of the body without organs, transposed in the critique of the major invariant. Constants are pulled from variables and are produced by universalization and uniformization. So, the constant is none other than a variable erroneously posing in the form of a transcendent universal.

> A constant is not opposed to a variable, it is a treatment of the variable that is opposed to the other treatment, that of continuous variation.[39]

The invariant, then, occupies a function of the constant, and variation is not Heraclitean flux, but the variable put into variation.

Creative stuttering

Even if all language is an exercise in minoration, not every speaker is a poet: stylistic success breaks with ordinary language use without appealing to transcendent or external factors informed by linguistics. This is an intensive definition of style as stuttering, which continues to approach literary and linguistic organization through the work of variation starting with becoming-minor: creation is a "treatment of language" that gives free reign to its intensive, informal power and thus transforms literature, including its genres and codes.[40] It aims to constitute a "foreign language" within language, which is a Proustian formula that is highlighted throughout Deleuze's works and is used as an inscription in his last book on literature, *Essays Critical and Clinical*: "the greatest books are written in a kind of foreign language." This creative stuttering, or foreign language, must not be confused with a speech disorder, but comes out of an intensive use that pushes language to the limits of the "agrammatical." It is a matter of putting language in variation *at the heart* of speech. From this point of view "the formula of stuttering is as approximate as that of bilingualism"[41] and turns out to be misleading if it leads us to believe that it is sufficient to write *in* a foreign language or to mimic disorganization in language, as if it is enough to manhandle a cliché in order to attain creative deformation. It is not a question of imposing an external rule on a poor use of speech, but of pushing language to the realm of variable constitution: "to cut" a "minor use" in it, and "to remove elements of power or majority."[42] This intensive definition and subtraction of style implies that "creative reality" is separate from "an individual, psychological creation." It is accomplished in "sobriety" and "creative subtraction" by "putting variables into continuous variation" that pushes language to its "continuum of value and intensity."[43]

This is why style is always described as a line of flight that implies an intensive, agrammatical variation, a becoming-minor or becoming-animal of language—a creative transformation of materials and conditions of enunciation that put language into contact with an intensive border, "its musical, deterritorialized scream that escapes signification."[44] Here, we touch upon the body without organs of language, and literature enforces its nonsignifying power and its semiotic efficacy. The minor affects the intensive border of phonetics and the political limit of proper grammatical use. Kafka impresses a Yiddish mannerism on Goethe's German and uses a Czech colloquialism that distorts German, not in the superfluous sense of Meyrink's Baroque mannerism, but in the sense of a kind of poverty, a kind of dryness, an "intense sobriety." Creation is always subtractive: style removes language from its conditions of stable convention in order to attempt a new assemblage and imposes a becoming-minor on it.

Collective assemblage of enunciation and the critique of power

This new assemblage must be understood in its triple determination: linguistic, stylistic, and political. Kafka's works are exceptional because their innovative style is only accomplished by exploring the previously unknown, real fabric of society (and is not "literary" in the sense of seeking to conform to major codes). Literature becomes a physics of affects, a social ethology. The writer is not defined by her preference for modifying rules (arbitrarily subjective), or by her designation as belonging to a linguistic or sociocultural minority, but by her capacity to express, without affectation, the ways in which he/she is affected by the social physics of time. "Two problems drive Kafka: when can we say that a statement is new? [. . .]—When can we say that a new assemblage has emerged? [...]."[45] This new assemblage is one of bureaucracy and power relations that Kafka describes in minute detail, which form the social assemblage, the collective assemblage of enunciation that he expresses. This is why the author-function is always collective.

> There is not a machinic assemblage that is not a social assemblage, and there is
> not a social assemblage that is not a collective assemblage of enunciation.[46]

The bureaucratic phenomenon that Kafka captures with dry and neutral prose forms a collective assemblage of enunciation (an apersonal author), and is creative because he "captures" previously unknown forces of social assemblage, so that the textual machine articulates the previously unknown enunciation in a clinical exploration of reality in the same assemblage. This is where the revolutionary impact of Kafka's text is located: it is not an individual refusal of social organization, but an exploration of the fields of social forces that impress this sober and dry system on language. The clinical analysis of power that Kafka achieves with his previously unknown processes is deemed revolutionary.

Here we have an objective parallel between Kafka and Foucault, who also performs "an analysis of power that reexamines all of the contemporary political and economic problems. Even though he uses a completely different method, his analysis is not without certain Kafkaesque resonances."[47] This is why writing has "nothing to do with signifying, but with surveying, and mapping."[48] Both Kafka the surveyor and Foucault the cartographer extract new sensations from the social body. For Kafka, the social body is treated as a kind of topography where he surveys recent territories of the Austro-Hungarian bureaucracy. For Foucault, the social body is treated as a kind of cartography where he uses *Discipline and Punish* to disclose the force relations that animate the apparently smooth space of knowledge.[49] The innovative analysis that Foucault devotes to power renders the extraordinary political machine that Kafka invents sensible. Reciprocally, Foucault releases a "Kafkaesque" tonality from the archive, since both refuse to make power and law an emanation of the State—the central, centralizing, sovereign organ—and they describe power as essentially unstable and local, diffuse, and inventive, as well as unknowable and positive.

The clinical strangeness of Kafka's work is thus attached to this analysis of bureaucratic power and its diffusion and dispersion on the social field. Kafka transforms the plot of the novel by rejecting the legendary model of power conceived as the act of a sovereign subject (the State) being exercised on social subjects. Since power is neither an external violence imposed on subjects, nor an internal mechanism (of the superego variety) that enslaves them, and is not at all reduced to the classic alternative, "violence, ideology, persuasion, or constraint."[50]

"The Great Wall of China" demonstrates that "the law has nothing to do with an immanent, harmonious, natural totality, but [. . .] on these grounds rules over fragments and pieces,"[51] and even traces this social coding into flesh.[52] In "The Procedure," power does not appear as the property of a class, even if classes exist, and it is not endowed with a homogeneity that could make it the property of a group. In Kafka, as in Foucault, power is not located in the State apparatus, but it is the State, on the contrary, that seems like a distant effect produced by the mechanisms of power of the "machine" that runs through different institutions and techniques (assemblage). Even if it is local, in the sense that it is not global, it remains unlocalizable and diffuse. It is not determined later by economic strata and is shown to be a producer: bureaucratic mechanisms are not separable from social factors, but they are not intrinsically determined by them and already govern productive forces and relations of production. Thus, power does not have an essence, it is operative; it is not an attribute but a relation, and on these grounds, sets itself up wherever force relations exist. Its action does not take the form of repressive violence or misleading ideology, and it "produces from the real" before repressing. Normative in nature, power is effective and productive, so repression and ideology always presuppose the real assemblage within which they operate, and not the reverse. A close correlation between illegalities and the law replaces the opposition between the abstract law and illegality that is based on the presumption that the law designates what is right. By managing the illegalities that it permits, creates, tolerates, or forbids, the law uses them as a means of domination.[53] These six traits of power profoundly transform the conventional analysis of law and do not allow Kafka's work to be reduced to a neurotic, transcendental law, or to an escape into the imaginary as a result of his inability to directly confront the established order, and this disavows both the psychoanalytic and the sociological readings of his work. The affinity between Foucault and Kafka attests to their visionary perspicuity, the beauty of their style, their clinical capacity, and their ability to create laughter in a strictly political context.[54]

The clinical and continuous variation

The definition of minor literature crosses into the theory of continuous variation. Writing is an asubjective impersonal assemblage, so that literature can "follow a path in the opposition direction" from personal phantasm, or the identification of a social person: "it only arises when uncovering the power of the impersonal beneath the apparent person," which is not general, but singular.[55]

> These are not the first two people to employ the condition of literary enunciation; literature only begins when a third person is born within us who gives up the power of saying "I" (Blanchot's "neuter").[56]

To become an author is to access this impersonal and singular mode that arranges active social machines and language traits at the same time, which Deleuze calls the "proper name," the signature of a machine of enunciation, the "K abbreviation" in the Bachelardian sense. One must not confuse the proper name with a personal mode, a private enunciation.

The proper name does not designate an individual: on the contrary, when the individual is opened onto the multiplicities that run throughout her, at the end of a more severe experience of depersonalization, then he/she acquires her true proper name.[57]

"Making a name" implies this kind of process of depersonalization. Thus, "there is not an individual statement, there never is one," and to become an author is to reach this apersonal point. This is why the statement is "always collective, even when it seems to be emitted by a solitary singularity, such as the artist." "This is because the statement never refers back to a subject": "it is useless to ask who K is."[58] The proper name does not describe the individual attribute, does not refer to the author as an individual, but refers to the collective, apersonal and remains singular as the "subject of a pure infinitive understood as such in a field of intensity."[59] This infinitive picks up the qualification of minor literature, but transports it onto the plane of intensive variation, without limiting it to the minoration of given codes. The proper name, the impersonal power of subjectification and "depersonalization," becomes the condition for art.

Minor literature marks this theoretical movement toward continuous variation by positing an epistemology of variation that places the norm in the related fields of art, language, and social norms, substituting the variation of variables for the invariant, major or minor. This shows the force of the analysis and the reasons why the minor or major qualification tends to disappear from Deleuze's writings after *A Thousand Plateaus*, letting the capture of forces take its place. The opposition of the major and the minor functions as a dualism and provides a binary description of the process of continuous variation. This is why Deleuze and Guattari always stress that one must not reify these tensors, as if becoming is actualized "between" the given poles of major and minor. On the contrary, the distinction engages the vibration of a process of becoming, which, in its assembling, is produced by the major, arranging social, linguistic, and literary norms at the same time that it arranges a minor margin: only the becoming that produces these two poles is real.

Minority, the polemical concept arising from the demands of the excluded, must, then, be conceived as inseparable from the majority. In 1978, taking up the concept of minor literature with respect to Carmelo Bene, then again in the article, "Philosophy and Minority," and two years later with Guattari in *A Thousand Plateaus*, Deleuze emphasizes the status of the major: majority is not an abstract archetype, nor a quantity, or even a numerical superiority, but a standard of measure, a variable erected into the position of a constant. The majoritarian, as a constant and homogeneous system does not exist any more than the minoritarian if we separate them as subsystems of the constitutive relation that produces both of them.

> There is no becoming-majoritarian; the majority is never a becoming. There is only minoritarian becoming. [. . .] There is a universal figure of minoritarian consciousness as the becoming of everyone, and creation is this becoming. [. . .] It is continuous variation that constitutes the minoritarian becoming of everyone, in opposition to majoritarian fact of Nobody.[60]

The dualist pair of the major and minor are replaced by continuous variation, which produces both of them. The major is put in a position of dominance by the process of minoration, which produces the minor at the same time. The only thing that is real is the process of minoration, and at the limit, the major is a creation, a product of the minor. Without a doubt, the major manifests a real effect of domination. What exists is thus not the major in itself, but the process of admiration, normalization, and domination that raises a given variable to a major position. Literature should, then, refrain from purporting to be minor in a moralizing gesture, claiming the heroic position for itself.

Rhizomes and Lines

Schizophrenia and Intensity

The theme of the major and minor transforms the status of schizophrenia, the experience of the dissolution of constituted subjectivity. Deleuze invented the concept of the body without organs at the intersection of schizophrenia, corporeality, and thought. For Antonin Artaud, schizophrenia provides an opportunity to fuel poetry and push it to the limits of language in a sublime manner. Artaud reconnects with the figure of the mad genius that he had helped to establish by calling Van Gogh the man suicided by society, and Deleuze considers his poetic breath to be irreducible to mental illness and makes schizophrenia an experience of definite intensity that escapes dogmatic modes of common experience.[1] He also takes up the positions that Blanchot adopted with regard to Hölderlin, without taking part in the diagnostic criteria for schizophrenia, which remains a pretty indeterminate term for a limit experience where thought no longer enjoys the position of conscious domination, but is confronted with its bodily materiality and radical immediacy. Even if he denies reducing Hölderlin to psychiatric diagnostic criteria, Blanchot readjusts his stance by adopting Jasper's position. Hölderlin fits well into the normal diagnostic criteria of schizophrenia, but he manages to "elevate the experiences of madness to its supreme form—that of poetry," and does so without understanding his own reason, while simultaneously understanding ours. If schizophrenia makes such extreme experiences possible, what is meant by the ecstatic, then pathology in itself is not sufficient for creativity: "schizophrenia is not creative as such. Only in creative personalities is schizophrenia the condition (if the causal point of view is momentarily adopted) for opening up the depths. A sovereign poet who was not mad would become schizophrenic."[2] In other words, a schizophrenic holds the key to such a breakthrough, but the experience can be reached by creative means by those who are already artists. One gives one's all in madness and art. Madness is only sublime through art. The nonschizophrenic artist lacks this supreme resource.

Literature and art serve a specific social function, getting society free of the Oedipal reference and presenting a source of intense experimentation for the fixed entities within culture. Both critical and clinical, art responds to the formation of the body and the significations of the subject by localizing the forces beneath forms, and by diagnosing the becomings and tendencies below roles and functions. Art dissolves organizations by presenting their intensive and vital side. Artaud the schizo tears down the wall of the signifier. He detects nonorganic life below social structures and renders the body without organs below stratified organizations sensible.

> But a molecular sexuality always boils up or rumbles below integrated sexes, a little bit like we see in Proust.[3]

Sexuality is going to be like all other substantive formations: the family, the group, the individual, the body, and society. The function of art always consists in making intensity move and revealing nonorganic life below the strata of organizations and structures, even if does not privilege sexuality but bears on the modes of psychotic and political subjectification in schizophrenia.[4] Sexuality is actually not flux, but a complex machine, an organization assembling individual, political, familial, and social elements. It no longer holds a privileged position for analysis, nor is it a vector for the exploration of social psyches. But art concerns nonorganic life and the intensive power of differenciation, which deals with living individuals. It is not a matter of there being a plane prior to individuation: intensive life is intimately connected to organic life, just as the virtual is to the actual, and the body without organs is to the organism. But the uniqueness of art consists in its ability to draw directly from theses zones of indetermination that organizations put into constituted forms.

> Only life creates these kinds of zones where living people are whirled around, and only art can reach into it and penetrate its project of co-creation. Only art itself lives in these zones of indetermination [. . .].[5]

The schizoanalysis that Guattari brings to Deleuze's clinic can be seen here. On the basis of its Nietzschean symptomatology, Deleuze formulated an analogous split between forces and forms, but his anti-historicism pushed him to separate creation, like the new, from all particular references to the historical arena, as if creative values were absolutely split between eternally new values and established values. Deleuze established a dualism following the axis of recognition and common sense, and in this way went back to the criterion of nonconformist creation. This rough opposition is not tenable, as we proved with respect to major and minor tensors. The merit of *Anti-Oedipus* consists in bringing a coextensive power of disorder to order, which is not secondary or first, but strictly interconnected, thus showing a potential to breathe becoming into history, and not in hopes of escaping from historical inscription. Undoubtedly, Deleuze and Guattari stress the opposition between schizophrenic creativity and Oedipal art, which is reduced to the status of pedestrian merchandise, anxious to recount its childhood memories and search for the Father.[6] The critique of common sense and established values transforms into a distinction between molar formations and molecular flows. Instead of placing these two modes in a binary conflict, the critique of molar formations is carried out in the name of the molecular process that forms them. And this is how the body without organs functions, by valuing the intensive side of a body that is nonetheless full of organs.

Molar and molecular

The Deleuzean distinction between lightning-like intensity and individuated differenciation is taken up again, but it is more firmly established through Guattari's lens regarding the polarity between the molar and the molecular. This distinction calls for the polarity between schizophrenia as a vital process and schizophrenia as a mortifying internal arrest, the catatonic effect of the institutional asylum. Just as with the virtual and actual pair, the molecular and the molar are two phases that affect the same elements, bodies, subjects, societies and organs. They are two tendencies that form all the material, psychological, organic, and social entities. The molar order corresponds to stratifications and the aspects of organizations that tend to harden, code, and limit subjects, orders, or forms. The molecular order arises out of flux, phase transitions, becomings, and intensities. Thus, the body without organs is shown to be molecular, while the organism exposes the molar tendency of a body individuating itself. For the first time, the polarity of the molar and the molecular meet the Deleuzean poles of the actual and the virtual, as well as intensive differentiation and stratified individuation. The actualization of an individual tends toward the molar; the virtual intensity of the body without organs is proven to be molecular. A presentation that identifies the molecular with the virtual and the molar with the actual immediately misunderstands the specific features that the distinction introduces.

Guattari adds the theme of desire to Deleuze's definition of power. He doubles the physics of intensities by making a distinction between two subjective modalities of organization, "subjected groups" and "subject-groups," which serve as the opposing figures of subjection and liberation. They reveal the mode by which power is exercised at the seat of desire in social productions of subjectivity. Subjected groups tend to be manipulated by a transcendent principle of organization established within a principle of domination, and that is where subject-groups maintain an immanent relationship to power. These two opposite tendencies of subjectification illuminate the opposition between repressive molar machines and desiring machines, which are molecular in nature.[7]

In Guattari, the distinction between subject-groups and subjected groups corresponds to two uses of code, as opposed to the metaphysical duality of the virtual and the actual. This coding is related to the definition of the desiring machine as a division of flux: yet, this division is accomplished through coding, so that the molar and the molecular are two sides of this coding. The molar always tends toward stratifying code, and the molecular opens coding onto flux. These coding relationships must be closely differenciated at the same moment, because every desiring machine and every real existent entity is coded. Tendencies of molecular coding, or, on the contrary, molar overcoding, that actually convey the relationship between the living individual and the organism are only added to the biological, psychical, or social codes that affect every actual individual. Guattari thus distinguishes between the recoding or overcoding movements for subjected groups, who double the real code through the representation of order and the determination of a transcendent system of reference, as well as the decoding movements for subject-groups who are capable of producing subjectivity without inflicting domination. The code itself, as we see, simultaneously introduces molar and molecular tendencies.

The tectonic movements of recoding and overcoding for subjected groups and movements of decoding for subject-groups are expressed with more finesse in Guattari's vocabulary of deterritorialization. Molar overcoding implies a violent movement of reterritorialization and assignation, whereas molecular decoding demands a deterritorializing movement. The relation to territory is always a provisional balancing act, a rhythmic formation of a milieu, so it must not be considered a place but an expressive habitation. This involves describing balancing movements that are formed from the outside (*de*territorialization), in an exploration toward (territorialization), or in a return to (*re*territorialization);

we would also be mistaken if we assumed that a territory is given. It is rhythmically constructed by movements that territorialize, deterritorialize, or reterritorialize— movements or vectors that either tend to stratify beings and things and contain their becomings by binding them in stratified organizations, or in movements that tend to undo them by placing value on their intensive axis. The body without organs is perfectly explained through this new terminology, since it consists in decoding, undoing, untying, or decomposing stratified bonds. It highlights the intensive limit of the organized body, and is not prior to desiring machines, since it is constructed from them as intensive sides of molar formations.

The molar corresponds to recoding groups and constituted organizations, while the molecular corresponds to decoding, micrological phenomena that affect molar organizations. The distinction between the molar and the molecular redivides the distinction between reterritorializing phenomena (overcoding) and deterritorializing phenomena (decoding), while it sets a third type of line into motion, the line of flight.

This distinction (just like the line of flight) takes up a distinction that Ruyer makes, starting with his earliest works, and which serves as a support in this situation. It is absolutely necessary to avoid defining the molar in terms of reactive force and the molecular in terms of beneficial tendencies, which Deleuze and Guattari expressly state. Ruyer establishes an inventive difference between statistical physical reality and microphysical reality, a distinction that is not established between two classes of objects—it is pretty clear that everything that is physical is also microphysical—but between two levels of effectuated reality and two kinds of epistemological analysis. This distinction between "organized bodies" at the physical level and the microphysical plane of vital molecular differenciation provides an important trajectory for the distinction between the molar and molecular in Guattari, but it also plays a clear role in Deleuze's theory of differenciation, as has been demonstrated elsewhere with respect to the similarity of terms, with Ruyer describing his project as a philosophy of differenciation beginning in 1938.[8] For Ruyer, physical bodies (individuals) are only statistical organizations, which he opposes to a strictly vital and microphysical plane of processes of differenciation, which he calls a plane of formation, distinguishing it from physical function. This matches up with the distinction between two modes of difference, the individuating growth and intensive differentiation in *Difference and Repetition*, and is particularly applicable to Deleuze's analyses of biology and, especially, embryology, which is the domain where formation is irreducible to function *par excellence*, and where nonformed matter, flows, and intensities do not link back up in organic strata.

This is how the opposition between the molar and the molecular must be understood, according to Guattari, which Deleuze integrates into his distinction between two types of multiplicity.[9] Molar physics arises from a multiple ordered by the one, a solely quantitative multiplicity. Molecular microphysics, on the other hand, responds to true multiplicities that are substantive and qualitative, irreducible to unity, and capable of creative differenciation. With Ruyer, it was a matter of adapting the outcomes of quantum mechanics to the vital domain, connecting microphysics and biology by developing an original theory of physical bodies, purely statistical wholes, group phenomena, and the "crowd," governed by loose rules and only probabilities of classical mechanics, whereas microphysics is applied to the real molecular movements that animate them. For Ruyer, vital and psychological microphysics is more real than molar statistical order, even if the two orders only actually convey a difference in perspective.

Deleuze and Guattari adopt this distinction, which transversally articulates material, vital, and cultural fields, but they assign these fields a political task that is a far cry from Ruyer's use. The molar tends toward order and subjection, and the molecular tends toward "decoding" and social liberation. The molar conveys the imposition of power, while the molecular conveys forces of resistance. For Ruyer, the molar order of function only arises out of causal modeling. The formative differenciation of a crystal, embryo, or cultural transformation do not bear on other phenomena, but consider them from the dynamic point of view of becoming, and not in terms of mechanistic causality. Deleuze and Guattari adapt this argument in order to distinguish between constituted wholes (molar) and molecular formation (desiring), and appropriate it through a sociopolitical lens. Besides, constituted forms show tendencies toward domination, order, and a conversion of order (subjected groups), which dismantle molecular movements (subject-groups). What Ruyer understood as a crowd phenomenon, in the purely statistical sense, becomes a mass phenomenon and is imbued with the political implication of the subjectification of crowds that are subjected to dominating powers which homogenize and divide them.

> These are the same machines (there is not a difference in kind): on one side we have technical, social, or organic machines that are apprehended in *their* mass phenomenon to which they are subordinated, and on the other, we have desiring machines that are apprehended in their submicroscopic singularities that are subjected to mass phenomena.[10]

So, the molar concerns real phenomena of a purely statistical order, subjected group involvements, wholes and people, bodies and subjects. The molecular encompasses micrological phenomena, "transversal multiplicities that treat desire as molecular phenomena."[11] The role of art is easily exposed: it takes molar formations back toward constitutive intensities; it dismantles subjects, bodies, and molar individuals in order to render intensive force relations sensible, namely, the affects and speeds that form the intensive side.

The two types of lines, molar and molecular, and their modes of territoriality, coexist in reality ("these are the same machines"). The molar arises out of paranoid movements of reterritorialization, codes, and rigid institutions, while the molecular is animated through the reverse movements of schizophrenic deterritorialization and intensive flows. But there is not a "difference in kind" between machines apprehended in their "mass phenomenon" or their "microscopic singularity"; there is only a polarity, a valence that opposes subordination, according to which a singularity is subjected to mass on the molar line, or mass is subjected to singularity on the molecular line. By moving toward a social theme, the functions and forms of Ruyer become the inverse of a single reality (which signals the doubling of the fold) that is animated by reverse polarities, as active and reactive poles of the will to power. The molar group expresses the reactive will and domination of the weak. This gives the opposition between molar and molecular a degree of critical Nietzschean evaluation of totalizing processes at work within constituted individuals, and also reveals that the "herd" instinct necessarily affects cultures.[12]

Artaud the schizo

The distinction between these two orders, molar and molecular, shore up the distribution of the concept of schizophrenia, according to the two thresholds or states of molecular process and psychotic collapse from internal illness that now emerge from the molar. From the perspective of the molecular, "schizophrenia" designates "process" in general, the indeterminate name of flux that desiring syntheses form, positively describing its active valence, while the artificial "schizo" signifies the suffering individual who is socially maladapted solely from the molar perspective of group phenomena, as he/she succumbs to a reactive disorder.

> Before it becomes the disorder of artificial schizophrenia, as personified in autism, schizophrenia is the process of the production of desire and desiring machines. [. . .] Jaspers provided the most precise information on this matter [. . .].[13]

This clarifies Artaud's status. An artist and bachelor machine, Artaud is exempt from social machines and is an anomalous figure on the margins of the group; he is the "true experimenter or hero."[14] In tribute to Duchamp, the figure of the Bachelor makes a brief appearance here and serves to theorize the anomalous position of the artist as a virtue of the minor.[15] It exemplifies his kind of impersonal singularity and conserves the position of the exceptional genius. This portrait of that artist as a Bachelor is designated with a strong sense of singularity, an impersonal, asubjective, nonfamilial singularity—the personal, dissolved individuality of genius. The notion of the Bachelor, which describes Kafka or Artaud, reveals an anomalous position, an unpredictable, special, solitary singularity, "an absolute solitude," whose marginal position explains the often teratological calling that amounts to a topological monstrosity and separation from the dominant track.[16] The Bachelor, who is exempt from social formations, is a schizo resistor who escapes family structure—Bachelor, not a son or spouse.

The critique of the forced Oedipalization of the rebel in *Anti-Oedipus* intersects with the theme of nonconjugal sexuality, developed through an analysis of homosexuality in Proust, which supports the relation of capture, the wasp and the orchid's "wedding against nature." This capture, which causes heterogeneous terms to converge, comes from animal ethology. The original example of this is the symbiosis of the wasp and the orchid that Deleuze borrows from Proust and from whom he pulls a complex theory of artistic creation: the animal series (wasp) that is captured by the apparition of the orchid ensures the function of the productive organ for the vegetable series. The improbable encounter of insects and flowers that ensures the fertilization of orchids blocks two heterogeneous series in a becoming that is interdependent and disjunctive, which Deleuze and Guattari call "a-parallel" evolution, or coevolution as suggested by Rémy Chauvin.[17] Each capture is at least double since it assembles disparate entities into a becoming that transforms them both without assimilating them ("a-parallel"). "There is not one term that comes from the other, but each one encounters the other." This mode of relating, which goes from biological reproduction to artistic imitation, undergoes an epistemological mutation when the critique of the social model of family, the structure of reproduction and major organ of domination, is applied to it.

The capture, then, essentially proves to be an encounter, which Deleuze theorizes as an extra-conjugal encounter in *Dialogues*, in particular, a disjunctive alliance and not a mixed, institutional conjugality. "An encounter is perhaps the same thing as a becoming or a wedding [. . .], a wedding and not couples or conjugality [...] a wedding against nature."[18] The Bachelor designates this relation of heterogeneous encounter, of capture by surprise, an abduction rather than an exchange, which is more of a theft than sharing and cannot be assimilated through fusion. With the description that Proust gives it in *Sodom and Gomorrah*, "the wasp AND the orchid" form a rhizome, an intensive model for the production of an effect, not "a common becoming of the two, since they have nothing to do with one another." "Between the two" there is "a bloc of becoming, an a-parallel evolution" that captures their codes. The orchid traps an image of the wasp, and the wasp fertilizes the flower. They undergo an evolution that remains disjunctive and does not fuse into a totality, but diverges through a disjunctive synthesis in the form of an "asymmetrical bloc."[19] The capture, a process that causes the terms of two or more heterogeneous series to converge, thus describes the way an assemblage creates a "neighborhood zone" between several heterogeneous elements taken together in a "bloc of becoming" that transforms them without identifying them. The expressive value of the schizophrenic artist relates to its clinical proximity to the molecular process of desiring machines, which naturally leads it to formulate the critique of social reterritorializations.

Therefore, is Artaud an artist or schizophrenic? It is no longer necessary to hesitate in responding. As with Freudo-Marxism, Deleuze and Guattari, at the end of a long debate that they inherit while opposing it, reject the choice of either literature *or* madness. It would be silly to claim that Artaud is "crazy," since he "writes" literature, or that because he was an inmate at Rodez he is a writer. It is no longer a question of aligning psychosis and literary talent, as Jaspers and Blanchot did, as if schizophrenia brought language to its point of incandescence. Artaud escapes the Oedipalization of the family and opposes the status quo while he is schizophrenic. In its own way, this radicalization of the themes from *The Logic of Sense* picks up the theory of genius as a sublime exception. But by shifting the argument to the plane of coexistence between the molar and the molecular in culture, a space opens up for a theory of minor art, and the line of flight calls for this theory.

We can call art schizophrenic in the radical sense where the revolutionary mission of art is removed from a critique of social formations. Thus, Artaud is a poet because he is crazy, and reciprocally, he is crazy because he is a poet in the sense that he occupies this *anomalous* position vis-à-vis the social, which he pays for with his confinement. The anomalous indicates a social maladjustment that settles into intensive affects, and we discover the function of genius, whose schizophrenic hypothesis again reinforces its martyrological aspect. Deleuze and Guattari write that Artaud's "suffering and glory," which was maintained in an extreme and perilous situation, denounces the fabrication of the psychiatric inmate along with the reduction that the familial hypothesis imposes on literature. Artaud seems like "the champion of great health," capable of denouncing the Oedipal process at work in capitalist society, which does not succeed in subjecting individuals without also threatening literature.

> Artaud is the achievement of literature, precisely because he is schizophrenic and not because he is not. It has been a long time since he tore down the wall of the signifier: Artaud the Schizo. From the depths of his suffering and glory, he has the right to denounce what society does to the psychotic in the process of decoding flows of desire ("Van Gogh, the Man Suicided by Society"), but also what it does to literature when it opposes it to psychosis in the name of a neurotic or perverse recoding ("Lewis Carroll, or the coward of belles-lettres").[20]

Artaud combats the signifier in its triple form: psychiatric and psychoanalytic, literary, and social. He is opposed to the psychoanalytic signifier, as well as Oedipal literature; in other words, the process of normalization that seizes literature while it becomes the vector of established vectors and is submitted to its merchandizing form. He literally takes sides against "*papa mama*" and finally declares war not just on organs (internal), but also on the organization of family and social bodies. On the grounds of molecular madness and the rejection of molar interiority, Deleuze can immediately pick up Foucault's hypothesis: "Artaud will belong at the ground of our language, and not at its rupture."[21] Artaud even talks about the ground of our language, and not from another place, because he serves as a kind of interchange between the "schism," the schizophrenic process or molecular flux, and the molar signifier.[22]

Art, schizophrenic or minor, serves to decode the strata that affect us by transversally traversing them. On our level, the main strata are organisms, as witnessed in the theme of the body without organs, the social strata of the signifier that codes the unconscious psyche, and subjectification, which produces political subjects. "Let's consider the three great strata that concern us, that is to say, those that bind us in the most direct way: the organism, significance, and subjectification. The surface of the organism and the angle of significance and interpretation."[23] Three tectonic valences that are characterized by liberation, virtual potential, and becoming-minor within the constituted body correspond to these three strata: the body without organs, the asignifier, and the asubjective.

Once and for all, this manifests the complicity between the artist's activity and the body without organs, since "the BwO opposes the disarticulation (or the *n* articulations) of the whole of strata." The body without organs is employed to critique the preponderance of strata by opening the body onto constitutive intensities, and is not employed to "de-stratify," which is a fierce break with organization. According to Artaud's poem, if the strata are described as a "true judgment of God," on the moral plane of judgment, transcendence, and major organization, then it is henceforth necessary to take the results of the analysis into account with respect to the tension between the minor and major.[24]

The body without organs is a limit, a tendency, and not a state. It does not impose itself like a mythical place where we would finally be delivered from strata, but is an act that valorizes the intensive, virtual side of reality in becoming. This allows art to be designated as enacting the deterritorializing virtue of the line of flight: art, as regards literature, painting, or cinema, entails dismantling strata and introducing their intensive axis.

The principles of a rhizome

The definition of art as a capture of forces, a machinic effect, and intensive decoding presupposes the logic of the rhizome. The dispositif of the rhizome is a weapon against dualisms and modes of internal functioning, and it applies just as well to every reading that reduces Deleuze to any of the following binary oppositions: the schizo and the paranoid, the artist and common sense, the genius and dominant taste, the molecular and the molar, the nomad and the sedentary, the minor and the major. He completely transforms dualism, and makes it possible for dualism to be effectively combatted: how can dualism actually be disputed without it being restored, since it cannot be opposed without instituting a binary split?

Rightly so, the rhizome develops the theory of real multiplicities and proliferations. It corresponds to the order of the multiple and initiates a mode of plurality that can no longer be traced back to binary logic of the One that becomes two, the "oldest and most tired" thought arising from arborescent dichotomies. Along with Bergson, Deleuze calls for a real and substantive multiplicity that is plural and cannot be reduced to unity or dichotomous binaries. This rhizomatic multiplicity refuses to bring real diversity back to a simple division. It only contests the pragmatic existence of revolving roots, logical trees, divisions, caesura, and oppositions that are activated in nature, as well as in thought. Furthermore, Deleuze and Guattari do not even bother to go back to *Anti-Oedipus* to fix the often clumsy propositions that can leave the reader thinking that the schizo is opposed to Oedipus, the molecular to the molar, and the body without organs to the organism. But that explains their outrage in *Rhizome*: "It is not enough to say 'long live the multiple!' [. . .] The multiple *must be done*."[25] How? Not by adding a higher dimension to the given; for example, an express correction of the sometimes simplistic statements in *Anti-Oedipus*, but rather, as is always the case in Deleuze, by force of sobriety and contraction, by removing the One from the reality in which it was believed to be used: in the species, the figure of exceptional genius, the figure of schizophrenia, the hero of culture, and the single artist.

"Such a system could be called a rhizome," the theory and practice of decentered systems, the logic of real multiplicities, whose characteristics involve the following: first and second principles of connection and heterogeneity; a third principle of multiplicity; a fourth principle of nonsignifying rupture; and fifth and sixth principles of cartography and transfer.

In accordance with the principle of coding and division of the machine, the first pair of principles does not restore a dualism, but actually suggests the active polarity of two principles in the plural, which puts the mixed principle into tension "between connection and heterogeneity." Here we find the principle of the rhizome's function. Just like the desiring machine, the rhizome transversally connects heterogeneous domains without beating them down into a unity on the same field; it pluralizes this connection by way of multiple relations, like a burrow or a proliferation of roots. The third principle is stated as the "principle of multiplicity" in order to name the model of a network lacking preferential order, which functions through semiotic connections. As with connection, the unifying link is immediately pluralized by the second principle of heterogeneity, and the third principle of multiplicity opens up to the fourth principle of nonsignifying rupture, which manifests the heterogeneity of these connections. Finally, the last dual principle, "the principle of cartography and transfer," in the singular this time, states the ethics of the rhizome on the epistemological plane: to treat multiplicities like open cartographies that are provisional and fluctuating, instead of erecting copies, fixed portraits, and abstract clichés that presuppose constituted organizations that are given force relations found at the level of forms, not forces. Thus, the rhizome serves as a methodological precondition for the definition of art as a capture of forces and the logic of semiotic sensation.

With the rhizome, the principle of mixed semiotics is ensured, because the diverse nature of articulated signals forbids the temptation to unify them under the primacy of linguistics, and it is no longer a question of instituting a radical division between sign systems and states of things. The sign becomes a force relation, the image.

In the rhizome, on the contrary, each trait does not necessarily refer to a linguistic trait: semiotic chains of all kinds are connected to very diverse modes of encoding, biological, political, economic chains, etc., [and] not only put different sign systems into play, but also the statuses of the states of things.[26]

Semiotic and machinic coding

What is this coding that works through heterogeneous connection, which already characterized the action of the machine and ensures a theory of the code that is emancipated from structuralism and the signifier? A code is thought to be like Markov's chain: it is "jargon," not a language, a capture of code.[27] He "returns to Lacan for having discovered this rich domain of a code for the unconscious"[28] and returns to Ruyer for having shown the fecundity of Markov's analyses, which make it possible to think about a code as statistical jargon of elements that function through an automatic, iterative method unlike a language. Deleuze and Guattari borrow Ruyer's use of Markovian chains, which enables a shift from Lacan's signifying symbolic order to statistical computation, which is as meaningful for life as it is for culture.[29]

Markov, a Russian mathematician, studies random phenomena that are partially dependent and that characterize the structure of languages, most notably, and he thinks that variables that govern the use and succession of these semantic, syntactical, or phonological entities can be statistically determined so they can be applied in an artificial, iterative, simple method (a code) that enables an "automatic pastiche" of language.[30]

Markov demonstrates the process with Latin. This type of statistical treatment remains independent of all significations, but still reproduces the traits of French, for example, where q is always followed by u or h, but is preceded by c 50 percent of the time, etc. Secondly, this jargon is applied to every linguistic entity in culture, language, style, or idiolect (by statistically studying key words), and does not take real occurrences or their significations into account. Just as he evaluates linguistic signs on plane of automated information, whatever works for all types of signals is also applied to the living domain. Ruyer coins the expression *"biological jargon"* to highlight the semi-fortuitous chain of themes evoked "without concern for the whole, according to the appeal of the previous sentence," through iteration and not signification, to determine chains (morphogenetic or behavioral) that do not refer to the unity of a form that is being developed according to a global theme.[31] The code's surplus-value phenomena are explained well from this perspective of semi-fortuitous chains. Ruyer makes several connections to schizophrenic language, and his jargon theory is important for the theory of creative stuttering and literature as a minor language. It goes without saying that such jargon is consistent with the syntactical disorganization that we encountered with Artaud. Deleuze uses this as an opening to develop the types of transformation that drive this telescopic style, this "code scrambling" that not only characterizes Artaud's texts, but also the jargoned texts that Michaux and Réquichot wrote.[32]

Ruyer uses Markovian chains to theorize a mode of open formation that is random and iterative, as opposed to thematically developed, and does so at every level of form. Open Markovian formation enables the crowd phenomenon to be understood, from Markovian cultural keyboards and historical hazards to biological mutations, and Ruyer does not fail to note that parasitism and symbiosis are striking examples of this.[33] Hence, for Ruyer, Markovian chains determine the mode forms use to communicate in a nonfinal way that is not devoid of order: this is because the animal is susceptible to taking signal-stimuli that interest it from pastiches, something that hunters know well. So, his analysis is integrated into the precise determination of the capture of codes between the wasp and the orchid, and it enables animal symbiosis to open onto all orders of phenomena.

Ruyer's use of Markov turns out to be pivotal for the theory of coding and the capture of codes: it presents a theory of discontinuous, not continuous, order. Signal chains are indifferent to signification, just as the homogeneity of its elements is indispensable for extending machinic coding to semiotics. Finally, his theory of pastiche is applied to the double becoming of the wasp-orchid capture, and gives a model of becoming to resemblance that works by way of capture and not mimesis.

The Markovian chain transforms the Lacanian signifying chain from the perspective of its articulation and composition. The coding of flux is not symbolic or signifying. It does not correspond to any linguistic rules, whether signifying or symbolic, and yet, it is not just anything whatsoever. Rather, it is similar "to a lottery drawing that sometimes causes a word, a drawing, a thing, or a piece of a thing to come out, each not depending on the others except for the order of the drawing."[34] It produces a semi-random order (a drawing) that Deleuze interprets as the "dice throw," a mix of randomness and dependence that makes it possible to think order without aligning it with continuity, and without succumbing to disorder at the same time. Markov's chain serves as a model for all problems of order, irrespective of the level where one is located, be it material, biological, cultural, or historic: it is a model for becoming as an emission of singularities.[35]

For Deleuze, it is a question of thinking about chains in a way that does not rely on causal or final succession, or structure. Markov provides the concept for this kind of chain, which is distinct from both continuity and the absence of order.

> It is not the case that anything is chained to anything else. Rather, it is a question of successive drawings, each operating by chance, but under extrinsic conditions that are determined by the previous drawing [. . .] as in one of Markov's chains. [. . .] Thus, chains are not made through continuity or interiorization, but through re-chaining over divisions and discontinuities (mutation).[36]

Like Markov, Deleuze maintains a dimension of order that operates randomly through discontinuous junction that is comprised of divisions, and also determined sections. In Deleuze, the nature of order is, then, semi-random. Furthermore, the connected elements do not signify and are not homogeneous. In other words, they are nonsignifying and heterogeneous. What is found assembled in an ordered section are mobile stocks of information that fit into a system of points and drawings, a nondiscursive, transcursive kind of writing, according to Deleuze and Guattari, which forms a pastiche with Simondonian translation in order to locate a process straight out of the real.

Markovian jargon enables the articulation of heterogeneous signs, which is particularly useful for their place in the code. The composition of different structural series that Deleuze studied in *The Logic of Sense* is heterogeneous: a word receives the same value as a drawing or a thing. On one hand, articulated signs are of any nature whatever, on the other hand, "a code resembles a language less than it does a jargon," or "an open formation"—a textual repetition of Ruyer.[37] We can even talk about signifying chains as Lacan did, as long as we emphasize that they signify since they are made of signs, but the signs themselves do not signify.[38] That is the essential definition of a theory of signs that is not indebted to the linguistic sphere. Unconscious, machinic coding crosses over into a nonsignifying semiotics that makes it possible to think about the articulation of a plural and discontinuous order.

> The code resembles a jargon more than a language and is an open, polyvocal formation. The signs here are of any nature whatever [. . .]. No chain is homogeneous, but a procession of different letters of the alphabet [. . .]. Each chain captures fragments from other chains from which it draws a surplus-value, just as the orchid code "draws" the figure of the wasp.[39]

Markovian code (Guattari) and Markovian jargon (Ruyer) form the middle road between order and disorder: here we discover the theory of transversal fragments that makes it possible to explain machinic production in a more determinate way. The machine is the unity of a function that codes, but that also detaches and takes from other code fragments, and it does so from an organic perspective (genetic code) in addition to social and neurological perspectives.[40]

> It was possible to stress [allusion to Ruyer] the common character of human cultures and living species, like "Markoff [sic] chains" (partially dependent aleatory phenomena). Because, in the genetic code as in social codes, what is designated a signifying chain is more of a jargon than a language, made of nonsignifying elements that only have meaning or an effect of signification in the large aggregates that they form through enchained drawings, a partial dependence and superposition of relays.[41]

Markovian code enables Deleuze and Guattari to escape the closing off of the human symbolic world while taking advantage of an opening that makes it possible to unify contemporary molecular biology and the discovery of the genetic code with economic theories and the cultural order, in general. They are unified in a fairly free variation that mixes political economy, the science of flux coding, and the theory of Marxian surplus-value, in particular, which is liberally interpreted as code surplus and capture. He introduces a semi-random order across disparate regions, which operates between heterogeneous chains, such as different strata that may be material, vital, or cultural.

Division and multiplicity

It is at this point that we discover the third and fourth principles of rhizomatic logic: the principle of multiplicity and the principle of nonsignifying division. The line is multiple and substantive; it is multiple in itself in the form of an assemblage that changes dimensions. What Deleuze calls a plane is not a two-dimensional surface but "an increase of dimensions within a multiplicity that necessarily changes in kind as it increases its connections": this was the principle of real multiplicity. The multiple is what changes and increases in dimensions; it is not divisible or indivisible, but *dividual*, as Deleuze writes in 1983: an aggregate that does not divide into parts without changing in kind each time, being neither divisible nor indivisible, but dividual.[42] The plane is thus "at increasing dimensions that follow the number of connections that are established on it": such a multiplicity is a rhizome.[43] But the rhizome does not have predefined articulations and it functions through nonsignifying divisions according to a chance mixture (drawing) and semi-random series in a Markov chain. The connection and heterogeneity of the rhizome thus implies the coexistence of lines that differ in kind, in the real as in thought, so that the molar logic of *Anti-Oedipus* seems like the binary phase in a theory in becoming.

> Every rhizome includes segmentary lines according to which it is stratified, territorialized, organized, signified, allocated, etc.; but it also includes lines of deterritorialization through which it endlessly flees.[44]

The movements of deterritorialization and the processes of reterritorialization are thus relative to one another and are in perpetual connection. The heterogeneous "wasp-orchid" rhizome provides the model for this. Deleuze and Guattari construct the theory of differentiated lines as understood in *Difference and Repetition*; that is to say, lines that are truly distinct but inseparable, which together form real bodies and translate different movements within them by returning to the cinematic determination of the body without organs as an egg—intensive and germinal matter that is stretched from movements and is comprised of gradients and thresholds.

If the line travels in packs, then they will not be distinguished from beings or states, just as territorializations and deterritorializations are not spatial concepts, but are kinetic and relative to movements that affect the territory.[45] Whatever is concrete, whatever exists, is the intertwining of all lines.[46] The haecceity takes over from the body without organs from the point of view of a kinematics of materials and is no longer a social determination. At the letter "C" in the index at the end of *A Thousand Plateaus*, "Plane of Consistency, Body without Organs," we learn that the plane of consistency is composed of speeds and slownesses, intensive affects, which form the plane's longitude and latitude.[47] "Bodies without organs (plateaus) are put into play: for individuation by haecceity, for the production of intensity."[48]

> Whether individuals or groups, we are traversed by lines, meridians, geodesics, tropics, and zones that do not beat to the same drum and differ in kind. These are the lines that form us, which we said were three kinds of lines. Or, rather, packs of lines.[49]

Even though lines are intermixed and given in concrete multiplicity, Deleuze and Guattari do not distinguish between fewer than three main kinds of lines that are animated by different movements. They are the line of flight, the molar line, and the molecular line, which we already encountered, but whose inflections and stresses can be used to theorize their mutual affiliation.

Molar lines, molecular lines, lines of flight

First, it is necessary to isolate molar lines—lines of stratification that have a tendency to ossify codes and segment them—and their inverse equivalent, molecular lines, which break codes and also distribute one code to another, between lines. As we recall, it is a question of modal difference. Just as is the case with Foucault's use of microphysics, it is not necessary to institute different levels or dimensions between rigid, mechanistic, molar structure, and molecular fluid, as if they refer to large or small forms, respectively. The molar and the molecular are "not distinguished by size but by the system of reference."[50] The molecular line and the molar line do not involve phenomena of different dimensions, but different modalities in the same phenomena, which either concern their virtual mode of differentiation or their historical mode of stratification. The molar and the molecular thus refer to the segmentary and the linear.

The line of flight imposes a third regime: it explores the intensive movement that draws constituted differenciations (individuals, bodies) back to differential movement (intensity), connecting the stratified molar form back to molecular flows. The line of flight could have easily been confused with the deterritorializing movement that animates the molecular line in *Anti-Oedipus*, as if the line of flight does not express anything more than a superior power. This is not at all the case, and *Rhizome*, just like the theory of minor literature that is developed in *Kafka*, says as much. The decisive pair that Deleuze and Guattari assemble from the dispositif is not the binary opposition of the molar and the molecular, but the necessary interpenetration of the molar and the line of flight, which is ensured by the molecular line of deterritorialization. The line of flight traces a new direction for a deterritorialization that flees and escapes, where the molecular line always interpenetrates the molar line, thus highlighting their true indiscernibility.[51]

Let's simplify these lines in terms of becoming, which is explained in *Rhizome* and *A Thousand Plateaus*. Three lines are intertwined and form every body. The hard line corresponds to molar formations, which is proceeded by generalized overcoding. The relatively supple line of tangled codes and territorialities, which corresponds to molecular lines, always moves across molar lines "as the molecular fabric that this assemblage dives into." The molecular line implies a movement of deterritorialization. Thirdly, the line of flight decodes and deterritorializes: art entails such a line of flight as it is pushes toward the excellence of genius, but just as lines of flight presuppose the territory that they deterritorialize, art, like other bodies, constantly mixes these three lines.[52] The desiring machines from *Anti-Oedipus* and the assemblages from *A Thousand Plateaus* are composed of these lines, forming a cartography of bodies.

The Violence of Sensation

Imperceptible, Indiscernible, Impersonal

The haecceity, which defines the theory of capture as becoming-molecular, becomes a model for art. Art, in all its diversity, for example, painting, literature, music, etc., is described by its ability to seize perfect individualities that do not arise from the nonassignable or the ineffable, but from the imperceptible. As such, the capture of forces determines the community of the arts, their common problem, whatever their differences and singularities may be.

Thus, there will be as many art forms as there are possible modes for capturing forces, which results from our sensory apparatus, the social assemblage that renders the forces perceptible, the essential plurality of force, and the haecceity of material.

The haecceity makes it possible to overcome the opposition between the molar and the molecular, an opposition it reconfigures by showing the molecular process (longitude and latitude) at work in every individuation, and by providing a positive formulation: the molecular is no longer conquered by a struggle of minoration with the molar; the haecceity shows the molecular to be present and available in all aspects of reality. Likewise, the haecceity enables a positive formation of the line of flight that is no longer presented as a somewhat risky, beneficial reaction to social stratifications, but as the simplest formulation of the vital. The articulation between the desiring machine from the second period in Deleuze's philosophy of art and the notion of haecceity is formulated quite simply in *Dialogues* (1977). Desire is a matter of affect relations, and as such, it is seized and replaced by the theory of haecceities.

> Thus, we said something simple [this we refers to the authors of *Anti-Oedipus*]: desire concerns the speeds and slownesses between particles (longitude) and affects, intensities and haecceities, below degrees of power (latitude).[1]

The haecceity makes it possible to move beyond the molar and molecular split seen in desiring machines, and meanwhile, the reference to desire disappears from *The Fold* and *What Is Philosophy?*[2] As a matter of fact, desire moves into perception. "Everything is a rhizomatic work of perception, the moment when desire and perception are confused."[3] Desire turns out to be like any other assemblage, and is conceived of less than other assemblages.

Art's task is to fight against the three strata of the organism, the signifier, and subjectivity. The theory of haecceities makes it possible to formulate this imperative in a positive manner: three modes of becoming now correspond to the three lines of stratification, which Deleuze and Guattari formalize in the tenth of *A Thousand Plateaus* in the chapter called "Becoming-intense, becoming-animal, becoming-imperceptible": the impersonal nature of the artist allows her to reconnect the actual movements that form haecceities, moving from the nonorganic to the imperceptible, from the nonsignifier to the indiscernible, and from the asubjective to the impersonal."[4] This is why art entails the creation of becoming and is opposed to the principle of analogy on the molar plane of organization which actually disguises stratifications: "forms and subjects, organs and functions are 'strata' or relations between strata," and "the plane of consistency is the body without organs, or the ethological plane of haecceities, speeds and slownesses."[5] Of course, becoming is sometimes called desire in *A Thousand Plateaus*, but it is a desire so removed from its usual coordinates that it falls under the single name of becoming, as a matter of convenience. This assemblage, or intensive becoming, concerns the ethology of the artist, most of all, and enforces the shift from imitation to becoming, as a connection and convergence of lines.

The following aesthetic imperative, which is borrowed from Miller, is thus employed:

> It is always the grass that has the last word [. . .]. It grows between and among other things. The flower is beautiful, the cabbage is useful, and the poppy causes madness. But grass is overflowing; it is lesson in morality.[6]

The grass' humility does not hide its vitality, and if there were a "lesson in morality," it would no doubt be better to discuss the ethical principle as it applies to culture. The disobedient, wild grass infiltrates domestic, agricultural plantations, and by using this reference to crazy grass, Miller, and then Deleuze, intends to graft the nonpoliced vigor of the most modest grassroots onto cultural productions.

This overflowing grass marks the assemblage of the rhizome and the capture of becoming. Art emerges from an ethology of existent force relations and draws up a map of affects. "Such a study is called 'ethology,' and it is in this sense that Spinoza wrote a true Ethics."[7] If ethology becomes ethics, then for Deleuze, art very classically inscribes this relationship into an incredibly innovative ethics. The rhizome's three virtues include the passage from the organic to the imperceptible, the signifying to the indiscernible, and the subjective to the impersonal. Becoming grass is to do as grass does—*as*, becoming and not imitation, real and not metaphorical, intensive variation and not analogy. The definition of a masterpiece is thus related to this triple rule: to shift from organic perception to its intensive edge, to move from the signifier to semiotics, and to pass from individuated subjectivity to an impersonal singularity that abandoned its human features in order to do "as grass" does.

> To be in time with the world. This is the link between imperceptibility, indiscernibility, and impersonality—the three virtues. To be reduced to an abstract line, a trait, to find one's zone of indiscernibility with other traits, and thus enter the haecceity and impersonality of the creator. Then one is like grass: one made the world and everyone a becoming [. . .] One combined "all," the indefinite article, the infinitive-becoming, and the proper name to which one is reduced. Saturate, eliminate, and include everything.[8]

The ethics of the creator combines the three virtues of creative, intensive becoming with a semiotic definition of art (abstract line, zone of indiscernibility), which requires correlating literature with the nondiscursive. Michaux, a painter and poet, demonstrates the move from literature to the pictorial, which does not mark the disappearance of literature, but the abandonment of its supposed supremacy. This change in status does not invalidate its potentiality in the least, but raises the dignity of the nondiscursive arts, and painting, in particular, which pushes beyond literature's signifying blockades. Writing now takes "the line of Chinese poem-drawing" as its model, the haecceity of the trace conjugating the graphic gesture into material expression.[9]

> It was Virginia Woolf's dream, and then Kerouac's, that writing be like the line of Chinese poem-drawing [. . .] "saturating each atom."[10]

The opposition between French literature, which is modeled on interiority and totality, and Anglo-American literature confirms this shift away from centralized literature toward nondiscursiveness at the very heart of literature. From then on, Deleuze opposes the Anglo-American grass-book to the French tree-book and challenges the sterile and abstract chaos of the open work, which he still used as a model for literature and philosophy during the time he wrote *Difference and Repetition*: in the end, "the most resolutely fragmentary work" comes back to "the Total Work or the Magnum Opus," whereas the majority of "modern methods" reconstitute a more intransigent Unity in hopes of attaining plurality, and the "abortionists of unity" show themselves to be "angel makers, *doctores angelici* [who affirm] a truly angelic and superior unity." Joyce, a Thomist, only breaks the unity of words to diffract them onto multiple roots with the intention of reconstructing the unity of the text or knowledge. Even Mallarmé is not spared this critique regarding the isolated Book: "it is a strange mystification, that of the book that is much more total than it is fragmented."[11]

> The isolated book, the total work, all possible combinations *inside* the book, the tree-book, the cosmos-book, all the reiterations that are so dear to the avant-gardes, which cut the book from its relations with the outside, are even worse than the chant of the signifier [. . .]. Wagner, Mallarmé, Joyce, Marx, and Freud are all still Bibles.[12]

In opposition to these figures of totality who command the Western Book, Deleuze calls for Real-literature.[13] While the French "too often think in terms of trees," the English or American concern is that of grass, "which grows in the middle of things, [which] itself grows through the middle [. . .] grass has its line of flight, and does not root itself." The rhizome's fasciculated growth is the opposite of the tree's unitary root structure. The grass figure refers biologically to the neural disposition, the "uncertain nervous system" that Deleuze borrows from Stephen Rose and who leads him to write: "the brain is itself grass."[14] Semiotically, it refers to Michaux's literary and pictorial experiments, especially the mescaline drawings that accompany the experiential methods that Michaux underwent, and who literally was no longer situated at the level of people or subjects, but who captures haecceities, "collections of intensive sensations," blocs of variable sensation, "individuations without subjects," "open packs of sensation, those collections or combinations that run along lines of fortune or misfortune."[15]

Michaux, captor of forces and affects

Michaux emerges as a figure between the passage of the tree and the rhizome, between the Total Work and the modest art of haecceities. Not only does Michaux propose a theory of creativity, which easily connects points to lines, forces to haecceities, but most importantly, he thinks about creativity from both sides of poetic writing and painting. In both these cases, regardless of the material differences employed (the word versus the ink stain, water versus the heavy pigment of ink, the fluidity of the paintbrush versus the dry incision of the pen), he makes creativity operate as a method of experimentation that comes even closer to imperceptibility, indiscernibility, and impersonality.

Michaux does not even have the time to dismantle the strata of organization, significance, and subjectivity, since he finds it positively urgent to capture variations of intensity and affects, and to write down molecular compositions. The artist of longitudes and latitudes categorically ignores the avant-garde trends of the time in order to devote all his efforts to the positive construction of "Knowledge through the abyss," which makes the practice of writing and painting pass through methodological experimentation at the limits of perception. From the 1950s, Michaux systematically experiments with mescaline use, which he transcribes in painting and poetry. Accordingly, he participates in that era's fascination with hallucinogens, but in a way that was recalcitrant and not remotely submissive, since he clearly only agreed to take them because, first and foremost, he was interested in the transformations in perception and knowledge that could be taken away from them. "Drugs bore us with their paradise. Let them give us a bit of knowledge."[16] The following notational methods attract Deleuze's admiration from the get-go.

> Insurmountable difficulties come from the incredible speed of the appearance, transformation, and disappearance of visions; the multiplicity, the proliferation of each vision; developments in spectra and sunshades, by autonomous, independent, simultaneous progressions (in some sense with seven screens); their unemotional nature; their inept, or even more so, their mechanical appearance [. . .]. I was stirred and I was folded. Dumbstruck, I stared at a Brownian movement, the panic of perception.[17]

This passage that Michaux writes in 1955 demonstrates an attention to impersonal individuation and the event of the haecceity, whose capture is shown to be an "insurmountable difficulty" as a result of its evanescence and "unemotional manner": it is situated far below forms (visions) and subjects (the panic of perception). While Michaux claims to be interested in the impersonal power that stirs and folds him, what is most at stake is the capture of haecceities and the creator's impersonality; the ego's falling away is only one of the consequences. "To be in time with the world," melts into "the abstract line," whereby the line follows an event as precisely as possible, and this precision results in the personal subject's obliteration for the sake of the fourth person singular that Ferlinghetti talked about.[18]

Michaux is devoted to pre-individual singularities and nonpersonal individuations. Nevertheless, this attention to incredible, unemotional speeds does not reveal praise for schizophrenia, and Michaux expressly separates himself from this elsewhere. His methods do not praise the mix of anthropology; the quest for ritual practices; the romanticism of the product, like Castaneda has for peyote; or the fascination with drugs during the beat generation.[19] We saw that in the 1970s Deleuze argues for an active schizophrenia and is interested in hallucinatory experiences, and in *A Thousand Plateaus* the reference to Michaux is used to shift the argument from the resistant charm of the schizo toward the meticulous observation of haecceities.

Deleuze knew perfectly well just how inept it is to reduce Michaux to limit experiences, as Blanchot does in his wonderful eulogy for Michaux. Realizing that he happened to be "against mescaline, then in a secret pact with it" in order to write "two of the most beautiful books" (*Miserable Miracle* and *Infinite Turbulence*), Blanchot adds: "it is not clear if we should regret or admire Michaux's wisdom, which, sketching a new form of literature, was renounced in a disgust with artifice."[20] Yet, this distinction between artificial method and literature fails to capture what makes Michaux a singularity. Mescaline is not an artifice; it is a conductor at best. Deleuze firmly emphasizes that Michaux tends to "get rid of rites and civilizations in order to institute methods for admirable and meticulous experiments, refining the question of the drug's causality, fully defining it, and separating it from delirium and hallucinations." In any case, the drug only seems like a creative vector for the perceptions it arouses: at best, it is a channel for transmission. What is important is that drugs make mad speeds and prodigious slownesses come out and play, which makes the haecceity's molecular becomings sensible by instigating a disorientation that overflows the ordinary conscious-perception system.[21] "Drugs make forms and people disappear," they transform perception and endow it with the molecular capacity to grasp micro-operations, just as they provide perceived material with "the force to emit accelerated or slow particles," which Deleuze and Guattari state when following Michaux's realizations and Castaneda's Don Juan teachings very closely.[22] Drugs take on "a floating time that is no longer ours." A transformation of style must respond to the collapse of normal spatiotemporal coordinates in conscious perception. Michaux thus reports "an unsteady style, bobbing and weaving" while transcribing mescaline's "immense churning in light."[23] The inscription in *Miserable Miracle* is eloquent: ". . . all in all, you find yourself in a situation such that fifty different, simultaneous, contradictory onomatopoeias that change every half-second become the most accurate expression of the experience." This concerns the intensive world that Deleuze calls the longitude and latitude of the body without organs, haecceity, and event, and in order to express this world of slownesses and speeds, Michaux resorts to what Deleuze calls "creative stuttering."

> There is nothing left but the world of speeds and slownesses without form, without subject, without a face. Nothing but the zigzag of a line like "the lash of the whip of a furious cart driver" who slashes faces and landscapes. All of it a rhizomatic work of perception [. . .].[24]

This zigzag—the lightning strike from *Difference and Repetition*—slashes faces and landscapes and represents the subjective (face) and objective (landscape) references to a perspective that captures the canonical coordinates of Western painting dating back to the Renaissance.[25] The rhizomatic work of perception slashes this sensitive fabric, which is rendered obsolete for "the linear acceleration that I had become," as Michaux says, which often falls back under the sway of the abstract line, the nomadic line that initiates this work in a simultaneous and distinctively graphic, poetic way.[26] Mescaline experiences can be said to describe the moment when distinct networks of pictorial movement—where the line's trace and writing as mental stenography converge—are supported while remaining distinct at the same time, and they do not emerge from illustration or commentary. These networks of pictorial movement enter a neighborhood that is not weakened at all by their real distinctness, but this distinction demands the exploration of the close relationship between the hand and the verb. When passing from writing to gesture, Michaux says we change "railroad tracks" and become "decongested" from the "speaking part" and the "word factory," which "quite simply" and "vertiginously" disappear.[27]

If drugs are valorized it because they allow us to perceive the haecceity's molecular features, which form us with what we perceive, but this is immediately put into perspective: it is not the drug that creates this passage of haecceities, and under the influence of drugs "the creative line or line of flight immediately turns into a line of death." Drug users "do not cease to fall back into that which they would like to flee": the "hardest segmentarity" of marginality, the most "artificial" territorialization of "chemical substances, hallucinatory forms, and fantastical subjectifications."[28] Neither Michaux, nor even Castaneda, refer to a drug causality or "artificial paradise." Deleuze's interest in drugs arises from the following principle: "follow the [intense] flows of matter" without reproducing them or imitating them.[29] The creative capture occurs according to the fifth principle of rhizomatic logic: trace the map, not the copy. Drugs can help catalyze a sober moderation for phenomena which they did not produce and which remain, as we saw, suspended in an art of precaution.[30]

Michaux thus affirms the theory of art as the capture of forces, and he affirms it from the dual perspective of writing and painting.

> I paint like I write. [. . .]
> In order to produce, not beings, or even fictitious beings, and not their forms, no matter how unusual, but to produce their lines of force, their impulses.
> [. . .]
> In order to show the rhythms of life, and if possible, the very vibrations of the spirit.[31]

Thus, art's job is not to produce real or imaginary beings, or even forms, no matter how unusual they may be, but to produce the truly unusual forces that animate them. The task is to make the haecceity last by fixing it to a support: the brevity of the perceived haecceity undoubtedly corresponds to the rapidity of the material haecceity (the speed of the ink's diffusion in the blotting paper), but its outcome is a work of art, a "monument" that endures. Mescaline, which Michaux always refers to as a perception accelerator, must be considered as "slow motion" from this point of view—a room of capture that gives a denser consistency to imperceptible, intensive movements, enabling these imperceptible forces to be rendered perceptible through these movements.[32]

Moreover, Michaux illustrates how his encounter with the pictorial sign made it possible for him to escape a language that signifies too much, and the way he values painting in his own career shows that through painting he discovered a connection to the haecceity's materiality, which enabled him to pursue his poetic interests in a quicker and more efficient way without decrediting them in the least.

Michaux's painting consists of an encounter with nonsignifying material: "not like words. Words always say too much. They lead you astray, words. Suddenly, you are led to complications." Painting liberates the "country from clouds and indecision, [. . .] from larval faces and phantoms of bodies or nature, but it always remains vague and ready to return to the clouds." Even better than capturing words, painting makes it possible to grasp rhythms and "electric traces,"[33] and this happens in the struggle between water and inkblots. Michaux calls himself a "tachist,[34] if I am one, who cannot tolerate blots," because they collapse into "huge splatters that are capable of spreading everywhere."[35]

So I fight with them, I whip them, [. . .] I would like [. . .] to galvanize them [. . .] and all the same, I want to monstrously combine them with everything that moves, the unnamable crowd of beings, non-beings, furies of being, and everything from here and elsewhere—insatiable desires or knots of force that are destined to never become concretized.[36]

This attention to electric intensities, this concept of art that prioritizes life takes Michaux into a process of becoming-animal again: "Animals and I have a lot to do with one another. I exchanged my movements for theirs, in a spirit that was opposed to theirs [. . .]. I invented impossibilities of the animal; I mixed it with man, not with its four limbs [. . .] but by producing extraordinary repercussions, which were spontaneously aroused by its moods and its desires, in an incessant morpho-creation."[37] It is a "new way of living in an explosive medium, in the very vitality of life."[38] There is an arrangement of nonorganic vitality and kinetic, transformational power in Michaux, which the fluid haecceity of pictorial or verbal matter liberates, and in beautiful prose he frames the conceptual dispositif that Deleuze systematizes almost 20 years later.

Painting sensation

Painting is not imitative or illustrative; it does not reproduce forms of objects, but captures forces: sensation is painted. The violence of Bacon's painting interests Deleuze, a violence that does not belong to representation. Instead, it expresses a taste for the sensational, the spectacle of tortured bodies, the effects of meat, homosexual struggle, an understanding of soiled mattresses, hypodermic needles, prosaic earthenware, bidets, sinks, dentist chairs, or mirrors with three faces, concentrated in the plastic work of pictorial materials, lines, and colors. Bacon stresses the distinction between the violence of the spectacle and that of sensation, "and that it is necessary to relinquish one in order to reach the other."[39] Ever since his study of Proust in 1964, Deleuze maintains that the violence of sensation is a criterion for creation. "Innovation is the sole criterion of every work of art," and it arises like violence and a process of seeing, as a relation of forces and affects; it is a shock to thought.[40]

It is through this unexpected, subversive, and intrusive method that the capture of forces must be conceived, which allows the arts to be defined as a pragmatic and aesthetic collective. Deleuze announces this definition of the arts in Chapter 8 of *Francis Bacon*, "Painting Forces," just after having determined that painting allows us to discover the material reality of the body, its "affective athleticism" and "howl-breath," cruelty that is not bound to the representation of a horrible spectacle, but is only bound to the action of forces on bodies, to sensation ("the opposite of the sensational"). This is where Bacon meets up with Antonin Artaud. The capture of forces necessarily speaks to the intensive plane of the body without organs, whereas represented form sticks to an organic cliché. This applies to music just as much as it does to painting.

> What is constructed is a very elaborate sonorous material that is no longer a rudimentary material that received a form. And the coupling occurs between this very elaborate sonorous material and forces that are not sonorous in-themselves, but that become sonorous or audible through the material that renders them significant.[41]

Music frees sonority from the ear and becomes disembodied, which makes it possible to talk about a sonorous body "with exactitude,"[42] while painting "puts our eyes everywhere," from the ear to the stomach, from the lungs to the mouth (the painting breathes, as Deleuze says).[43] Music and painting rise to distinct sensorial systems, and their effects neither modulate the same forces, nor the same materials, which leaves the analysis of the singular arts open. Even if it is treated differently according to specific circumstances, the problem of the arts always involves producing sensation by exposing it in its energetic or intensive dimension, and thus increasing it by allowing it to capture nonsensed forces. Thus if painting and music differ in their methods and their effects, even if it is maintained that "music starts where painting leaves off," both deal with sensation.[44] Force is the condition of sensation, and sensation, as a relation of forces, produces an "image," a percept, and an affect. The longitude of force relations unfolds and curves into a perceptible latitude. This is why art is a capture of forces. A force must act upon a body in order for sensation to exist, without, however, being sensed by itself since "sensation 'produces' everything else from the forces that condition it." Thus, painting must be defined as a visible expression of invisible forces.

> How could sensation sufficiently turn back onto itself, expanding and contracting, to capture the non-given forces that it provides us, in order to make insensible forces sensible and raise itself to its own conditions? It is in this way that music must render non-sonorous forces sonorous, and for painting to render invisible forces visible.[45]

Painting differs from music because it "establishes itself upstream, where the body escapes, and in escaping discovers the materiality that forms it." Its task is to discover "the material reality of the body, with its system of lines and colors and its polyvalent organ, the eye."[46] In this regard, Bacon belongs in the history of painting, which he resumes and recapitulates in a unique way, in his own way, transforming it, and returning to question of the portrait and the human figure. "It seems that throughout the history of painting, Bacon's Figures are one of the most wonderful responses to the question: How do you make invisible forces visible?"[47]

Francis Bacon's figures

What Deleuze calls a "Figure" is the method that Bacon uses to disclose the forces, expectations, and thrusts of the body. In several places, Deleuze insists that it is not a question of transforming forms, but of deforming bodies. Bacon does not stick to the reproduction of past forms, or the discovery of new forms, but manages to capture the body's forces and deformations, which must be accomplished from the perspective of the materials, lines, colors, and haecceities in painting, along with the affects that it produces.[48] This is because sensation is shown to be a "master of deformations, an agent for deforming the body."[49] Deleuze states that the capture of forces entails this extremely different individuation that does not fall back into the combination of form and matter. Like Simondon, he calls this the haecceity of material, which makes it possible to define rhythmic characters: material itself makes it possible to render forces that are not present sensible. The forces that concern Bacon's painting are the powers of the body that are rendered visually sensible within the very work of material.

Thus, Bacon escapes figuration, illustration, or anecdote, and the accepted representation of the body. Deleuze opposes figuration to the "figural," which he borrows from Lyotard.[50] The figural is not narrative, but is a figural event: something happens or takes place, and something moves in the sensible appearance of the "Figure." It arises from the intensive register of the body's deformation ("figural") and not from the abstract illustration of formal transformation ("figurative"). Yet, it is not enough to simply destroy clichés in order to escape the figurative, just like it is not enough to enact syntactical disorganization to attain a poetic moment. While a form concerns the brain and acts as an intermediary for conscious perception, and ultimately functions as a cliché, like a pre-established, fixed, generalized image, provoking a pre-established sensory-motor response, the Figure, a sensible form connected to sensation, enables the nervous system to be grasped by producing a shock, a violent sensation that characterizes the masterpiece.

Since the Figure is said to be a sensible form, it is less a matter of repudiating forms than proposing a new conception of form, such as material, sensible, variable, and intensive form in modulation, and not as given, abstract form. For Deleuze, form entails force relations, and strictly speaking, there are only forces. Forms are a becoming of forces. So, the Figure does not reproduce a molded body with its individual form, but tries hard to attain all the drives of the body, the nonorganic vitality of the body without organs. Bacon can then confine himself to a preference for the human body, the portrait, or classical genres, and he is no less innovative in the context of painting. His creative potential does not have to be measured by the "subject" of the painting or the destruction of the genre, but by the violence he invokes to recast the question of the portrait from the perspective of the Figure. Form is thus a question of forces when it is related to sensation, whereas it remains a clichéd reproduction when it is confined to a copy or an opposition of previous pictorial formulas. Since "form is related to sensation (Figure), it is contrary to a form that is related to an object that it is supposed to represent."[51] The Figure, then, is an Idea, in a very singular, nonmental sense, a term which Deleuze uses beginning with *Difference and Repetition*. An Idea is a problematic field of differentiated virtualities, a field of forces and pre-individual singularities. "What I call Ideas are images that produce thought," force relations that are expressed as sensation.[52] The task of the logic of sensation becomes clear: to establish the function of painting through empirical details, such as the appearance of the Figure in Bacon.

Movements of the figure

Thus, Deleuze outlines the pictorial elements that combine to form the logic of sensation in Bacon. First, he focuses on the Figure, the seated or standing person, or people, who are more or less identifiable; second, he focuses on flat surfaces with vast, often monochromatic zones that separate, like colored lozenges, creating the Figure of depth; and third, he focuses on the place, track, or contour, and minimal decoration—a play of features that allow the Figure to take place.

These three groups function as elementary categories for a classification that would take Bacon's colored semiotics as an object of analysis. These three composites are: humanoid characters or painterly (*malerisch*)[53] surfaces, abstract panels in clay, and pieces of rudimentary perspectives or larval decoration that stage bodies and connects them to colored areas.

What Deleuze calls a Figure is not truly a human person, a head or a body that is put into a painting, but it involves an invisible, dynamic play with forces of isolation, deformation, and dissipation that affect the relations between these three pictorial elements. The Figure, taken in its immediate sense, often signifies the humanoid person that stretches across and falls onto the painting, but the "Figure event" always refers to the dynamic play that causes color and the coloring sensation to converge in these three categories. The term Figure applies less to the "person" in the classical sense than it does to the rhythms and flows that the painting discloses. The logic of sensation entails this dynamic, and semiotics comes back to extract these three elements from canvases and examines their primary relations, which provide the capture of forces and the violence of sensation with definite content.

These three actors are flat, colored surfaces, the *malerisch* bodies or heads, and the rudimentary patterns that bind them together. The flat surfaces, which are the material structure of coloring emptiness, are confronted by the place, sidewalk, contour, arena, puddle, or mattress that emerge from them. Place delimits the person, the fact of the body, which is the Figure in its immediate sense, and causes it to emerge. It can be said that place expels the event from the Figure, so that it literally becomes a Figure, which is not simply a person, but its movement of expulsion from the flat surface. Consequently, contours, abbreviated perspectives, and vibrant, monochromatic flat surfaces take place through rudimentary processes on an operative field so as to define the relation of the Figure with its isolating place, and to make it possible for the Figure event to appear. These three distinct elements converge through color and are grounded in a coloring sensation that configures individual colors from a painting in a process of rhythmic sensation. The painting's effect is entirely a result of color modulation; that is, the relation between forces and materials. The Figure is animated by two simultaneous movements, a dynamic double, an alternating rhythm, a heartbeat that defines its athleticism as a powerful deformation, a violent body-to-body fight with sensation.

The first movement rolls out from the material structure, the flat surface, toward the Figure, and expels it by contracting it and imprisoning it: this is the Figure's place, not so much a spatial place than the act of taking place, an event that Deleuze calls a fact, "the fact of the Figure." It coexists with a second, inverse movement, which goes from the Figure toward material structure, or the flat surface, around which the Figure tends to move spasmodically in a contour, "dissipating in the material structure."[54] This "second direction of the exchange," the second form of athleticism, conveys the rhythm and beat of the painting.

Through an onsite deformation, a static quiver that courses through the body in an intense movement, the Figure not only takes place but appears as an event, a "deformed and deforming movement that transfers the real image onto the body at every moment in order to constitute the Figure."[55] This beating animates sensation in the painting and constitutes a rhythm: a diastole that relates the Figure to its isolating place in a deformed way (the movement of the flat surface toward the Figure), and a systole that expels the Figure from the painting. There is a dynamism vibrating in the canvas, showing that the contour between the flat surface and the Figure acts as a membrane that ensures communication in both senses. What passes between the Figure and the material structure, this beating that simultaneously alternates between systole and diastole is rhythm. At the same time, the systole contracts the body of the structure into the Figure that the diastole expands and dissipates the body of the Figure toward the structure. Deleuze remarks that the coexistence of these two movements forms a rhythm that leaf through or make sensation either synesthetic or synthetic, "forcing it to move through different levels under the action of forces."[56]

These two movements can be traced back to the primary forces of becoming: individuating actualization that propels structure toward the Figure expresses the rise toward form; the screaming deformation that expels the Figure with a scream, an upsurge into structure, implies intensive becoming and the insistence of the virtual in the actual. Thus, it is necessary to emphasize this outcome: the body without organs designates the virtual, intensive side of every corporeal organization less than the rhythmic coexistence and sensible beating of the virtual in the actual. Bacon's painting contains a unique contact with the forces of bodies, because it turns out to be a trap for becoming, or the modulation of the actual (systole) and the virtual (diastole) palpitating alternatively. Painted sensation is thus temporalized, distanced between the individuating actualization (the taking place of the actual) and the intensive differenciation of the body without organs (the virtual event). It becomes vibration.

Vibrations and the body without organs

The rhythm of a painting, which is given through the empirical inventory of its movements that are enacted between elements, reveals sensation to be an intensive vibration and deformation of the body. What moves through and qualifies the Figure are the very movements that animate it and capture the potentiality for the deformation of a body, which are not worn out from a narrative reproduction of the cliché, but produce what Bacon calls a shock to the nervous system. To paint sensation is to paint the relationship between force and sensation, the point of birth between vibration and sensation, which is capable of being transformed from pictorial material into a spectator. Color becomes tactile. This process of sensation defines the Figure. In accordance with the intensive definition of a masterpiece that is capable of producing such an effect, the shock makes it possible for the theory of the body without organs to find its last phase of development. Deleuze first develops the theory of the body without organs on the poetic field located in Antonin Artaud, and then develops it on the field of the life sciences in a remarkable analysis of Geoffroy Saint-Hilaire and Canguilhem.

An intensive movement runs through the body as it connects with the forces that traverse it—this movement is none other than sensation, which demands that the body be thought without organs.

> Bacon can be said to have encountered Antonin Artaud at several points: the Figure is distinctly the body without organs (dismantling the organism in favor of the body, the face in favor of the head).[57]

Bacon's high spirituality leads him outside the organic toward the encounter of elementary forces of corporeality, which allows him to escape the organic cliché and reach this "deformed and deforming movement that transfers the real image onto the body at every moment in order to constitute the Figure."[58] That is how he reaches the Figure and escapes the figurative. "Bacon did not stop painting bodies without organs, the intensive fact of the body."[59] Sensation shatters the limits of organic activity, is liberated from the mold of organic form, and exposes itself to intensive forces in action. In 1981, Deleuze rediscovers the same tendencies that he found when discussing Artaud in *The Logic of Sense*: affective athleticism and scream-breaths in Bacon correspond to those in Artaud. Sensation ceases to be representative when it is related to the body and can be qualified as real.

Bacon shows himself to be capable of making powerful, nonorganic life that animates the sensed body, and the forces that he captures are those of the body without organs, which Deleuze also calls intensive becoming, or "becoming-animal," in order to note the same intensive power of deformation and movement at the limit of the human with regard to the Figure.[60] The Figure "experiences an extraordinary becoming-animal in a series of screaming deformations."[61] Here we have the deformation of the body, the body without organs, becoming-animal, and the modulation of organic form under the action of forces that construct it and elongate it, which it responds to and resists. This is why "the Figure is not only a body isolated" in flat surfaces and contours, "but [is] the deformed body that escapes," and this body is not so much devoid of organs as it is trembling with temporary, transitory organs. It is no longer a matter of taking place, but a matter of appearance, the Figure event and its intensive force.[62] This rhythmic vibration, which is reinforced by the dynamic interactions between the Figure, structure, and the ground, endows Bacon's painting with sensible potentiality. That is what makes it possible for him to "surpass figuration," the figurative, the narrative, the anecdotic, and the dogmatic, in accordance with the unique perspective of the nonfigurative portrait.

Surpassing figuration, painting sensation

Nonetheless, the distinction between the figurative and the figural, and the injunction of surpassing figuration, should not at all be understood as an accomplishment of modern painting. If it were just about pulling painting away from the figurative, ancient painting succeeded in doing so perfectly well, whereas contemporary painting struggles to accomplish it, besieged as it is by clichés, readymade images, and constituted form. Surpassing figuration works on different levels: ancient painting accomplished it by making the coordinates of the organized body pass through the liberated presence of disorganized bodies; contemporary painting is split between the abstract approach, with its unique intellection, and the nonfigurative, figural approach that Bacon opens up in its material dimension with vital, nonorganic potentialities that run through the body.

As such, the definition of painting that Deleuze develops in *Francis Bacon* is both disarmingly simple and a great entry into actual painting. Beyond genres and techniques, far from discourses on form, painting is a matter of sensation. Moreover, what painting paints is sensation. The approaches that painting uses to attain this production of sensation are extremely diverse and span across various formulas in the history of painting. Each instance involves an aesthetic shock that must be situated precisely within the nervous system, which is a bodily event, since sensation is captured in the materiality of painting.

Art and Immanence

Becoming versus Resemblance

The intensive conception of form as relations of forces and affects definitively breaks with all hermeneutic interpretation by positing art as image, affect, and percept in *The Movement-Image, The Time-Image*, and *What Is Philosophy?*

The critique of interpretation, continued by Guattari, was essential for a philosophy of immanence, which began with the first Spinozist studies in the refutation of eminence and analogical equivocity in favor of univocity. The Spinozist critique of analogy occurs in conjunction with the clinical reduction of the signifier. There is no transcendent sense in the text, and no analogically figurative, eminent intelligibility in materiality. Art cannot be the object of hermeneutics if hermeneutics designates the search for some true, invariant meaning that is introduced by way of analogy in the material sign-system within the body of the work. Along with Spinoza, Deleuze launches a critique against all attempts to reduce art to the expression of a meaning that would involve abstracting from the materiality of the work. The nondiscursive arts, painting, and cinema are not reducible to discursive meanings that would be circumscribed by analogy. It is not that they are devoid of intelligibility, since thought is produced by the image. At the same time, this notion of thought, which is also Spinozist, is not an act of private consciousness, but the ideal singularity of a differentiated virtuality. By choosing Spinoza's ethics rather than judgment by analogy, Deleuze replaces signifying forms of analogy with an expression of real forces in ethology.

Every analogy relies on transcendence, hierarchy, and the separation of form and matter. This critique of analogy drives the critique of the humanities and reconstructs the status of art: analogy depends upon imaginary resemblance or structural homology. Both the humanities (e.g. Lévi-Strauss' ethnology and Lacan's psychoanalysis) and discourses on art and literature suffer from this analogical conception of form, which attach the meaning of the work to the author's, reader's, or spectator's imaginary intentions, or on the work's formal properties. When all is said and done, structure is nothing more than a composition of relations, and not analogical correspondence. "What constitutes structure is a compound relation of movement and rest, speed and slowness."[1] When formally reducing structure to haecceity, Deleuze has no problem demonstrating that this composition of forces requires an understanding of resemblance as becoming.

The critique of analogy, which is first developed in *Spinoza and the Problem of Expression*, also attests to this important realization. Instead of applying the analogical theory of the copy that imitates a model to art and literature, Deleuze shows that it is necessary to understand this relation as a becoming, from the perspective of the capture of forces. It is not the copy that imitates the model, but rather, the act of imitation that creates the model, as was shown in the analyses of the minor and the major levels. The imitative act raises the model to the major level, thus constituting the model much more than the reverse. If all bodies are relational compounds, then one moves from one body to another in a simple, intensive variation that ensures the formation of a new haecceity, which corresponds to the effective relations of this new encounter. Thus, imitation does not occur between two terms that preexist the relation in question, as if they are independent and given ahead of time; instead, the encounter literally forms a zone of indiscernibility and a new body—a haecceity of neighborhoods that provisionally reunites these terms as they are truly taken up into a "bloc" of becoming. The famous example of the wasp and the orchid serves as a model for this theory of becoming that delivers art from an analogical theory.

> Ahab does not imitate the whale; he becomes Moby Dick, he moves within the zone of neighborhoods where he can no longer be distinguished from Moby Dick [. . .] it is no longer a question of Mimesis, but of becoming.[2]

What applies to the relationship between man and animal in Melville's work also applies to the relationship between the work and the forces it captures. Deleuze rejects models of interpretation that conceive of the figure as an imaginary identification or relational correspondence. Deleuze replaces the metaphor, which presupposes the word's transition from a zone of literal meaning to figurative meaning, with continuous variation, or a becoming of forces. As such, there is no longer a literal meaning or a figurative meaning, but an intensive circuit and a "distribution of states within the word's range."[3] The figurative meaning falls away with the literal meaning, without excluding literature from the movement of thought. But this movement becomes a transformation, a metamorphosis that occurs through the deterritorialization of sense and sound.

If there is a figure it is in the sense of real metamorphoses, not metaphors or analogical correspondences in structure. Becoming-animal, in painting or literature, illustrates this metamorphic capacity that is neither metaphorical nor allegorical. When describing Gregor Samsa's metamorphosis into an animal, Kafka explores a becoming that affects entities having to do with literature at the same time that literature innovates his style. Symbolism, imaginary identification, and structural homology do not affect style in different art forms—including their form or content—but real transformation manages to do so. "A thing is no longer designated according to its literal meaning, or an assignation of metaphors according to a figurative meaning," but a "sequence of intensive states," "a circuit of intensities," which subjects entities in art to the same, intensive deterritorialization. This applies to grammatically formed words, musical sounds, and literary characters (e.g. Gregor Samsa), regardless of whether they happen to be pictorial or cinematographic.[4] The image is thus captured in a neighborhood and an arrangement between different terms that nonetheless remain distinct. In this encounter with a zone of indiscernibility the image comes to know a "becoming-dog of man and a becoming-man of the dog, and a becoming-monkey or beetle of man, and vice versa."[5] The shift unleashes the deformation of forces onto a single plane—a single zone of immanent transformation—instead of superposing two separate meanings, as analogy does when enacting a substitution of forms. Success in art is measured by this ability to make new forces sensed in a vital, powerful deformation that is necessarily nonorganic, since it is confined to the level of constituted forms (organic cliché), but acts at the level of forces (body without organs).

> A thing is no longer designated according to its literal meaning, or an assignation of metaphors according to a figurative meaning. But the thing *as* images forms nothing more than a sequence of intensive states [. . .]. The image is this very process; it became while becoming.[6]

Literature, then, crosses into a zone of intensity "where contents are freed from their forms as much as they are freed from expressions, and from signifier that formalized them."[7] Literature produces the same visionary capacity on the syntactical plane, the same informal potentiality as the nondiscursive arts, and like them, it evokes an experience of the body that redistributes thought. Colors and lines for painting, sounds for music, verbal descriptions for the novel, and movement-images and time-images for cinema: all of these methods converge in the arrangement of elements of sensation. Blocs of percepts capture an hour of the day, a smile, the quality of a breath, and affective variations turn force onto itself, causing it to vibrate in the image.

The expressivity of art is thus intensive, and art's success is measured by the encounters that it arranges for the spectator, and in the way art's materiality forms or reforms our lived relations. This is why the critique of art is strictly a matter of cartography, and requires what Deleuze calls "the art of *Ethics* itself," in honor of Spinoza: "organizing good encounters, constructing lived relations, forming potentialities, and experimenting."[8]

The plane of immanence, the plane of transcendence, and the critique of structuralism

Deleuze replaces metaphor with metamorphosis. Bacon and his faceless heads, the gaseous perception of Vertov's camera, and Michaux's cacophonies: nondiscursive art and literature are established on the plane of immanence of speeds and slownesses, making subjectification explode with an affect in the force relations that animate the materiality that they employ.

The theory of art as a relation of forces thus necessitates distinguishing between two planes, opposing reproduction to itineration, resemblance to cartographic endeavor, and a transcendent conception to an immanent conception of art. There is only one world, and the art's effect is produced in the real. This very surprising theory of reference rejects all analogical *mimesis*: art, which is the real, *follows* matter, and arranges new encounters with it.

> *Following is not at all the same thing as reproducing*, and one never follows in order to reproduce [. . .]. One is forced to follow when one is searching for the "singularities" of a material, or rather, a materiality, and not the discovery of a form [. . .].[9]

All the arts move from machinic assemblage to affectology, including literature, architecture, cinema, and the Baroque fold. Simondon's principle of modulation reinforces Spinoza's rejection of analogy and transcendence: it is no longer a question of "imposing a form onto a material, but of developing a richer and richer material [. . .] apt to capture more and more intense forces."[10] All of the arts arise out of an ethological map of affects, because it is not known what a body can do when it is not pulled back to the affects that traverse it, which "may or may not be arranged with other affects, with the affects of another body, in order to either destroy it or be destroyed by it, or in order to exchange actions and passions with it, or to construct a more powerful body with it."[11] Accordingly, art sticks firmly to this plane and interchange, this circulation of affects, and is a body like other bodies, an image, made by force relations, percepts, affects, and potentiality.

This conception of art as an image, which separates the transcendental moral plane of analogy, on one hand, from Spinoza's plane of consistency, which is formed by speeds and material transformations, on the other hand, leads to this outcome. Art is not a different body from other bodies. Since it arises out of a plane of immanence and not transcendence, a reconstruction of its status begins from the moment it is thought apart from a spiritual or anthropological essence, or when its functions are confiscated by human subjectivity. This paradox thus must be maintained: since art is a body like other bodies, it requires that the immanent or transcendent uses that it makes are shared, and that it cuts across these manifestations, discourses, modes of production and reception in art, along with the immanent ethics of the affect and the transcendent morality of judgment. Since art is immanent, it is necessary to reject any understanding of it that is established from a transcendent perspective, and any separation of art and life must be combatted, as well as any evaporation of art into a metal, recreational, or inoffensive circuit.

Deleuze takes up Artaud's Tarahumaras by splitting them into two planes where one "is denounced as the source of all evil."[12] In *The Age of Suspicion*, Nathalie Sarraute also distinguished between two "planes," where one finds an ordinary scope of familiar characters from the previous century; or one can proceed as Proust does and liberate characters from "the minute fragments of an impalpable material," the tropisms and affects.[13]

These instances fuel the separation between the transcendent plane of individuated organization and the immanent plane of affects and forces that Deleuze sets up in *Dialogues* and *A Thousand Plateaus*. This distinction helps affirm the critique of analogy, which favors imaginary resemblance or structural homology. The "plane of immanence objects to analogy" and fights against resemblance from a perspective that is just as vital (regarding theories of the living, for the philosophy and science of life) as it is social (for the humanities, and the analysis of cultural works).[14]

The dual refutation of the imaginary and the structural that Deleuze continues to affirm with Foucault, from 1970 onward, finds its point of application and extends beyond the theory of enunciation into the ontology of becoming, allowing it to be applied to all cultural and vital forms without being exclusively restricted to the order of discourse. Analogy, whether serial or imaginary—where Deleuze bridges analogy and Thomist proportion—or structural and rational— the analogy of proportionality—conceives of "Nature as an immense *mimesis*."[15] Analogy's inability to think in terms of becoming forms the core of Deleuze's critique of structural methodology. Of course, the analogy of proportionality, which substitutes the work of the Understanding for the resemblance of a solely imaginary relation, can be "considered royal." Nevertheless, it is not less abstract or derivative than imaginary resemblance, and like imaginary resemblance, the analogy of proportionality rests on the imitation of a model.

Deleuze thus administers his ultimate critique of structuralism in the tenth of *A Thousand Plateaus* under the heading of "Memories of a Naturalist," in the context *mimesis* and the vital symbiosis that was used to develop the theory of capture. Contemporary humanities rediscover the controversies that disturbed the field of life sciences at the turn of the nineteenth century, notably the dispute between Cuvier and Geoffroy Saint-Hilaire, which already demonstrated the theoretical superiority of structural homology over imaginary resemblance. Structuralism was established on the ashes of the imaginary. Deleuze grants theoretical privilege to the structuration of differences, which is founded on the equality of relations and internal homologies. On the other hand, the series of resemblances, which approach the identification of terms through simple, external resemblance, and through identification with an eminent model, possess a modicum of scientificity. The imagination, even if it is pushed to the "the highest cosmic or dynamic level, as in Bachelard or Jung," can always be refuted by structure, as Lévi-Strauss demonstrates.[16] According to a series, progression and regression cannot explain becoming any better than imitation or the imaginary contribution to types. From this point of view, structuralism will always be more correct than imaging interpretation, and could easily substitute "metamorphoses in the imagination, for metaphors in the concept."[17] At the same time, Deleuze shows that he can be ironic with respect to structuralism's "great revolution" and its preference for rationalization: "the entire world becomes more reasonable."[18] The heroic effort of structural intelligibility and its appetite for formal domination finds itself definitively dismissed. This so-called intelligibility turns out to be an anthropological leap, and the superiority of the Understanding poorly hides the European consciousness' will toward domination that lifts the real up to intelligibility. Structure thus values its formal consistency even more and establishes itself against series, because metaphor cannot fight against homology, but also because its epistemological efficacy accompanies a pragmatic program of domination in the order of knowledge.

Even if it is theoretically stronger, symbolic structure is not any more adequate to becoming than imaginary resemblance. These two theoretical adversaries find themselves disproven by the same argument, because they both abandon becoming for the sake of correspondence.

> Neither of these two figures of analogy is adequate to becoming: neither the imitation of the subject, nor the proportion of a form.[19]

Now, according to Deleuze, "a correspondence of relations does not make a becoming," and this implies that the concepts of resemblance, correspondence, and progress in imitation are eradicated from the arts.[20]

The distinction between these immanent and transcendent planes is thus determinate for the status of resemblance, as well as the history of art. The analogical plane reduces becoming to an eminent term of a development, or establishes proportional relations of structure.[21] This is what Deleuze calls a plane of organization, as we saw, a plane of judgment, or sometimes a theological plane when noting that it refers to a transcendent principle, which concerns forms and formed subjects, such that the archetypal imaginary of Jung, Bachelard, or Durand, and the structural homology of formalists can be referenced back-to-back. Instead of studying the material plane of the image and sticking to the longitudes and latitudes that map a body, they postulate a readymade copy and reduce real variations to developments of form in history, or subject formations in styles.

Historical genesis and formal structure, which Deleuze sought to articulate in *The Logic of Sense*, finds itself brought back to the same analogical tendency, and their differences seem inessential in this respect: the plane can be said to be structural or genetic, or "as much as is desired, structural *and* genetic."[22] The local opposition between ideal structure and imaginary resemblance arises from the same identification with a plane of transcendence that relegates forms and subjects, and always adds a supplementary dimension to the given. The plane of immanence itself remains strictly within the given, that is, within force relations, the speeds and slownesses between particles, nonformed elements (longitude), and the anonymous affects that fill them (latitude).

By dismissing the reversible figures of relational correspondence and serial resemblance throughout the critique of natural history, structural anthropology, and every aesthetic theory founded on the imitation of nature or the proportion of form, Deleuze redefines the arts' mission: to think in terms of becomings.

Semiotics must not depend on either the imaginary resource of metaphorical resemblance, nor on the detection of intelligible formal structures; these are two processes of interpretation that unburden art from its efficacy and confine it to the inoffensive planes of the symbolic or the imaginary, depriving it of its diffusion as a force in the real.

> Ah, the poverty of the imaginary and the symbolic, the real always being put off until tomorrow.[23]
>
> [Art] is neither analogy, nor imagination, but an arrangement or speeds and affects on this plane of consistency: a place, a program, or rather, a diagram [. . .].[24]

Regarding the differences between the arts

The theory of art as a relation of forces can thus seem to favor a new dualism, which is erected between two tendencies in art: the kind of art that concerns substances and subjects, and the art of images, which is attentive to haecceities. The theme of the image shows that this is not the case at all. Of course, when recalling the Hegelian determination of Greek art as the triumph of subjectivity, Deleuze often considers Western art to be an art of individualities, from its very origins, which is numb to the art of tropisms and haecceities characteristic of oriental art on the other end of the spectrum, and Chinese art, in particular.

> Throughout examples of civilization, the Orient has many more individuations by haecceity than by subjectivity or substantiality [. . .].[25]

Yet, this is not a matter of abstractly opposing the Orient to the Occident, but about revealing a kind of tension between organizational growth, or stratifying territorialization, and points of deterritorialization, a concern that also affects Western art. This tension determined the opposition between French literature and Anglo-American literature, and during the time of *Difference and Repetition* it allows Deleuze to accord priority to the methods of contemporary art with sympathy toward actual problems of creativity. The true principle of discrimination between the arts comes from the intensive virtues of the haecceity: the destratification of the subject, the signifier, and the organic body. The same opposition between stratifying growth and virtual intensity vitalizes the two volumes that he devotes to cinema. *The Movement-Image* in classical cinema creates its plots by following an ordered narrative, by defining individuated characters whose perceptions cross over into actions, and who can be thought to transform the world. On the other hand, impersonal and floating individuations of neorealism are more engaged with descriptions than actions, just as they are more concerned with incomplete sketches than reactions. It is a question of moving from a narrative model to a descriptive model. *The Time-Image* moves from epic narration, which centers around a triumphant subject that acts within a readymade world, toward neutral description, a ballad where partial and floating subjectivities experience the intensive and virtual power of sensation in the relaxation of their sensory-motor connections. The crisis of the action-image, which corresponds to the war's historical caesura, separates these two types of images: the movement-image focused on the victorious action of the Western, for instance, or the film noir, and the time-image of a face, an intensive surface filmed in close-up shots, or by wandering through town at night. These two images are separated by the considerable political fracture of the World War II. But this historical event only introduced its caesura by naming a turning point and articulating two streams of cinematographic creation. And if the war's irruption of history is not the only reason for neorealism's innovativeness, it is not because it is indifferent from the point of view of its social and political actuality, but the event has to produce its effects from a cinematographic perspective. Without minimizing the force of the political events, Deleuze understands art to be a creation of new types of signs and images, not as a reaction or commentary. The virtual becoming of the neorealist description is not explained by the event of the war, but it responds to it, and opens characters and actions onto their intensive becomings for the war.

True art would thus be able to make the body without organs sensed, along with nonsignifying breaths, asubjective relations, forces of time and affects of material, as we see with Virginia Woolf, who precedes each chapter of her novel *The Waves* with a sequence on the waves' eddies, hours, and becomings. Deleuze prefers nonformal art to the art of subjects and forms, with dreamy material that will be vigorously distinguished from formlessness, and which is characterized by its ability to capture the event's haecceity.

> Cross the wall, the Chinese maybe, but at what price? At the price of a *becoming-animal*, a *becoming-flower or rock* [. . .].[26]

Art is no longer qualified by its function as a line of flight with respect to constituted assemblages, but by a positive becoming that defines the triple principle of this Ethics of the haecceity: becoming-imperceptible, becoming-indiscernible, and becoming-impersonal. Tearing down the wall of the signifier did not imply imitating the schizophrenic, but reaching intensive force relations through a stylistic work that puts art into the world as a force among other forces:

"to be in time with the world." Art is the instrument of intensive becoming, and it produces its effect for reality.

> But art is never an end, it is only a tool for tracing life lines; that is to say, all of those real becomings that are not simply produced *in* art, all those active flights that do not involve fleeing *into* art, or seeking refuge in art, and those positive deterritorializations that are not going to be reterritorialized on art, but are swept away by it toward nonsignifying, a-subjective, and faceless regions.[27]

Deleuze can thus invoke an Oriental aesthetics that knew how to garner importance to haecceities, much more than Western aesthetics, recommending an impersonal withdrawal for the creator. Chinese thought, in fact, values haecceities, the kind of relations like "winds, undulations of snow or sand," and chooses to privilege whatever "has neither a beginning nor end, nor origin or destination" but "is always in the middle," if the middle is understood as an empty median.[28] But he perfectly integrates this dimension of Chinese thought into the definition that he gives to Bacon's flat surface, for example, and its "chronochromism"; that is to say, its ability to fold and vibrate time in a block of color.

> The colored void, or rather, coloring void, is already force.[29]

Here the void receives the status of sensation in accordance with the precepts of Chinese art. In order for a painting to become a work it is necessary, "as the Chinese painter says, [that] it keep enough empty spaces for horses to gallop (if only through the variety of planes)."[30] This dynamic tension of empty space as force implies that the figure is no longer opposed to it according to the hylemorphic schema that opposes the ground (the material force and empty median) and form. In its own way, Chinese art responded to the refutation of a dualism between the trace and empty space by releasing the point from its subordination to the line: the point seems like a kinetic concentration of the line, just as in Michaux's great ink drawings. The movement and the level of signs, most of all, are given in the irruption of projectiles—the miniscule projection of droplets that keep the nervous viscosity of Chinese ink intact, and which, on the contrary, provide slower ink blots with coordinates on their axes. From the point of view of Chinese art, the middle corresponds to the empty meridian's respiration, which circulates between traits, just as lines conform to the principle of *ch'i-shih*, the "momentum, growth, and lines of force" that control the articulation of traits, including their skeleton and respiration.[31]

A monument, but a monument can include a few strokes or even a few lines, as in a poem by Emily Dickinson. From a sketch about an old, worn out ass, "How marvelous! It is done with two stokes, but placed on immutable bases" [. . .].[32]

Of course, the haecceity in Deleuze applies to every level of reality, but its methodological relevance is easier to pinpoint for this kind of assemblage, which "requires an extraordinarily fine topology," such as a mist or fog, which pertains to smooth spaces—as opposed to striated spaces that are squared when put into form—and that do not rely "on points or objects, but on haecceities, and relational sets (winds, undulations of snow or sand [. . .])."[33]

Even if it is easy for the Ink-Paintbrush to paint the Visible, the Full, it is even more difficult to represent the Invisible, the Empty Space, Between Mountain and Water; the light from smoke and the ink from clouds are endlessly changing.[34]

Thus, the Chinese tradition introduces an explicit theory of the haecceity, stressing its dual aspects of tension and virtuality, even if it integrates it into a cosmology that remains foreign to Deleuze. Oriental art and the nomadic line are at stake, whose functional properties transform the use of space and the status of the line, becoming a circulation and plastic movement that no longer follow points. Nomad art, circulating in an open space that becomes more and more connected, foretells the distinction between smooth and striated space, which Deleuze and Guattari adopt from Boulez. It concerns two uses for measure: smooth space applies to a numbered rhythm and is not subjected to external measure; striated space applies to homogeneous measure that squares an ordinate space in advance. This makes it possible to distinguish between the abstract line, which unfolds its smooth space in dynamic turns, and the line that is standardized by a striated space where it takes place and the external measures to which it is subjected.

What Worringer called the abstract and infinite northern line comes to us from the depths of time; the line of the universe that forms ribbons and strips, wheels and turbines, an entire "living geometry" "*raising mechanical forces to intuition*" and constituting a powerful, non-organic life.[35]

Classical ornamentation (Greek or Renaissance, for example) prefers a wise, moderated line that is subordinated to symmetry—the repeated star, the centered rose. However, the nomadic line adopts the turbine, peripheral movement, and the speed of a proliferation that breaks free.[36] What distinguishes the nomadic line from classical ornamentation is the criteria of speed, proliferation, and accelerated transformation that characterizes smooth space. In itself, the line frees itself from representation, metrics, but also from repetition and symmetry, which characterize classical ornamentation in striated space, subjecting it to systems of external coordinates. With Worringer, Deleuze distinguishes ornamentation that is subjected to striated space of regular metrics, which is characterized by the repetition of a motif in reverse, such as symmetrical alternations that calm and close off rhythm while provoking an additional effect in Greek or renaissance ornament; that is to say, unity or closure. He prefers the Nordic line that puffs up through indefinite iteration. Organic ornament is characterized by its stability, its levelheadedness, which "keeps elusive, mechanic mobility in check," as Worringer says. It restricts the northern line, which changes through internal proliferation that follows a fluid, noncrystalline model, and both Deleuze and Worringer consider ornamentation part of the organic repertoire. As a result, we have the concept of elusive and mechanical mobility that is repetitive yet infinite, which runs through barbaric art on the Gothic line, and which makes it possible for Worringer to formulate the concept of a "powerful, non-organic vitality." Deleuze emphasizes this tendency, which opens up the space for a kinetic, deterritorializing line. Thus, Deleuze uses "The infinite melody of [Worringer's] the northern line" freely in *A Thousand Plateaus*, *Francis Bacon*, and *What Is Philosophy?*, in the context of tension between the organic and nonorganic, smooth and striated space, nomadic and sedentary values, and in defining the Figure's process.[37]

Solving the problem of dualism and transformation in the arts

Oriental art and the nomadic line are of vital importance, but one must not overestimate their relative importance in Deleuze's work, and the same goes, in principle, for the opposition between the Orient and the Occident, or between the nomad and the sedentary. Furthermore, whatever value Chinese art may have, Deleuze's analyses of them are fewer and less in depth than those that he devotes to the becoming-haecceity in Western art, cinema, the Baroque line, or the nomadic northern line. The theme of the haecceity endows art with a becoming-imperceptible line that our Western gaze discovers in Chinese or Japanese art, as we are guided by the problematic of abstract art. The contemporary status of classical Chinese art also depends on this liberation of the line, which Michaux found in Klee, and that Deleuze also thinks through, after his encounter with

Worringer, and it depends on the becoming-line of the point that is unfolded in a trajectory.[38]

In fact, art is an excellent terrain for experimentation for a philosophy of variation that seeks to escape discrete oppositions and binary Manicheism. By taking nomadic art into consideration, Deleuze definitively escapes polemical cleavages and the logic of a *Defense and illustration* in contemporary art, which was the case during the 1960s. The plastic domain, in particular, lends itself to this practice of the major and minor poles' gradual dissolution, so it is difficult to liken Piero della Francesca or Michelangelo to the servile execution of a norm, or the imposition of a model of domination. At the same time, the short history of cinema forbids the theme of major art from being applied to the classic works of Vertov, Eisenstein, or Dreyer. This is because cinema now concerns semiotics, and not the polemics surrounding the status of art or the discourses that it creates. Deleuze's interest bears on textures and materials, meaning, the operations by which art produces its effect. It would be completely mistaken to think that Deleuze applies an historical and geographical criterion to creativity, which misunderstands Ancient or French art.

Moreover, Deleuze addresses Ancient art and Baroque art when he discloses the movement from the minor to mannerism. Baroque painting and statues establish a mannerist object that is no longer essentialist as an event, but as a force field and an object in the process of constitution, and not like a readymade form. So, Deleuze adopts Gilbert Simondon's definition of modulation, which helps him, as always, affirm the move from form to force, and he relates it to Georges Canguilhem's anomalous variation. The object must not be related to a spatial mold, but to temporal modulation: it is no longer determined from the center of an organized figure, but only from the point of view of variation. "The fluctuation of the norm replaces the permanence of a law."[39] This concept of mannerism, which Deleuze defines in *The Fold*, literally adopts Simondon's notion of modulation: "The new status of the object is no longer related to the status of a spatial mold; that is to say, to a form-matter relation, but to 'temporal modulation,'" Deleuze writes before citing Simondon: this "temporal modulation implies a continuous variation of material as well as a continuous development of form."[40] There is no longer an object or a subject "when the object takes place in a continuum through variation," and is given as an arrangement of forces, speeds, and slownesses, and not as a formed subject.

The modulation of forces and materials, which informs the definition of the haecceity and the reality of the image, turns out to be a stronger and more definite criterion than a chronological distinction that separates historical periods and privileges contemporary art, or than a symptomatology of civilizations that distinguishes between Anglo-Saxon and French literature, the Orient and the Occident, or the nomadic and the sedentary. Furthermore, these different cleavages are not cut again. This is because it is not a matter of eluding a classification of objects, but of valuing respiration, a nonformal tendency, and preferring the play of forces to a repetition of forms. As such, national qualifications remain extremely equivocal, and Deleuze and Guattari do not ignore this. "Profound dangers and ambiguities [. . .] coexist with this endeavor, as if [. . .] each creation were confronted by a possible infamy": the attention to race, territory, and national characteristics can easily be perverted as racism or dominating fascism, while the Orient threatens to turn to Western fanaticism.[41] Deleuze and Guattari already deployed this critique in *Anti-Oedipus* by mocking the Oriental fanaticism of people like Laing.

At the same time that he uses the haecceity as a polemical criterion for differentiating that which holds most of his attention in art, along the axis of a masterpiece's classificatory criteria, Deleuze formalizes the philosophical conditions of his work and solves the problem of binary dualism in 1977, in *Dialogues*.

> It would not be enough here to oppose the Orient to the Occident, the plane of immanence that comes from the Orient to the plane of transcendental organization that was always the Occident's sickness: for example, Oriental poetry or drawing and martial arts, which so often proceed by pure haecceities and grow through the "middle." The Occident itself is traversed by this immense plane of immanence or consistency, which takes forms and tears indications of speed from them, and dissolves subjects and extracts haecceities from them: leaving nothing but longitudes and latitudes.[42]

Deleuze does not posit Chinese painting as being superior to Western painting, but instead gets ready to devote a study to Western painting—Francis Bacon— who epitomizes the history of Western painting. Deleuze's literary analyses no doubt bear the mark of a preference for contemporary novels and poetry: his references are almost exclusively situated on the field of recent literature, from the eighteenth century to our time, and he certainly confirms that Anglo-American literature is better than a certain kind of French literature—a defamatory category that he immediately violates for *every* French author that interests him: Artaud, Proust, Mallarmé, and Céline—Michaux is Belgian. His pictorial analyses, on the other hand, absolutely dismiss the criterion that grants privilege to the methods of contemporary art, so it is absurd to oppose Giotto to Dubuffet, for instance.[43] The history of plastic art manifests the oscillation between traits that can be considered nonformal and those that bear on subjective forms instead (individuated faces or landscapes), if this fragile and futile criterion is maintained once the haecceity is reached. As always, the polemics in Deleuze serve as a provisional relay for the exploration of a certain domain and turn out to be futile once the theory is achieved.

The haecceity brings with it a new theory of the subject that requires that it be located on the plane of forces and not forms. Thus, from this perspective it is absolutely pointless to oppose the haecceity to the subject, because even if most conceptions of the subject actually adopt a transcendent mode, in reality, the subject is formed though force relations, and the image that we have of it is a subjectified force.[44] This is the same for other universals in philosophy. In reality, subjects, objects, things, and substances are haecceities. At the very most the haecceities of assemblages will be distinguished from interassemblages; in other words, between the analyses focused on a particular individuation (a body, considered as longitude and latitude) and haecceities of interassemblages, whose analysis crosses several packs of lines.

> It is every assemblage in its individuated entirety that is located between a haecceity; the assemblage is defined by a certain longitude and latitude, by speeds and affects, independently of forms and subject that only belong to another plane.[45]

This is the case for haecceities as for multiplicities, as they are evaluated according to the relative stability of their assemblage, or according to the lines of flight that also traverse them. The haecceity possesses all of the characteristics of a multiplicity, which is always a multiplicity of a multiplicity, and it necessarily overlaps different individuations across diverse levels. Thus, it is inseparable from its neighborhood, which Deleuze takes in the topological and quantum sense to note the indiscernibility of forces, independently of considered subjects and determined forms.

The relation of forces in the haecceity serve, then, as a provisional criterion for formalizing modes of informal subjectification, which could seem more unstable or more delicate in its theorization. Deleuze uses it as an aesthetic claim and determines modes of expression through it, which overcomes the alternative of forms and forces. Just as subjects, people, things, and organs are actually formed by haecceities, longitude and latitude, spatio-temporal coordinates, and variation in power, the haecceity is not attributable to subjects, things, or constituted individuals: subjects and things should not be attributed a plane of composition in terms of being prior to a foundation. One must avoid this simple understanding, which reestablishes an opposing dualism of subjects, forms, and identifiable things on one hand, and their floating, spatio-temporal coordinates that maintain the subject-form, on the other, only varying their predicates, just as one must avoid valorizing the politics of becomings-animal, the body without organs, or all the becomings-intense that always remain "extremely ambiguous," if they are extracted from their polemical context in order to transform them into prescriptions.[46]

Hence, the haecceity has to do with capture and not resemblance, with becoming and not identification with a subject or a symbolism of form. It has to do with rhythm and not measure, if measure is understood as a given and coded form, while rhythm does not operate in homogeneous space-time, but in heterogeneous blocs and changes in direction. "Every haecceity is formed in the passage from one milieu to another," and is formed with other milieus and is subjected to intensive movements of deterritorialization and reterritorialization. As such, the haecceity is an image, a capture of forces, and a variation of affects.

The affection of the image

The same formal montage runs through the analysis of cinema. *The Movement-Image* details different kind of montage that classify cinema, focusing on prewar cinema. According to the movement-image, different tendencies are attained that correspond to different kinds of montage, movements, or schools, which Deleuze specifies as American, Soviet, French, or German. In this case, as well, one must not ascribe a prescriptive role to this classification, or be shocked by its lacunae and the absence of Italian, Japanese, African, or South American schools. It is only a question of moving partitions, or descriptive categories that help with the conceptual creation of new types of signs, making it possible to cut out, classify, and index new kinds of images. The second volume, *The Time-Image*, corresponds to the chronological, postwar caesura, and is ordered as a function of a new image regime. Recall that the movement-image unfolded into a wide range of perception-image varieties, from the affection-image to the action-image. With the time-image, a new image regime digs a mode of becoming into the heart of the movement-image, which is no longer suspended in the actualization of a movement understood as a shifting of parts in space. This is how cinematographic art is written into a Bergsonian universe. It no longer treats movement like a displacement of a stable object running along a trajectory in an all-encompassing space, but rather, an intensive transformation and real vibration of qualities in time. Cinema, in its own way, exhibits what Deleuze considers to be the most decisive metaphysical result of philosophy: the coexistence of the actual and virtual in the image.

By moving from *The Movement-Image* to *The Time-Image*, not only does cinema move from one period to another, but it moves from a mode of individuating narrative to intensive description, from a regime of qualified, ordered space and time to a direct experience of becoming. This is how cinematographic art explores Bergson's philosophical advancements on its own terms: spatial movement and actual shifting always presuppose intensive and virtual vibration, in reality. Time palpitates behind movement. The intensive becoming of time doubles the actual movement of history at every point.

> What Bergson discovers beyond translation is vibration, radiation. Our error consists in believing that it is any element external to qualities that moves. But qualities themselves are pure vibrations that change at the same time that the so-called elements move.[47]

Using the shift from the movement-image to the time-image, cinema explores the movement from forms and subjects toward intensive forces. It implies a relaxation of the sensory-motor link that redoubles and intensifies the interval, distension, and cerebral fracture that already qualified vital images. Recall that subjectified images are stretched between actions and reactions and hollowed around a vital "center" of indetermination, separating the subjected action from reaction, which took the subjective color of the perception-image and the action-image, respectively. This characteristic relaxation of the subjective movement-image emerges as a superior potentiality in the time-image.

In accordance with Bergson, Deleuze already conceived of the movement-image as a subjective transplant between action and reaction. From this point of view, every image opens up a perspective specter that oscillates between motor reaction and sensible affection. But, the affection-image condenses an intensive pool in the sensory-motor circuit that drives perception to action, which the time-image makes even denser. For the affect of the time-image corresponds to this characteristic experience of thought in modern cinema: "the image ceased to be sensory-motor."[48] As such, the time-image distends again, and it even pushes the interval that separated the movement-image to the breaking point. Unhinged from the actual, the affection-image already developed this sensitive and vibratory disturbance within the circuit that drives perception to action. The time-image makes the affect vibrate even stronger, and from then on severs the sensory-motor link that already united perception to action in the movement-image.

It is less a matter of abandoning the sensory-motor mechanism, or of overcoming it, than it is a rupture that affects the movement-image itself, taking place within it. The sensory-motor link is not moved or replaced, as Deleuze notes, but is "broken from within," and is so distended that it ruptures. It concerns a rupture that affects the sensory-motor system of the movement-image and breaks it in two; which is to say, literally, that it stops the motor output from corresponding to the sensory input. If Deleuze, following Bergson, conceives of the sensory-motor system as a living image that mechanically doubles actions and reactions of a sensible lining, then the bankruptcy of the sensory-motor system opens the image's living circuit onto an experience of time.

As such, the modern cinema of the time-image does not refer to the image's progress or the triumph of cinematographic art, but the subversive intrusion of the virtual, the affect of time, into an image that is no longer affected by living responses. These two contradictory aspects must be conjoined within appearance. The time-image does not replace the movement-image: it coexists with it and even preexists it from the spectral perspective of the "always already," since becoming, well understood, is always already in history, just as time is in movement. And if it delivers "a little time in a pure state" better than the movement-image, it is still not better than realist cinema. First of all, the time-image does not come after the movement-image according to a chronological axis, but it is immanent in a certain sense, as a fracture, an interstice that always palpitates within it. That explains why the Japanese filmmaker Ozu serves as a privileged example of postwar cinema. Next, the movement-image itself also introduced this distinction between actions and reactions, since it made the affection-image and its current peak of intensity appear between the poles of the perception-image and the action-image. The affect's interstice, which separated the subjective perception-image from the subjective action-image, makes the time-image appear in the movement-image as its breaking point. The time-image is thus not the "inside" of the movement-image; it is outside it as its intensive lining, not "hidden," or deeper, but different and direct. It is true that it is taken from the rupture of the sensory-motor link. It is in this respect exclusively that the time-image presupposes the movement-image.

In art, it is never a question of conceiving a dialectical sublation, an historical succession, or a causal progression of two types of images; at the very most, it is a matter of fracture, interstice, or interval.[49] It is essential to avoid the aesthetic trap that consists of conveying the privilege of the time-image in terms of a "more profound," "more beautiful," or "truer" reality.[50] However, the time-image is presented in the fracture of the movement-image, a fracture that presents two sides. The ruptured sensory-motor link refers to a new political relation between man and the world, and the interstice, or interval, that inhibits perception and is immediately prolonged into action and producing movement, putting thought into direct contact with time. These two properties are intimately linked, as Deleuze demonstrates at the end of *The Movement-Image* and in the first chapter of *The Time-Image*, "Beyond the movement-image."

If the time-image introduces a "beyond" of the movement-image it is because it maximally distends the relation between image and movement, and within the interstice it puts perception into relation with thought, not with motility. Perception ceases to be prolonged in action and is put into contact with thought; from then on, the image is subordinated to the signs that make it overcome its motor state. The affection of thought replaces motor output. At the same time that perception is put into relation with thought instead of being prolonged in action that the image ceases to be confined to movement when coming into time. The sensory-motor circuit is severed because the political conditions of action are no longer given in the current assemblage, so "the modern fact is that we no longer believe in this world."[51]

But this political pessimism is doubled by the necessity for art, and especially cinema, the art of masses and potentiality, opposing pedagogy of the image to pervasive mediocrity, and calling for a population that has yet to exist. The sensory-motor rupture finds "its condition" in the "rupture of the link between man and the world," the political and historical rupture that is not internal to cinema but is limited to sociopolitical, postwar conditions. As a result, situations are no longer prolonged in actions but redouble their perceptive situation: we reach the process of seeing, that is, the prevalence of the affect on the action in the image. Deleuze establishes these conditions of sensory-motor rupture with precision: perceptions and actions "are no longer enchained."[52]

Perceptions and actions no longer form the sensory-motor chain that binds the image to movement. It unrolls a profound mutation of cinematographic style from it, which moves from organic narration toward crystalline description. Spaces cease to be places to coordinate or fill; characters are transformed into seers. Sensory-motor conditions face and transform the spatiality and modes of possible subjectification within these spaces. The transformation systematically touches on perceptions and actions, fields and modes of subjectification, or the characters that affect these fields.

That means that perceptions and actions are no longer enchained, and spaces are no longer coordinated or filled. Taken in pure optical or sonorous situations, characters find themselves condemned to wandering or walking. These are the pure seers [. . .].[53]

Thus, neorealism invents a new mode of subjectification for a new kind of relation between man and the world. As such, the cinematographic invention of a new realism corresponds to a new political relation, which is no longer sensory-motor without being outside of the world, which is a "seeing" relation with the world that corresponds to the contraction of the crystal image.

The crystal-image

Every image dilates and envelops a world, so the action-image of realist cinema referred to a world where action could transform an initial situation and produce measurable effects. Neorealism puts the image into relation not with its dilation in space but its contraction in time, so the crystal-image corresponds to the densest circuit of forms possible, as well as their intensive actualization. What, then, is the difference between a crystal-image and a crystalline description? It is a question of haecceities, or force relations giving the greatest possible actuality to the intensive insistence of the virtual. The polarity of the virtual and the actual contain the reality of permanent oscillation with the crystal-image, so that the privilege of the virtual vanishes: the crystal-image is a consolidation of the actual and the virtual, and the virtual as such turns out to be completely dependent on the actual.

Without question, the actual object dissolves in the process of individualization with the time-image, but the physical presence of the image also indicates that every virtual expresses its process of actualization. With his analyses of cinema, Deleuze is able to explain his most difficult thoughts. The virtual is not more valuable than the actual, as could easily be believed with the constant privilege given to the intensive realm and the dissolution of form into force. In fact, "the actual is the complement or the product, the object of actualization, but one that only has the virtual as its subject."[54] So, if the time-image can seem more important than the movement-image it is not because neorealist cinema comes after postwar cinema in historically successive order, or because the virtual proves to be superior to the actual in terms of ontological priority, but because the time-image pushes thought to its intensive limit. For "time is this formal relation that affects the mind as a result."⁵⁵ The time-image allows us to experience the affect of force.

> It is not time that is inside us, or at least it is not particularly inside us; it is we who are inside time, and thus are always separated by time from what determines us when affecting it.⁵⁶

The rupture of the sensory-motor link transforms the image's circuit, which puts us into direct contact with the nonorganic potentialities of life. While we are deprived of our motor protection, we subject potentiality to a vision. Instead of being reduced to action, the image is redoubled in the process of seeing. This is why the condition of this affection goes back to a rupture of man and the world, a rupture that transforms man through seeing. As such, this opposition between the agent and the seer defines seeing because of the inversion of the possibility of action in the world.

> Yet, this sensory-motor rupture finds its highest condition and goes back to a rupture of the line between man and the world. The sensory-motor rupture turns man into a seer who finds himself struck by something intolerable in the world, and is confronted with something unthinkable within thought.⁵⁷

Yet, the rupture of the sensory-motor link indicates that "something became stronger within the image."⁵⁸ That is why the rupture of the sensory-motor link comes close to the sublime and the intense experience of the limits in which Deleuze is always interested, from the body without organs, to schizophrenic stuttering and becoming-minor. From this point of view there is a romanticism of intensity in Deleuze. "Romanticism already proposed this goal: to seize the intolerable or the unbearable, the empire of misery, and through visionary becoming create a means of knowing and acting with a pure vision."⁵⁹ Yet, Deleuze just as soon declares that this new process of seeing no longer makes use of the consolations of the sublime that restores human subjectivity within its parameters once the experience of the terrible is overcome. The intolerable overcomes the conditions of ordinary subjectivity, but is no longer overcome through dialectical inversion. The unbearable is not strictly the largest or the highest, but is shown to be ordinary, mediocre, vile, or banal under the sole condition that it strikes us with the intolerable and confronts us with the unthinkable, and it thus pushes thought to its extreme limit, while making it sense its impotence.

> This is because what happens to them does not belong to them, and only half concerns them, because they know how to separate the irreducible piece from

what happens within the event: this piece of inexhaustible possibility that constitutes the unbearable, the intolerable, the visionary piece.[60]

The process of seeing the image concerns an image that is deprived of its motor releases and its active escape. This is why it is necessary to avoid turning the time-image into a more profound or a more beautiful image, since it only concerns an image that opens up a new view of the real. Contemporary cinema exposes new modes of subjectification, transforms conditions of spatiality and habitation within space, and calls for a new kind of character, a new kind of actor. The character is no longer the sovereign actor, or the subject of her action, but the passive and enchanted vector of a particular perception. We move from a motor image, which slips away into adumbrations of movement, toward what Deleuze calls pure, sensible affections.

Cliché and vision

The preponderance of perception ensures the supremacy of the time-image over the movement-image: *opsigns* and *sonsigns* designate purely optical or sonorous images, and not motor images, for Deleuze. These optical and sonorous visions cut out "a new kind of character for a new cinema," which are characterized by the "weakness of their sensory-motor links," "weak connections" that are able to "release great forces of disintegration" because of their impotence; in other words, great visionary potentialities.

In fact, Deleuze, like Bergson, contends that the perception that is resolved into action remains a common, stubborn, statistical perception, following the path of ordinary action. Inversely, the time-image delivers perception from common action and liberates it for a superior, sensorial exercise. In *The Time-Image* metaphor is definitively critiqued in a more moderate form, it seems, without appealing to the judgments to which it is subjected in *Kafka* and *A Thousand Plateaus*, where metamorphosis is preferred. The critique is more nuanced as well as subtle. Metaphor is technically a cliché, a sensory-motor evasion that releases sensation into motor reaction. The sensory-motor link releases an established, social mode, an apprehended reaction, or a behavior. As such, the movement-image is still an interest or participation squeezed out of a thing, or the thing recovered from an action, and it remains metaphorical because it pulls us out of a behavior by use of a signal. Following Bergson, Deleuze often emphasizes that our sensory-motor schemes are the sole processes that control what we perceive through cliché alone. The cliché, the readymade image, and the metaphor are thus not mediocre or worn out images in reality, or weakened with use, but on the contrary, they are prescriptive images that immediately elicit a response. They directly speak to our muscles and the backs of our knees, and we have already been pushed to react before even having been able to "feel." The cliché is thus "a sensory-motor image of the thing" that inspires a particular scheme within us, an affective scheme, whereby what is perceived immediately releases the interested action as a function of multiple social interests that we judge and to which we are subjected. Metaphors, sensory-motor images, and behavioral clichés all turn out to be modes of subjection.[61]

Just as we only perceive what interests us in the thing, what we are interested in perceiving for multiple reasons involving economic, ideological, or psychological subjectification affecting us, which intersect within us in a contradictory manner, the sensory-motor system remains a captive, vulgar, and social image from a uniquely reactive perspective. Under these conditions it is understood that a new mode of perception arises out of the fragments of the sensory-motor image: seeing contradicts the immediate action and is liberated from subjected sensory-motility. Thus, in order to make this process of seeing possible it is necessary for the sensory-motor scheme to break apart, to rupture the reactive chain that immediately disperses us in action, instead of focusing us on perception.

> But our sensory-motor schemes are jammed or broken, so that another kind of image can appear: a pure optical-sonorous image, an entire image without metaphor, which makes the thing in itself, literally, appear [. . .].[62]

This seeing cinema proposes to "tear a true image out of clichés" that possesses intensive characteristics from reality and not from fiction, the imaginary, or the metaphorical.[63] The relation of the time-image to the movement-image also specifies how the superiority of the time-image must be understood. The movement-image ultimately remains a cliché, because it is confined to metaphor, the privilege of individuated action and preestablished response. If movement's relation to time corresponds to the relation between the sensory-motor cliché and the image, then the image's inchoate potentialities are understood to make it possible for the cliché to be dissolved, and it makes us directly experience the force's temporal affect instead of it dissipating into movement.

The relation between the image and the cliché, which Deleuze describes in *The Time-Image*, informs his analyses in *Bacon*, along with the conclusion from *What Is Philosophy?* A cliché, a readymade image, is a social channel, and image that molds behavior. As such, every image disintegrates into a cliché according to a process of vulgarization that corresponds to a loss of intensity, and to the entropy arising from use that affects the givens of a culture, as an inverse result of their diffusion. At the same time, the image incessantly fights against the cliché. Even if the cliché degrades the reified image into behavior, as the cliché enters the image, every image dreams of the cliché's efficacy. Thus there is a complete coexistence between the cliché and the image, even if it is pointless to want to attain one without the other. Every cliché is capable of being an image, and every shocking image risks becoming the indication of a certain kind of behavior. But the inverse is equally true, and if every image is condensed into a cliché, then every cliché also weakly vibrates within an image. The pacified coexistence of the virtual and the actual is discovered between the image and the cliché.

This complete coexistence does not impede the cliché from following popular opinion, even as the image attempts to open up a new process of creation. When discussing Cézanne and Fromanger, Lawrence says that both affirmed the role of painting as a battle against the blank canvas.[64] The cliché preexists creation: painting does not function in the void of an image; on the contrary, the canvas is full of clichés that must be gotten rid of, subtracted, and torn out. Creativity is actualized within the hurly-burly of opinion—it is a Bachelardian memory.

> It is a mistake to think that the painter stands before a blank surface. [. . .] Figuration exists, it's a fact; it is even a precondition of painting. [. . .] There are psychic clichés just like there are physical clichés, ready-made perceptions, memories, and phantasms. There is a very important experience for the painter here: all categories of things that can be called "clichés" already occupy the canvas before painting begins.[65]

These clichés concern reflexes, conditions, and sensory-motor traces, and not images, but image channels. The image wins over the cliché with a true violence of sensation, at the place where the cliché procures the solace of a conventional reaction. As such, the relation between image and cliché is one of perusal and collusion, since the image deprives the cliché of its preferential motor impulses, but always remains complicit with the active, pragmatic virtue that it might use on occasion and that it could help take place. Like metaphors, clichés judge us, instead of exposing us to the forces of sensation. Images are so rarely neutralized that it remains bearable within the cliché. The relation between image and cliché thus restages the relationship between taste and genius in Kant: the cliché imitates conventional taste, and the image awakens new potentials, and like genius, breaks into new processes that are not satisfied following prescriptions in culture. Yet, genius and taste, image and cliché, ultimately only demarcate the intensive poles, thresholds, or tensions between which creativity is developed.

Thus, the distinction between cliché and image comes back to the necessary polarity between individuation and becoming-intensive, but it also engages the fracture between creativity and opinion that is essential for societies. And so, Deleuze rediscovers the Nietzschean polarity between active and reactive forces. The necessary coexistence of the actual and the virtual should not weaken the battle for creativity, which is always threatened by social powers, and it should not be distracted from the political imperative to think and create for the sake of the new. Clichés stick to the dominant tastes of convention; images look to awaken new forces. "That is to say that the artist fights less against chaos (which, in a certain way, s/he calls forth with all her desires) than against the 'clichés' of opinion."[66] Art thus struggles with chaos to make "a vision appear that illuminates an instant, a Sensation."[67]

Conclusions

The Four Principles of Semiotics

For Deleuze, articulating thought with respect to life is what matters, and to think about their disjunctive encounter as an irruption of creativity. From there, the relations between philosophy and art can be condensed into four principles that signal the guiding force lines of a system in a state of continuous variation. That makes it possible not only to condense the previous analyses in a systematic way, but also to return to the method of periodization that was employed when evaluating its prospective and retroactive power for the system of categories that transformed them. Finally, it is important to diagnose the results and problems that can now be drawn from this cartography with respect to the question of art.

Above all, Deleuze's semiotics is *noetic*: it takes art to be a problem for thought and first considers the creation of thought, which actualizes a sensation (the preparation of the work and its reception) or a concept (philosophy). But it is also *vitalist*, as thought actualizes itself in an intellectual way, while art arises out of an expressive capacity of life that modulates along with its territory, positing the becoming of forms as kinetic transformations. These outcomes reveal Deleuze's primary methodological orientation, which defines philosophy as a critique of transcendence, a refusal to consider universals or invariants of thought as anything other than variables whose content must be explained. Philosophy's primary task involves the logic of immanence. The third principle follows from the previous principles: semiotics is a *doctrine of material effects*, because art is a body that produces real effects: the haecceity of materiality determines the sign as force and affect with symptomatological value. Deleuze substitutes real becoming and metamorphic variation for metaphor or imaginary resemblance.

He turns art into a composite of sensations by introducing real transformations for collective receivers. The fourth proposition summarizes the previous ones: semiotics is a doctrine involving the *sensible genesis of thought* under the effect of an image, in the very unique sense that Deleuze gives to this term, which is composed of speeds and slownesses and variations of power.

These four propositions sketch the primary intertwining forces of art in Deleuze, but they are articulated in a mobile montage that undergoes many variations, which we have outlined in a few stages in order to conveniently freeze the becoming of concepts: the body without organs, schizophrenia, and clinical critique. A key to the work of art's cartography corresponds to plateaus and scansions: thinking, living, and creating, which give rhythm to the different stages of Deleuze's thought. The first plateau reveals the question of the genesis of thought under the violent action of the intensive sign and lasts until *Difference and Repetition*. Guattari's contribution leads Deleuze toward a vitalism that articulates anomalous madness and social critique in a movement that integrates art into political force. At the heart of the ethology of culture, art is endowed with a special power of critical and clinical elucidation related to the processes of subjectification that social bodies put into action. Lastly, the problem of creativity, which inscribes becoming within history, carries the philosophy of art toward the theory of haecceities, the becoming-intense of materials, and the semiotics of the image.

The cartography of concepts and the examination of method

The role of a particular periodization is pragmatic, above all else. It is not transcendent with respect to the materiality that it articulates, especially in Deleuze's philosophy. Instead, these thresholds must be used as problematic knots, radiating from a retrospective point of view, as well as a prospective point of view, so that the ruptures or continuities will be alternatively emphasized along the chosen problematic axis. From our perspective, it was urgent to establish these divisions in order to provide a sufficient determination for the semiotic concepts that outlined determined trajectories that were important to follow within the work. It is not that the elements of periodization seem objectionable to us, but they remain relative to the chosen perspective, and they never stop moving: they are variable divisions that make it possible to better follow conceptual ramifications that help discern and stabilize concepts by noting their connections. They are justified in this primary orientation, which functions as a hinge point that conveys the tension in Deleuze's thought: immanence, conceived as the auto-consistency of thought, then increasingly as an outright empiricism and heterogeneity. Thus, the very constructed, formal characteristic of the first studies bask in an annoying atemporality, whereas his encounter with Guattari transforms the theoretical regime, which falls into a whirlpool of theoretical sections and joyous, transversal constructions, even though the last works pick up a more constructed regime. These divisions allow the becoming of concepts to be observed, but their chronological basis remains relative to the chosen problematic, and obviously does not prejudge other potential periodizations. It is a question of thresholds, which have no value for the objective determination of thought, but only for prospective supports.

Deleuze's writing, in particular, lends to such a cartographic reading, resulting from its resolutely affirmative character and the treacherous play of masks that he wears when taking up other authors, not to mention his method of rereading through varying and successive versions. The real becoming of concepts in his work compensates for his method of exposition, which is more thetic than it is explanatory. Thus it is the movement of concepts within the work that justified the employed method: to draw up a table of spatiotemporal coordinates for concepts, which is not a substitute for the theoretical examination of their conceptual connections, but which must form the first step, without excluding analysis.

Deleuze's thought is a system in a process of becoming. The method that he applies to authors that he studies in his first works is transposed in his own work with only moderate difficulty, because it grazes conceptual variations that scan the development of problems. He is not unbiased, so concepts like "the line of flight," or "the body without organs," have a range that is limited to the treatment of problems that they help to resolve. Analyzing the intensive variation of concepts in Deleuze requires considering the thresholds of their constitution, their internal ramifications, and their zones of dissipation, as well as their external rhizomatic development, which requires that the assemblage that connects them to a body of reference—which is also variable, dense and often surprising—be taken into account: this method of investigation was used for a few concepts here, while an extended analysis remains to be done. The explication of concepts is not reducible to an internal reading, in accordance with a rhizomatic principle according to which a concept forms an assemblage with its contextualization—a complexity that is redoubled again by the very specific way that Deleuze aligns disparate references in order to produce his own determinations through differentiation. These referential complexes form intersecting and very characteristic dispositifs in Deleuze, where notions are decontextualized and reconnected in distinct problems according to the principle of connection and heterogeneity in the rhizome. The haecceity makes Nietzsche and Spinoza intersect with Simondon's individuation and Foucault's subjectification, along with Bergson's image and medieval notions of longitude and latitude. One can multiply these instances of references, echoes, appropriations, and bifurcations that Deleuze always conceives through a model of neural cartography, an effective trajectory of thought that digs and traces grooves into intellectual material. The rhizome is less of a vegetal model than it is neurobiological, which is convenient since it cuts the binary model of the tree and plays a pedagogical role, borrowing axons and dendrites from the neuron, as well as its emission of chemical or electrical impulses. The same applies to the work of references, and we can assume that it applies to this study, too, which is obviously only indicative and not exhaustive, even though it simplifies the compilations and erudition that are employed most of the time. Deleuze is an author who thinks through external references. To give an example of a complex that remains to be studied, the analysis of the emission of a singularity aligns the cast of the die in Mallarmé, the eternal return in Nietzsche, the mixtures of chance and dependence in Markov reread through Ruyer, with Jean Wahl's reading of Whitehead. The properties of an open system are ramified by noncentered iterations.

Thus, it is not pointless to apply Deleuze's theory of assemblage to his corpus and consider the constant use he employs in his readings as essential. This art of intersecting references is never applied to the explication of an author, but instead looks for the production of the new through disjunctive synthesis, a process of collage and distortion. It is a slow but capable method for seizing these two characteristics of Deleuze's thought from life: the continuous variation of concepts, the dispositifs of intersecting references, and the external connections that characterize each new case. This conceptual mannerism varies in accordance with what it is considering and engages a particular situation within thought; it is a perspective that illuminates and transforms the referential apparatus. We saw it operating each time, as it was a matter of responding to new problems. It is an effect of its casuistry, which requires considering the individuation of concepts in adequate detail, as we noticed with the body without organs and the haecceity. It was a long and costly investigation, precisely because it is subjected to transformation: the body without organs in *Anti-Oedipus* does not have the same definition that it has in *The Logic of Sense*, or in *Bacon*; the fold in

Difference and Repetition is not the same in *Foucault* or in *Leibniz*. Deleuze often compares the history of philosophy to portrait art in painting, or even more so to collage. In fact, that is how he proceeds in his philosophy, and he transforms his references, most notably, when citing them out of context, and from a perspective of discourse that is indirectly open. His method of transformation through capture marvelously applies Montaigne's formula:

> Like those who disguise their horses, I stain their mane and their tail, and sometimes I poke out an eye.[1]

On the other hand, there is another scholastic preference in Deleuze for abbreviated naming, and a tendency for contraction that also explains the variation within his concepts. When he says that a text must be flattened like an egg and avoided from all sides, he should be taken literally: the conceptual diagram of a problem is affected by a cinematic folding, stretching back to Geoffroy Saint-Hilaire. There is a theory of folding in Deleuze that can be reduced by synchronically summarizing it: a theoretician of becoming requires an attentive study of the system's transformations and their internal logic of movement and migration. An empirical meticulousness must be applied to his texts, all the more because his method of reappropriation releases living forces that work within the system through an approach involving variation. A reading of the concept's coordinates must be extended to theoretical segments and diverse practices that are put into relation. The assemblage of the concept must understand the texts it rejects just as much as it understands the diverse authors that it depends upon in constructing its collage. The scrupulous examination of the mutation of concepts demands that the *context* of their development be taken into account, including debates of the era, the chronology of readings, and authors being referred to; in other words, the *ethology* of the problem must be taken into account: its constitutional milieu. Thought itself is produced through an external encounter.

This casuistry favors differential reappropriations of the same motif, and the formative methodology of incessant reappropriations in Deleuze show the systematic power of thought and its "points of becoming," to borrow the expression that he applied to Foucault. The meticulous analysis of the strata constituting the body without organs, for instance, serves as a spectograph for thought within the work. The variation of overtones and conceptual mutations testify to the debates, returns, and confrontations within the same references that are dealt with on a different field, or the appearance of new references that transform the previous field.

It is time to move from a mechanical to a dynamic system, which examines points of tension, cases for solving, and cinematic vectors that appear at such and such a point under the pressure of such and such a problem. Schizophrenia is such a problem, or the desiring machine perfectly adapted to its role, provisionally, that is, until its function is fulfilled and it is replaced. This mannerism has an extreme singularity of concepts as a consequence that is dated and localized: the temporal layer can be identified solely by the notion of the complex that it puts into play. Deleuze theorizes about it in *What Is Philosophy?* when positing concepts as haecceities, as intensive variations of forces and potentiality that have an endo-consistency as well as an exo-consistency, which proceeds through heterogenesis, an "ordering of its components through zones of neighborhood."[2] Even if he puts this method into action in his readings, he does not always apply it to these precise readings—what we were tempted to do here, since our approach is pedagogical while its approach is always endogenous.

This conceptual mannerism accepts two styles of reading that were both conducted: a cursive reading, which spells out the transformation of names, references, and problems from book to book, and a systematic reading that nonetheless presupposes the results of the previous method of investigation.

Diagnostic of art

Deleuze's first principle is noetic, and he is the one in control of his initial encounter with the arts, from the form it takes as a literary contribution to a transcendental aesthetic of sensation. Even though he leaves the first noetic principle in order to elaborate a new semiotics, he encounters the problem of thought with attention to artistic experience, and responds to the problem by appealing to the epistemological elements that help develop a philosophical system. This calls for a few remarks on the interactions between art, science, and philosophy—the three dimensions of creative thought in Deleuze.

Deleuze often appeals to epistemology and not poetics when theorizing the effects of art. For example, he uses Bachelard's epistemological work and not his poetics, and the same applies to Simondon's notion of modulation. Reciprocally, the apprenticeship of signs in Proust, or symptomatology in Masoch, minority in Kafka, and the body without organs in Artaud serve to rectify, amend, and establish philosophical statements. Not only is semiotics interested in scientific categories, but the analysis of artworks fuel epistemological discussions whose goal is the ensuring of a philosophical method. In this way, the philosophy of art is always qualified by experimentation, experimentation that art undergoes for its own sake, but it is always experimentation for the sake of philosophy, as well.

By applying this function of experimentation to the arts, Deleuze continues a long-debated theme and situates himself amidst the prolongation of a century's worth of discourse about the avant-garde, which is a continuation of the romantic position. This experimentation is understood as a necessity for innovation that transforms the content of art as much as it transforms its status. This is affirmed in literature, the plastic arts, cinema, and music through a variety of ways, but sufficiently redundant so it can be considered a major norm, reduced to the most impoverished social conventions. Deleuze picks up on this convention without discussing it, but he offers his own theory of the effects of art, which revitalizes the debate.

The aesthetics of effects is appropriated from Bachelard's phenomenological technique, Simondon's individuation, and Canguilhem's normativity, endowing art with a singular, realist function. And if art exists, its effects cannot be limited to the imaginary, but they must be seized on the physical plane of an ethology of force. This realism is stimulating for a philosophy of art and makes it possible to grant definite attention to the haecceity of materiality, instead of and in place of the typical, empathic protest that so often condemns philosophical aesthetics to weak exhortation and subjective contemplation. Deleuze does a good job of challenging the divorce between the critical and the clinical, and he does so in the context of a physics of intensity. This functionalism understands art's affect to be a kind of electric passage through intensity. Such a theory only escapes from the suspicion that it is metaphorical on the condition that it really thinks about semiotics as a physical effect. As a result, it exposes itself to the inverse objection, reducing aesthetic emotion to a simple pretext for a philosophy of signs. The complex and concentrated taste found in the monographs animating *The Movement-Image* and *The Time-Image* provides a sufficient counterexample.

It is possible to return to the method of appealing to science and art in Deleuze, which pays a lot attention to science, but it is not on the same register as the attention he gives to art. Where sciences of matter and life play a role on the terrain of investigation and explication of effects, art serves as a terrain of validation. It would be interesting to do a study on the role of mathematics, compared to physics and the life sciences in the constitution of this differential method. And yet, it is as a clinician and critic, not epistemologist, that Deleuze establishes the methodological conditions for an empirical reworking of transcendental critique. He finds these conditions in a given novel, a repertoire of zoological forms, or even in spatiotemporally localized cinematographic production—and finally, in the repertoire of an era that marks the end of the classical age. The validating instance of the arts is actualized in the form of blocs of sensations, percepts, and affects conserved within materiality in the exact way that they modulate with their receiver and produce their effect. From the novel to painting, cinema to architecture, the approach is always the same: art is experimental in the strongest sense. It climbs up a material dispositif in order to produce a real effect, an effect "for seeing" that results from a chance adventure and a dangerous capture of forces. Ever since his reading of Nietzsche in 1962, Deleuze stresses the becoming of forces, but he only gradually specifies that this theory of art is about capture, and he incessantly redevelops the nature of these intensive forces, especially the relationships they enter into; that is to say, the variable *forms* that they construct. We move from the capture of forces as physical intensity (thinking) to the theory of symbiosis and becoming-animal (living) in order to arrive at the subjective, Baroque fold and the production of seeing in Foucault (creating). Thinking of art as an exchange of forces from the perspective of Simondonian modulation fixes the conditions of semiotics as a critique of art: works of art are symptomatologies. Their clinical capacity concerns the forces with which they put us into relation, forces that works of art are capable of "capturing," thus confirming their social diagnostic function. And while the task is to inspect the methods put into action, Deleuze varies, moving from Proustian essence to haecceities, from images in cinema to the Baroque fold of textures: each case imposes its own mode and its own method. There is also an effect on the receiver, moving her from the mental (*Proust* in 1964) to processes of subjectification, at first sexual (*Proust, Masochism . . .*), then corporeal (*Artaud*), social (*Kafka*), in the sense of an exploration that goes from the mental to the collective, from noetics to pragmatics and from the actual to historical duration (*Leibniz and the Baroque*). But the articulation of the relation between science and art remains stable, and for the Baroque, as well, where Baroque mathematics continues to serve as a reference.

Proust provides the matrix for this reference to the sciences: for the first time art captures the intensity of sensation. Deleuze understands the first stage in this "artistic experimentation" as a kind of "electric, electromagnetic" function, which forces him to determine a philosophy of nature that is informed by the science of his time.[3] But this effect is developed from the physical to the vital, from the vital to the political, so that the intensive physics of *Difference and Repetition* becomes becoming-animal and the collective assemblage of enunciation. In both cases, the end of the individual and personal opens us onto an intensive, vital border (animal) and a social border (collective assemblage).

Deleuze challenges every separation of science and art. The artistic model mobilizes knowledge, but it does not see as its task to find the means of "treating literary texts [or any other complexes of signs] scientifically."[4] On the contrary, it puts this rule of extrinsic interference into practice, the theory of which is given in the last pages of *What Is Philosophy?*: "the interfering discipline must always proceed with its own means."[5] And in this case, the interfering discipline is not science, but it is philosophy that interferes with science to solve the problem of art "with its own means." Thus, it can be assumed that there is a double interference: philosophy uses the sciences to solve the problem that the experience of art created for philosophy. Here also, the study of cinema is paradigmatic for this method. Hence, the explication of the arts requires Deleuze to put a semiotics in place, a philosophical invention of concepts that does not reflect on the arts, or describe theories, but proceeds with an intensive cartography of categories that are mobile and necessary. The idea that such a semiotics perishes on the terrain of pure thought can be rejected, while the question remains very complex. It is actually within systematic philosophy that Deleuze redirects art *quid juris* toward its conditions authorized by science. But he subjects philosophy to a casuistry of scientific specimens, using art as a laboratory for the creation of thought. The problem can be assembled from these noetic aesthetics by maintaining that literature, then the nondiscursive arts, serve as a singular drive to reform the categorical, philosophical apparatus. Reciprocally, this singular use of the arts is shown to transcribe poetics into the form of a theory of signs that Deleuze slowly outlines in its historical and political dimensions, with the use of concepts like the collective assemblage and the body without organs.

Thus, the difficulties of the noetic position reveal the limits of this analysis and the points at which the entire problem must be reevaluated. Effectively, if thought is produced through a violent irruption of a material sign, then analysis must stop focusing on thought alone and think about it in terms of connections. The status of the multiple, conceiving of thought as a rhizome, is what drives Deleuze to these important discoveries. The noetic, then, ceases to be posited as a separate order, and thought diffuses into the social and vital.

The becomings and histories of art

Vitalism was implied by symptomatology in two ways: art evaluates a type of forces, contending with the social sciences (psychiatry and psychoanalysis, linguistics, politics); this rivalry relies on its diagnostic capacity with respect to modes of subjectification. The practice of co-writing changes the regime of thought in facts, carrying Deleuze from a multiple that was only ideal toward concrete multiplicity. It not only transforms philosophical practice, but also opens each concept onto a concrete assemblage and onto a network of semiotic systems that include practices, powers, and sensations in a rhizomatic logic. The real turning point in Deleuze's work is located at this shift from architectonics to pragmatics.

Not only do continuities exist between knowledge, powers, and empirical conditions, but discontinuities also take place between theories that "reconnect"—as Deleuze said about the transitions in Foucault's work—without forming a closed totality. Art escapes from this purely mental physics of intensity, which gave the arts the status of a model of investigation for relations between thought and the sensible. Effects, like affects and percepts, are not only noetic acts—thinking—although they always presuppose it. The effect is now shown to be a vital and creative operation—living and creating. The vital terrain makes it possible to land the effect of art in culture, forcing it to move from the critical to the clinical. The ethology of culture assigns this function of investigating the vital speeds of the social to art by positioning it on the empirical plane. Apart from a physics of intensity and a transcendental philosophy of relations between thought and sensation, the effect implies that the investigation be carried into these new directions: a theory of the social; the resistance to dogma, major norms, and constituted powers; a table of categories for works that also provides a recapitulation of images and signs, a display of creativity through affects and percepts.

The vital ethology of thought endows art with a political function, and Deleuze discovers a process for accessing historical actuality, which he begins to consider as more than a reified and dogmatic field that thought would have to avoid if it were to become creative. The Bergsonian opposition between the actual and the virtual was formed when taking empirical actuality into account. With Guattari's help, and also that of Foucault, Deleuze discovers a new theoretical field: instead of thinking about creativity as being radically lateral with respect to constituted strata, he is interested in the becomings at work within the movements of stratification. The theme of an art that reformulates its norm connects the goal of creating the new with a critique of power that increases norms, which applies just as much to the poetics of artworks as it does to social normativity.

This pragmatic dimension transforms the philosophy of creativity. Without question, Deleuze always privileges the irruptive virtue of becoming and brings it to bear on historical contingency, which is considered doubly suspicious, owing to its successive dimension: succession, which is reifying and transcendent, absorbs real, immanent, virtual becoming. History reveals a succession that reifies time, and Deleuze aligns Bergson's analysis of the virtual past with Nietzsche's distinction between the historical and the untimely. Above all, history seems to him to be the very place for a teleology of progress that operates through negativity. However, the problem is deeply transformed by the outcome of his Foucaultian studies such that historical strata, which were neglected in his early works, take on an increasingly clear consistency in order to become essential as a philosophical problem in the later works. *Foucault, The Fold,* and *What Is Philosophy?* attach increasing importance to this new philosophy of history, which is henceforth capable of forming a crystalline alliance with the ontology of becoming. The history of forms in Deleuze doubles the becoming of forces. From there, the extraordinary tension between systematic thought, constantly vying to dehistoricize its categories and posit them as being untimely while claiming a logic of immanence, which plunges them like concrete assemblages into the empirical and historical reality of a given society.

This problem traces an impressive diagonal throughout Deleuzean metaphysics and signals a fundamental difficulty: the polarity of the virtual and the actual has a tough time giving rise to a theory of relationality, because it can be said to proceed with a perpetual fulguration of the actual, which is not easily manifested from a duration of assemblages. But the embedding of the time-image in the movement-image and the crystal of the actual and the virtual respond to this precise difficulty. The crystal-image does not posit a relation or even a circuit between the actual and the virtual, but the indiscernibility of a palpitation of time within matter. That is what shows the passage of the movement-image to the time-image.

Deleuze moves from an instantaneous vision of differentiation to a slower, cinematic one, and *A Thousand Plateaus* marks the irruption of this historic temporality, which entails the study of a long duration that affects the bodies of cultures and their processes of subjectification. The category of the historic should now be added to the categories of the noetic, the vital, the material, and the empirical, which would specify the modes of individuation of these haecceities that are slower than genres, norms, and "abstract machines." Thus, the appearance of art and its individuation in European culture would also be established. Deleuze is a good example of the expansion of art in contemporary culture, but he does not apply the results of this normative variation to art, genres, or mannerisms. Under the aegis of Geoffroy Saint-Hilaire, he brings oscillation and perpetually singular actualization from the same plane of immanence to a variation of place. Yet, the teratology and perspectivalism that begin with Leibniz and Nietzsche demonstrate how to think about the individuation of these assemblages, which Deleuze clearly explains are historical in *A Thousand Plateaus*. History never returns to a reification of teleological succession, as Deleuze demonstrates with respect to Foucault. But he never sought to think about art's enunciations and visions within his own thought, thus constantly posing them in the form of Kant's schematism. It would be interesting to conduct a study of genres and mannerisms, not as universals of culture, but as assemblages themselves participating in the individuation of the objects of art and the doctrines that explicate them. Deleuze poses problems more than he solves them, remaining faithful to his creative method, which rebels against the empirical examination of archives.

But it also shows from what point of view the question of art must be resumed, by examining the historical individuation of categories this time, which Deleuze, on the contrary, considers from an untimely perspective in such a way that his casuistry allows him to avoid any reflection on the history of forms: since the nomadic line is diversified in a way that acts like a hinge, a zoomorphic interlacing, or like the presence of nonsignifying traits in Bacon, it is given an empirical but untimely actuality that does not allow for a study of connections between forms. Deleuze does not proceed in this investigation because he maintains the opposition between becoming and history, a fecund opposition in the way it insists on the reality of transformation. Even if he becomes increasingly interested in empirical contingency, he rejects causal chains, and holds that history introduces the whole host of necessary but not sufficient negative conditions into an achronological breach of untimely becoming. Experimentation is empirical, but it is not historical in the sense that is not produced by a causal chain, and so it remains "something that escapes history." In order to avoid determinist causality, Deleuze accentuates the achronological actualization of the virtual, the "diagnosis of actual becomings," and not their historical effectuation.[6]

As such, Deleuze could scarcely be interested in the history of art, the movement of individuation from art to culture, where his semiotics nevertheless directly proceeds. This would be the sentiment of an epistemology of art that takes up the question from this angle, essential elements of which Deleuze can be assumed to have carried with him.

His emphasis on the haecceity of materials, his critique of a personal subjectivity, his way of positing the processes of subjectfication as encounters at the interstice of intellectual and material planes, the creation of haecceities, images and tables of signs, constitute fecund entry points for taking up the question of the diversity in the arts. Deleuze makes it possible to think about the arts as phenomeno-technical effects, material yet not imaginary effects, and social effects that interact with the modes of subjectification in culture. It is a fecund process for the philosophy of art, which turns out to be programmatic.

Understood as nonorganic vitality and the conservation of sensation in material expression, art establishes a monument that is inseparable from the complex of forces into which it is taken. Aesthetics, as the philosophy of art, conquers its empirical dimension: it starts an investigation that simultaneously bears on the becoming of materials and the variation of forms in culture. The nomadic line is inseparable from its social assemblage, the Baroque materiology of its European moment, even if, once posited, their formal criteria can swarm outside their fields under certain conditions. Thus, Deleuze demands that "the means of the material" be exposed with all available resources, from the practice of a gesture to scientific explanation. In addition, he maintains that the affects of materiality depend on social conditions and are not given independently of the variable circumstances where they can become expressive. There are conditions of true empiricism here, accomplished by the ethology of cultures.

Notes

Chapter 1

1   Of the 26 books that make up his bibliography, 10 are devoted to art, while 9 books are devoted to the explicit examination of the work of a particular philosopher, and 9 are coauthored. Philosophizing on art, on philosophy, writing as a pair, through juxtaposition, as we will see, or through co-writing (with Guattari, Parnet, or Fanny Deleuze): these three modes of exposition are systematically linked.

2   Deleuze and Foucault, "Introduction générale," F. Nietzsche, *Le Gai Savoir, et fragments posthumes*, from *Œvres complètes*, G. Colli and Montinari (eds), Fr. trans. P. Klossowski (Paris: Gallimard, 1967), I–IV, reprinted in Foucault, *Dits et Écrits*, under the direction of D. Defert and F. Ewald (Paris: Gallimard, 1994), 561–4. The citation is located on 563–4. Also see "Michel Foucault et Gilles Deleuze veulent rendre à Nietzsche son vrai visage" (an interview with C. Jannoud), *Le Figaro littéraire*, issue 1065, September 15 (1966), 7, reprinted in Foucault, *Dits et Écrits*, 549–52.

3   Deleuze, *Foucault*, 1988 (cited herein as F), 50.

4   Deleuze decided to categorically oppose semiotics—the non-linguistic theory of signs—to semiology. He rarely talks about semiology in the sense of "semiotics," except in specific instances. For example, he does so when discussing Peirce, who invents a non-linguistic logic of the sign that he calls "semiology," or when he addresses an Anglo-Saxon audience that is accustomed to Peircian terminology. In all other cases the term semiotics takes precedence and semiology is understood in terms of semantics, the linguistic theory of signs that Deleuze so vehemently criticizes. For example, in the preface of the English edition of *Nietzsche and Philosophy*, when referencing Peirce, Deleuze writes semiology, but he writes semiotics everywhere else. See Gilles Deleuze, *Deux régimes de fous. Textes et entretiens 1975–1995* (Paris: Minuit, 2003), ed. David Lapoujade, cited herein as RF, 188, and *L'Image-mouvement*, cited herein as IM, 101.

5   Gilles Deleuze, "Description de la femme. Pour une philosophie d'autrui sexée," *Poésie* 45.28, (October–November 1945), 28–39; "Introduction," Diderot, in *La Religieuse*, (Paris: Collection de l'Ile Saint-Louis, 1947), vii–xx.

6   Gilles Deleuze, "Mystère d'Ariane" (on Nietzsche), in *Bulletin de la Société française d'études nietzschéennes*, (March 1963), 12–15, reprinted in *Philosophie*, 17, (Winter 1987), 67–72. Reprinted in revised form in *Magazine littéraire*, 298, (April 1992), 21–4, prior to its publication in *Essays Critical and Clinical*.

7　The text on Spinoza is spread out over an 11-year period: *Spinoza. Textes choisis* (Paris: PUF, 1970). The expanded second edition has a different title: *Spinoza. Philosophie pratique* (Paris: Minuit, 1981) cited herein as SPP. Three chapters are added (III, V, and VI whose "Spinoza et nous" was published separately in the *Revue de Synthèse*, 3.89–91, (January–September 1978), 271–7) and he cuts out the selected extracts from Spinoza's works. Thus, there is a history of the book which appropriately experiences a transformation from its literary genre, an academic piece, to an ambitious monograph. We can observe the same phenomenon with the text *Foucault* from 1986, which takes up and modifies Deleuze's successive reviews of *L'Archéologie du savoir* (1969) and *Surveiller et Punir* (1975), and he presents the material in a newly assembled structure, which constitutes the first few chapters. The development of the book takes place over the course of 16 years, while the diachronic reviews are transformed along the way in conceptual moments: "Un nouvel archiviste" (review of Michel Foucault's *L'Archéologie du savoir*), in *Critique*, 274, (March 1970), 195–209, reprinted for the first time in a separate volume (Paris: Fata Margana, 1972), and "Écrivain? Non: un nouveau cartographe" (review of Michel Foucault's *Surveiller et Punir*), in *Critique*, 343, (December 1975), 1207–27.

8　Gilles Deleuze and Félix Guattari, "La synthèse disjonctive," *L'Arc, Klossowski*, 43, (1970), 54–62, which is taken up again and revised in *Anti-Oedipus*.

9　Félix Guattari, *Les Années d'hiver 1980–1985*, (Paris: Barrault, 1986), 287. The moment that Deleuze himself stopped using the notion, Guattari suggests a definition for this term that is so illuminating that it merits a reproduction here. "Collective enunciation: linguistic theories of enunciation ascribe linguistic production to individuated subjects, although language is essentially social, or rather, diagrammatically connected to contextual realities. Beyond individuated instances of enunciation it's best to update the definition of what we know to *collective assemblages of enunciation*. The collective does not need to be understood merely in the sense of a social group; it also implies to the entry of diverse collections of technical objects, material and energetic fluxes, incorporeal entities, mathematical idealities, aesthetics, etc.," ibid., 289. With his Marxian inflexion, and his relatively weighty vocabulary, the concept is characteristically Guattarian. In *The Years of Winter* Guattari offers a very illuminating glossary of different concepts that are integral to his coauthored works with Deleuze: body without organs, rhizome, assemblage, territoriality, etc.

10　Gilles Deleuze and Carmelo Bene, *Superpositions*, cited herein as S, (Paris: Minuit, 1979). The book appears in Italy in 1978, but is not published in France until 1979.

11　Gilles Deleuze and Félix Guattari, *Rhizome* (1976), cited herein as R, and also see F, 68–9.

12　Gilles Deleuze, *Essays Critical and Clinical* (1993), cited herein as CC.

13 Gilles Deleuze and Gérard Fromanger, *Fromanger, le peintre et le modèle*, (Paris: Baudard Alvarez, 1973). The connection to Foucault is interesting here, as always: See Michel Foucault, "La peinture photogénique," a small volume written for Gérard Fromanger's exhibition, "Desire is Everywhere" at the Galerie Jeanne Bucher, 53 rue de Seine, Paris 6, from February 27 to March 29, 1975.

14 This expression is used for the title of the conclusion in the first version of *Proust* in 1964. It is kept in the current edition, but from then on it is the title of the conclusion of the first part of the book.

15 Gilles Deleuze, *Proust et les signes*, (1964, 1970, 1976), 118, cited herein as PS.

16 Ibid., 195.

17 Ibid., 24. According to Jean-Pierre Faye, the occasion of this meeting resulted from a review of *Difference and Repetition* and *The Logic of Sense* that Lacan was supposed to accept in his journal *Scilicet*, but that he didn't publish and that Guattari brought to Deleuze. Faye finally published the article "Machine and Structure" in his journal *Change*, (October 1972), 49–59, republished in Guattari's *Psychoanalyse et Transversalité. Essai d'analyse institutionelle*, (Paris: Maspero, 1972), 240–8. See Faye, "Philosophe le plus ironique," in *Tombeau de Gilles Deleuze*, ed. Y. Beaubatie, (Tulle: Mille Sources, 2000), 91–9, (92, 95).

18 Gilles Deleuze, *The Logic of Sense*, (Paris: Minuit, 1969), cited herein as LS.

19 Félix Guattari, *Les Années d'hiver*, 82.

20 See the beautiful text that Deleuze published with Guattari, "Mai 68 n'a pas eu lieu," *Les Nouvelles*, (May 3–10, 1984), 75–6, republished in RF, 215, and F, 123, n. 45.

21 Lacan reevaluates the category of psychosis, which Freud abandons to psychiatry while restricting the psychoanalytic perspective solely to the treatment of neuroses, and dedicates his medical thesis to him in 1932: Jacques Lacan, *De la psychose paranoïque dans ses rapports avec la personnalité* (1932), republished (Paris: Points/ Seuil, 1980). For information about Lacan's role, see Guattari's statements in *Pratique de l'institutionnel et politique*, by Jean Oury, Félix Guattari, and François Tosquelles, (Vigneux: Matrice Éditions, 1985), 47–50.

22 François Tosquelles withdraws to Saint-Alban during the war in the 1940s. He participated in the resistance and created institutional psychotherapy. Tosquelles claimed that he walked on two legs, one Freudian leg, and one Marxist leg. Ten years later, resulting from the aftershock that traumatized the few who were loosely connected by their experiences in the Resistance and Liberation, Jean Oury joins La Borde and carries on Tosquelles' research in a modest group of about 40 people, including retirees. For information on institutional psychoanalysis see *Pratique de l'institutionnel et politique*, by Jean Oury, Félix Guattari, and François Tosquelles. The term "institutional psychoanalysis" was created by Guattari, who was thinking about what could be "another analytic path [. . .] an expression that I didn't really use in this context but that arose from outside" (ibid., 48). On La

Borde, see *La Borde ou le droit à la folie*, writted by J. C. Polack and D. Sivadon-Sabourin, the preface written by F. Guattari and J. Oury (Paris: Calmann-Lévy, 1976). See 116.

23 Gilles Deleuze, *Trois Problèmes*, reprinted in *L'Île déserte et autres textes. Textes et entretiens 1953–1974*, (Paris: Minuit, 2002), ed. David Lapoujade, cited herein as ID, 273.

24 Deleuze, *Trois Problèmes*, ID, 272.

25 "Behind Marx and Freud, behind Marxology and Freudology, there is the shitty reality of the communist movement and the psychoanalytic movement. That's where we should start and that's where we should always return. And when I speak of shit, it is hardly a metaphor: Capitalism reduces everything to a fecal state, to the state of undifferentiated and un-coded flux, out of which each person in his/her private, guilt-ridden way must pull out his/her part." Félix Guattari, *La Révolution moléculaire*, Paris, *Recherches*, "Encre" (1977), reprinted in UGE, "10/18" (1980) 9. We should compare this icebreaker with the beginning of *Anti-Oedipus*.

26 Deleuze, PP, 24–5, 186–7; Deleuze, *Dialogues*, (Paris, Flammarion, 1996), 23, cited herein as D.

27 Deleuze and Guattari, *L'Anti-Œdipe*, 453 (cited herein as AO).

28 Deleuze, "L'éclat de rire de Nietzsche," (interview with Guy Dumur), in *Le Nouvel Observateur*, (April 5, 1967), 40–1, reprinted in ID, 180.

29 Deleuze, "L'éclat de rire de Nietzsche," ID, 180.

30 Ibid. The article, signifying a "return to Nietzsche," welcomes the publication in France of the translation of the *Nietzsche's Complete Works*, ed. G. Colli and M. Montinari, a widespread editorial undertaking that Deleuze and Foucault performed for Gallimard in France. It also refers to the conference at Royaumont that was dedicated to Nietzsche, where Deleuze was chosen to give the keynote address, the proceedings of which were just published: *Cahiers de Royaumont. Philosophie, 6: Nietzsche*, (Paris: Minuit, 1967), reprinted in ID, 163–77. Also see "Sur Nietzsche et l'image de la pensée," reprinted in ID, 187–97, and Gilles Deleuze and Michel Foucault, "Introduction générale," Friedrich Nietzsche, *Le Gai Savoir, et fragments posthumes*, in *Œvres complètes*, ed. G. Colli and M. Montinari, trans. Pierre Klossowski, (Paris: Gallimard, 1994), 561–4. Unfortunately, this important text is not reprinted in *Desert Islands*.

31 "The essence of art is a kind of joy, and *this is the very point of art*. There can be no tragic work of art because there is a necessary joy in creating: art is necessarily a liberation that shatters everything, especially the tragic." Gilles Deleuze, "Mystique et masochisme" (interview with Madeleine Chapsal), in *La Quinzaine littéraire*, 25, (April 1–15, 1967), 12–13, reprinted in ID, 186.

32 Deleuze, "L'éclat: de rire de Nietzsche," ID, 180–1.

33 Deleuze, PP, 230.

34 Deleuze and Guattari, *Kafka*, (1975), 32, 48 (cited herein as K). We should compare this with the previous article, "According to Nietzsche, the masters are the 'Untimely,' those who create and destroy in order to create, not to conserve," ID, 181.

35 Deleuze and Guattari, MP, 9.

36 Deleuze, PP, 187; see also PP, 15–16 and Deleuze, D, 23–5.

37 Deleuze, RF, 199.

38 Ibid., 194–5.

39 Deleuze, *L'Image-temps*, (Paris: Minuit, 1985), cited herein as IT, 44; RF, 168–9.

40 Deleuze, *Francis Bacon. Logique de la sensation*, (Paris: La Différence, 1981), republished (Paris: Le Seuil, 2002), 54.

41 Deleuze, IT, 44.

Chapter 2

1 Foucault, *Madness and Civilization: A History of Insanity in the Age of Reason*, (Paris: Plon, 1961), published by Gallimard in 1972; *Raymond Roussel*, (Paris: Gallimard, 1963), and the same year, *The Birth of the Clinic*, (Paris: PUF, 1963); also see "La folie, l'absence d'oeuvre," *La Table Ronde, Situation de la psychiatrie*, 196, (May 1964), 11–12, which reappears in *Dits et Écrits*, I, 412–20, and the collection of writings on literature from 1960–70.

2 Pierre Macherey, "Présentation," Foucault, *Raymond Roussel*, (Paris: Gallimard, 1963), later published in "Folio essais" (1992), IX–X. One might wonder how Foucault could have committed the blatant error of writing a commentary on the works of a literary figure—the very man who criticized the exegesis and position of the commentator in his methodological preface to *The Birth of the Clinic* the same year in the "Galien" collection, which was edited by Canguilhem. Macherey claims that Foucault uses literature as a laboratory where the status of an experiment/experience must be connected to: Kant, for an evaluation of the transcendental conditions of the clinic; Bataille, for experience/experiment as the production of subjectivity; and Canguilhem, for the experience of fundamental fluctuations and relativity regarding the categories of that which is normal and pathological.

3 Deleuze, "From Sacher-Masoch to Masochism," *Arguments*, 2, (1961), 40–6, reprinted in *Masochism: Coldness and Cruelty and Venus in Furs*, (Paris: Minuit, 1967); "Raymond Roussel ou l'horreur du vide" (a review of Foucault's *Raymond Roussel*) in *Arts*, 933 (October 23–29, 1963), 4.

4 Georges Canguilhem, *Le Normal et le Pathologique*, (Paris: PUF, 1966), republished in a collection (Paris: Quadige, 1993), 81–2, cited herein as *Le Normal* . . . It is telling that Canguilhem refers to Isidore Geoffroy Saint-Hilaire here, whose

teratological studies continue his father's work, Étienne Geoffroy Saint-Hilaire, a very important reference for Deleuze. Geoffroy is the one who provides the idea of an animal plane of composition, which helps Deleuze formulate the concept of a "body without organs," because it serves as a way of thinking about the animal as an *anomalous* variation, an intensive, continuous variation.

5 Deleuze and Guattari, MP, 298. This is a direct commentary from Canguilhem, *Le Normal . . .*, 81–2.

6 Foucault, "Préface à la transgression," *Critique*, 195–6: *Hommage à Georges Bataille*, (August–September 1963), 751–69, in *Dits et Écrits*, 233. Foucault completely corroborates this Nietzschean reading of Canguilhem, see Foucault, *Dits et Écrits*, 434.

7 Canguilhem, *Le Normal . . .*, 179.

8 Deleuze, "Coldness and Cruelty," in *Masochism: Coldness and Cruelty*, (Paris: Minuit, 1967), cited herein as SM. Deleuze text serves to introduce Masoch's novel, *Venus in Furs*. To complete the file on Sacher-Masoch, we must add the interview by Madeleine Chapsal entitled "Mysticism and Masochism," in *La Quinzaine littéraire*, 25, (April 1967), which is reprinted in ID, 182. A third article, printed for the new edition, appears 22 years later: "Re-presentation of Masoch," in *Liberation*, (May 18, 1989), 30. It is reprinted in 1993 in the collection *Essays Critical and Clinical*, chapter VII, 71–4.

9 Richard von Krafft-Ebing, *Psychopathia sexualis* (Stuttgart: 1886; Paris: 1907), published by Dr Albert Moll, (1923), trans. Fr. René Lobstein, Preface by Pierre Janet, (Paris: Payot, 1950). This is the edition Deleuze consulted. For the first time Krafft-Ebing "describes the troubles of sexual life in a complete way" (Janet, *Preface*, 3) and hands over a passionate anthology of sexual "perversions" to the public (all of sexuality that does not refer to heterosexual, adult genital sex).

10 Deleuze, PP, 195, CC, 10, 71.

11 Deleuze, ID, 185.

12 Krafft-Ebing is the inventor of "masochism" (Krafft-Ebing, *Psychopathia sexualis*, chapter IX, 236–311). Moll states on 143: "The noun *masochism* is derived from the name of the writer Sacher Masoch." Schrenk-Notzing suggested replaced the proper noun with a more neutral neologism, *algolagnia*, from the Greek "*algos*," pain, and "*lagneia*," pleasure, but Krafft-Ebring refused.

13 Krafft-Ebing, ibid., 143.

14 Deleuze, "From Sacher-Masoch to Masochism."

15 What does the masochist say? Deleuze often returns to this question, notably in *A Thousand Plateaus*: "Sexuality passes through the becoming-woman of man and the becoming-animal of the human: an emission of particles," Deleuze and Guattari, MP, 341.

16 Deleuze, SM, 195.

17 Deleuze, SM, 31; LS, 327. Deleuze defers to Klossowski on this matter, CC, 72; PP, 195.

18 Deleuze, CC, 72.

19 The legalism of the contract is absolutely distinct from the law, according to Deleuze. We can align Kafka and Masoch on these grounds and assume that the name of the narrator in *The Metamorphosis*, Gregor Samsa, pays homage to Masoch (Deleuze, CC, 72, n. 2).

20 Deleuze, PP, 229.

21 Deleuze, SM, 113.

22 Deleuze, LS, 325–6. Among the works devoted to Sade, let's first recall Bataille, *Eroticisme*, (Paris: Minuit, 1957), "Arguments," whose effect can be measured by the simultaneous publication of the following works: Blanchot, *Lautrémont et Sade*, (Paris: Minuit, 1963), "Arguments"; Klossowski, *Un si funeste désir*, (Paris: Gallimard, 1963); Lacan, "Kant avec Sade," *Critique*, 191, (April 1963), even if Lacan justifiably specifies that the article was written in 1961 . . . and obviously, Foucault, "Préface à la transgression," *Critique*, 195–6: *Hommage à Georges Bataille*, (August–September 1962), 751–69, in *Dits et Écrits*, I, 233–50.

23 Deleuze, LS, 326.

24 It is in 1977, in chapter 3 of *Dialogues*, that Deleuze definitively separates himself from transgression, and thus from the concept of perversion, which is still taken seriously in his work on Masoch. It is in this text that Deleuze turns Freud into an emulator of Geoffroy Saint-Hilaire: treating perversions, Freud puts all of his energy into "polymorphism and developmental possibilities" that he is neglectful when in comes to neurosis (SM, 40). At this time, Deleuze considers the terrain of perversions in psychoanalysis to be favorable to a truly differential analysis—a hope that he will abandon as soon as he will have systematized his critique against transgression and the authoritative domination of the signifier. In 1967, it could have seemed to Deleuze that sexual transgression could import a value of metamorphosis, a multiple becoming. In 1977, sexuality no longer seemed to have revolutionary value, and above all, the very mechanism of transgression had broken down.

25 Deleuze, D, 58–9.

26 Deleuze, SM, 15.

27 Deleuze, PP, 195.

28 Deleuze, SM, 11.

29 Ibid.

30 Deleuze, PP, 195.

31 Deleuze, LS, 102.

32 Deleuze, PP, 196.

33 Deleuze, SPP, 144.

34 Ibid.

35   In 1968, Deleuze writes: "The notion of sense can be the refuge of a renewed spiritualism. What we occasionally call 'hermeneutics' (interpretation) took over from what we used to call 'axiology' (evaluation) after the war." This runs the risk of denaturing the Nietzschean or Freudian notion of sense, which Deleuze characterizes by two properties here: it is effect and not essence, reality in its surface and not depth; it is produced and not given, and consequently, it is a matter of demarcating the laws of production. "One talks about 'original' sense, forgotten sense, erased sense, veiled sense, recycled sense, etc. Under the category of sense ancient mirages are re-baptized, Essence is resuscitated, all of the religious and sacred values are rediscovered. In Nietzsche and Freud it's the opposite: the notion of sense is the instrument of an absolute refusal, of an absolute critique and also of a determinate creation. Sense is not a reservoir at all, nor a principle or an origin, nor even an end; it is an 'effect,' a *produced* effect, and the laws of the production of which must be uncovered," Deleuze, ID, 189.

36   Deleuze, SPP, 35.

37   Deleuze, CC, 158.

38   Ibid., 169.

39   Deleuze opposes every interpretive position that arises from a high version of hermeneutics where the text itself makes itself a world, but functions like a verb, as we see in Ricoeur and Gadamer. Such a move traces sense onto the power of the verb, a "major" interpretation of transcendent sense in place of a minor interpretation and a becoming of sense, which is unacceptable for Deleuze. From this fundamental divergence, Deleuze and Ricoeur reconnect with respect to polemics: they both reject that art be its ultimate goal. But Ricoeur insists on the productivity of the metaphor as a re-description of the world, while at the same time, Deleuze substitutes metamorphosis for metaphor (Ricoeur, *La métaphore vive*, (Paris: Seuil, 1975), 115 and 247). The work on "reference," continued in *Time and Narrative* in 1983–5, shows that literary processes (metaphor, as a miniature poem, the novelistic *muthos*) produce not an aesthetic judgment of the essence of art, but a second reference, an acquired resemblance, a creative *mimesis* of sense, which imitates speculative reflection. During the same period Deleuze devotes himself to an analysis of the relationship between time and cinema, which demonstrates the relative proximity of the objects studied, while depicting the divergence concerning sense and the status of hermeneutics.

Chapter 3

1   Haecceity concerns "a mode of individuation that is not to be confused with that of a thing or a subject" (Deleuze and Guattari, MP, 318, n. 24). Deleuze borrows

the concept from Duns Scotus, but above all, he leans on the beautiful theory of *ecceité* developed by Gilbert Simondon. The tribute is nuanced because, as the note indicates, it's erroneous to write "ecceity" by deriving the word from *ecce*, "here," thus Duns Scotus creates the concept from *haec*, "this thing," but this error is fecund since it enables Simondon to determine individuation as a process, an appearance, the occurrence of an event, by placing the emphasis on the temporal appearance and not on the constituted individual. The Simondonian "ecceity" weighs heavily in the Deleuzean theory of haecceity, and concerns thought as much as the production of signs or signals, since it theorizes the appearance of a singularity at any level it is defined: human thought, molecular encounter, distinct atmosphere, or "five o'clock in the evening." See Simondon, *L'Individu et sa genèse physico-biologique, L'Individuation à la lumière des notions de forme et d'information*, (Paris: PUF, 1964), "Epimethee" collection, republished by Grenoble, J. Millon, "Krisis" collection, (1995), cited herein as *L'Individu . . .*, 47, and the analysis of modulation, 103. Also see Sasso, Robert, Villani, Artnauld (eds), *Les Cahiers de Noesis No. 3: Vocabulaire de Deleuze*, (Nice: University of Nice, 2003), 170–80.

2   Deleuze and Guattari, MP, 318, 320–1.

3   Deleuze, RF, 188.

4   Deleuze, *Nietzsche et la philosophie*, (Paris: PUF, 1962), 7, (cited herein as N); RF, 188; F, 131.

5   Deleuze, PS, 118–19; ID, 180.

6   Deleuze, RF, 189.

7   Deleuze, PS, 22.

8   Deleuze, RF, 142.

9   Deleuze, PP, 195.

10   In the 1983 preface of the American edition of *Nietzsche and Philosophy*, Deleuze talks about semiology to designate the categories of signs in Nietzsche, as an assignation of forces. Such a "general semiology considers linguistics, or philology, rather, to be one of its sectors." Since he is addressing an Anglo-Saxon audience in this instance, Deleuze uses the term semiology synonymously with semiotics (even though he often opposes these two terms, identifying semiology with semantics, a theory of the sign that depends upon linguistics).

11   Deleuze, SPP, 111.

12   Ibid., 166.

13   Deleuze, RF, 144.

14   Deleuze, SPP, 166.

15   Deleuze, FBLS, 57.

16   Ibid.

17   Deleuze, SPP, 166; Deleuze and Guattari, MP, 318–19.

18 Deleuze and Guattari, *What Is Philosophy?* (Paris: Minuit, 1991), cited herein as QP, 156.

19 Deleuze, RFF, 269.

20 Deleuze and Guattari, QP, 158.

21 Deleuze, IM, 7; 83.

22 Deleuze, PP, 62.

23 Deleuze, RF, 194.

24 Deleuze, PP, 62.

25 Deleuze, IM, 89.

26 Ibid., 88.

27 Deleuze, *Leibniz. Le Pli ou le Baroque*, (Paris: Minuit, 1988), cited herein as Pli.

28 Deleuze, PP, 62.

29 Bergson, *Matière et Mémoire, in Oeuvres*, Édition du Centenaire, (Paris: PUF, 1959), republished in 1984, 180 and IM, 90.

30 Deleuze, IM, 89 and 93, citing Bergson, *Matière et Mémoir*, 186.

31 Deleuze, IM, 94.

32 Ibid., 95.

33 Ibid., 97.

34 Ibid.

35 Deleuze, F, 127.

36 Deleuze, PP, 62.

37 Deleuze, RF, 250.

38 Ibid.

39 Deleuze, CC, 167–8 and SPP, 189.

40 Spinoza, *Éthique*, III, post. 1 and 2; and Deleuze, SPP, 70.

41 Deleuze, SPP, 126–7.

42 Deleuze, RF, 266.

43 Deleuze, IM, 241.

Chapter 4

1 Blanchot, *Le livre à venir*, (Paris: Gallimard, 1959), republished in "Idées," (1971), pp. 55–9, IT, 218.

2 Deleuze, *Différence et Répétition*, (Paris: PUF, 1968), 192, cited herein as DR.

3 Artaud, *Correspondance avec Jacques Rivière, Œvres complètes*, Vol. 16, (Paris: Gallimard, 1970–94), pp. 9–11.

4 A discussion of the relationship between Geoffroy Saint-Hilaire and the body without organs can be found in Sauvagnargues, "De l'animal à l'art" in P. Marrati, A. Sauvagnargues, F. Zourabichvili, *La philosophie de Deleuze*, (Paris: PUF, 2004), 179.

5 For organology and its role in the problem of embryogenesis and phylogenesis, see G. Canguilhem, G. Lapassade, J. Piquemal, J. Ulmann, *Du dévelopment à l'évolution au XIXe siècle*, (Paris: PUF, 1962), and republished in "Pratiques théoriques," (1985). This study is important in order to understand the plateau devoted to the "Geology of Morals," MP, 54.

6 Deleuze, LSFB, 47.

7 Deleuze and Guattari, MP, 186: the event lends its title to the sixth of *A Thousand Plateaus*: "November 28, 1947—How Do You Make Yourself a Body without Organs?," 185.

8 Artaud, "Pour en finir avec le jugement de Dieu," in *Revue 84*, 5–6, (1948), 101. Deleuze devotes several analyses to this poem, with Guattari in AO, 15; LSFB, 47; MP, 196; CC, chapter 15.

9 Artaud, "Pour en finir avec le jugement de Dieu," in *Revue 84*, 5–6, (1948), cited in Deleuze, LS, 108; FB, 47–51; AO, 15; MP, 196, also reprinted in *Critique et Clinique*.

10 "The organic strata do not wear life out: the organism what life opposes in order to limit itself, and there is a life all the more intense, all the more powerful, for being anorganic," Deleuze and Guattari, MP, 628.

11 Deleuze and Guattari, MP, 197.

12 Deleuze, FBLS, 50.

13 Deleuze, F, 129.

14 Deleuze, LS, Preface: "From Lewis Carroll to the Stoics," and 102.

15 Deleuze, LS, 108: "the body without organs is only made of bone and blood." We also find the expression "the head without organs," LS, 110.

16 Deleuze, LS, 108.

17 Deleuze, CC, 16–17.

18 Deleuze, LS, 102–3.

19 The power of Artaud's translation will be verified by comparing it with Parisot's translation, from Carroll, *De l'autre côté du miroir*, in *Oeuvres*, Lacassin ed., (Paris: Robert Laffont, 1989), 125. Also see Deleuze, "Le Schizophrène et le mot" (on Carroll and Artaud), in *Critique*, 255–6, (August–September 1968), 731–46. And Artaud, "L'Arve et l'Aume, tentative anti-grammaticale contre Lewis Carroll," *L'Arbalète*, 12, (1947), and *Lettre à Henri Parisot, Lettres de Rodez*, (Paris: G.L.M., 1946), cited by Deleuze in LS, 103. We are indebted to Parisot, one of the translators of Lewis Carroll in France who seeks to render *Through the Looking Glass* and *Jabberwocky* in French and was worth Artaud's wrath. "Since *Jabberwocky* is no more than sugar-coated and dull plagiarism of a work written by me, which was made to disappear in such a way that I myself barely know what is in it." Incredulous, Parisot wonders: delirium or phoniness? Artaud's fury does not enter into his system of comprehension (Artaud, *Lettres de Rodez*, cited by

Parisot, "Preface to *De l'autre côté du miroir*," in Carroll, *De l'autre côté du miroir*, in *Oeuvres*, 125).

20 Deleuze, LS, 103. This is what Artaud says about Carroll: "I do not like surface poems or surface languages that breathe of happy leisure and the successes of the intellect, this particular intellect relied on the anus, but without putting any heart or soul into it. The anus is always terror, and I cannot accept someone losing a bit of excrement without also tearing and losing a part of his soul in the process, and there is no soul in Jabberwocky . . . One can invent his own language and make this language speak with an extra-grammatical sense, but this sense must be valid in itself, to come from torment . . .," Artaud, *Lettre à Parisot*, cited by Deleuze, LS, 103. It is clear that Artaud denies that Carroll knows depth or the real tormented experience of a body without organs.

21 Deleuze, LS, 108.

22 Ibid., 129.

23 Ibid., 135.

24 Ibid., 109. The conception of a-grammatical style will later appear in *Anti-Oedipus*, and especially *A Thousand Plateaus*, as a linguistic, non-psychopathological opposition to Chomsky's *grammaticality*. The expression appears in AO, 158.

25 Mounin, *Dictionnaire de linguistique*, (Paris: PUF, 1974). Agrammatism. Agrammatism appears in motor aphasia and in the evolution of Broca's aphasia: the subject, who does not suffer from problems of comprehension, is perfectly conscious of his or her grammatical defect.

26 Artaud, *Le pèse-nerf, Œvres complètes*, I, 95; LS, 108, see AO, 160, 250. Artaud's expression is discussed in a more brutal way in the 'caca de l'ètre', LS, 255, reproduced in the first provocative lines of *Anti-Oedipus*.

27 Deleuze, "Schizologie," in Wolfson, *Le Schizo et les langues*, (Paris: Gallimard, 1970), 5–23, cited herein as LW. A revised version of the same article appears in 1993 in chapter two of *Essays Critical and Clinical*. See LW, 8; CC, 21. Foucault cites this text in the preface that he wrote for Brisset's *Logical Grammar*. Brisset is another author and exceptional predecessor to whom Breton drew attention, and Foucault wrote an article on him at the same time he was working on Roussel (Foucault, "Sept propros sur le septième âge," in Brisset, *La Grammaire logique*, (Paris: Tchou, 1970), 9–57). On the contrary, the figures that Foucault studied, including Wolfson, Brisset, and Roussel, are three representatives of *procedural writing*, or psychotic writing. Deleuze follows Foucault's lead, and even if he does not consider Wolfson a poet, he does consider Brisset and Roussel poets. The three authors, Brisset, Wolfson, and Roussel introduce three types of procedure based on homonymy (Roussel), synonymy (Wolfson), and paronymy (Brisset). Deleuze draws a parallel between Brisset's linguistic humor and Alfred Jarry's pataphysics, which enables Deleuze to treat the very serious question of Heideggerian etymologies with caustic

humor ("En créant la pataphysique, Jarry a ouvert la voie à la phénoménologie" in *Arts*, 974, (May 27 to June 2, 1964), reprinted in a radically modified form 23 years later in *Essays Critical and Clinical.*)

28 Deleuze, LW, 8; Deleuze cites "the student of schizophrenic language" in *The Logic of Sense* when drawing a parallel between Wolfson and Roussel.

29 Deleuze, LS, 104–5, 109; LW, 5–9; CC, 18, 21.

30 Wolfson, *Le Schizo et les langues*, 70.

31 Deleuze, LS, 104.

32 Deleuze, LW, 8, and reprinted in CC, 21.

33 "Too often still we consider that a writer provides a case to clinical psychology, and while this is important, it is what he/she provides herself as the creator to clinical psychology. The difference between literature and clinical psychology, what makes an illness not the same as a work of art is the type of *work* that is done on the phantasm. In the two cases, the source—the phantasm—is the same, but from there the work is very different, beyond comparison: artistic work versus pathological work. Oftentimes, the writer goes further than the clinician and even the patient," written by Deleuze in 1967, "Mystique et masochism," ID, 184–5.

34 Artaud "confronts *letters* and *organs*, but in order to make them move to the other side, in inarticulated breaths and an indecomposable body without organs. What he tears out of the maternal language are breath-words that are no longer from any language, and from the organism he tears out a body without organs that has no more generation. [. . .] Wolfson is not on the same 'level,' [. . .] So much so that he remains trapped in a condition of resemblance between sound and sense: he lacks a creative syntax. And yet, it is a combat of the same nature, the same suffering, and should also cause us to move from hurtful letters to lively breaths, from sick organs to cosmic bodies without organs." Deleuze, CC, 28.

35 Deleuze, CC, 22.

36 Deleuze comes back to the question of the novel and the symptom when discussing Lewis Carroll, and not Artaud, in the preface of *The Logic of Sense*: it is a question of the novel, not of poetry, and the relationship between the novel and neurosis and perversion (not the relationship between poetry and psychosis), but the argument is clear, even if his argumentation is like that of Marthe Robert (*Roman des origines, origines du roman*, (Paris: Grasset, 1972), republished by Gallimard in the "Tel" collection, 1976) and does not directly address the status of the schizophrenic (whose conceptual carrier is only sketched out). The symptomatologist is a novelist. Deleuze is referring to Charles Lasègue, the psychiatric "inventor" of exhibitionism (*Études Médicales*, 1877) 692–700, just as he did with Krafft-Ebing and masochism, pointing out that the doctor who isolates the symptom performs the act of a novelist. "The symptom is always taken up in a novel, but sometimes the novel determines the *actualization* of it, and on the contrary, sometimes it releases the

event from it which it counter-actualizes in fictitious characters," Deleuze, LS, 277–8, n. 2.

37 Deleuze, LS, 101: "It is hardly acceptable, under the pretext of portmanteaus, for example, to see children's nursery rhymes mixed with poetic experimentation and experiences of madness. A great poet can write in direct relation with the child [. . .]; a madman can carry the most immense poetic work along with him, in direct relation with the poet that he was and that he does not cease to be. That does not justify in the least the grotesque trinity of the child, the poet, and the madman."

38 Simondon, *L'Individu . . .*, 122.

39 Deleuze, RF, 145.

40 Deleuze and Guattari, MP, 508.

41 Ibid.

42 Ibid., 424–5. Also see the theory of material, which is directly inspired by the Simondonian haecceity: MP, 426.

43 Deleuze, RF, 145.

44 Deleuze and Guattari, MP, 406.

45 Deleuze, FBLS, 126. This is the definition that is found in Simondon: "a modulator is a *continuous, temporal mold* [. . .]; to modulate is to mold in a continuous and perpetually variable manner," Simondon, *L'Individu . . .* , 45.

46 Deleuze, IM, 39.

47 These determining notions, which are thematized from *Kafka* onward, are necessary to understand the substitution of becoming-animal or becoming-minor for a theory of imitation. They engage the detailed analysis of relation between Deleuze on biology and Uexküll, notably, on ethology, and give a well-defined sense to the frequent example of the wasp and the orchid, which Deleuze borrows from Proust. Let us be content to note on this point that the theories of becoming-animal and the capture of the wasp and the orchid are articulated in precise terms of modulation: like modulation, they help determine form as intensive, and art as becoming. See Deleuze and Guattari, MP, 17, and Deleuze, D, 13.

48 Deleuze, IT, 41; FBLS, 57.

49 Deleuze, IT, 41.

50 Ibid., 43.

Chapter 5

1 "It is curious; I was not the one who got Félix to leave psychoanalysis, he was the one to get me to leave. In my study of Masoch, and then in *The Logic of Sense*, I thought I had revealed things about the false unity of sadomasochism, or even about the event, that did not comply with psychoanalysis, but which could be reconciled with it. On

the contrary, Félix was a psychoanalyst and remained so, a student of Lacan, but as a kind of 'son' who already knows that reconciliation is impossible. *Anti-Oedipus* is a break that is made all alone [. . .]," Deleuze, PP, 197.

2 Deleuze, ID, 364. Deleuze is a recognized author who has no fewer than nine works behind him when Guattari, who had only published half a dozen articles, meets him. "I had made certain strides, for example, regarding the necessity to interpret neurosis using schizophrenia. But I did not have the logic that is necessary for this connection. I had written a text entitled 'From One Sign to Another' in *Recherches*, which was very marked by Lacan, but where there was no longer any signifier. Nevertheless, I was mired in a type of dialectics. What I expected from my work with Gilles were things like this: the body without organs, multiplicities, the possibility of a logic of multiplicity with connections to the body without organs," Guattari, PP, 26. Guattari presents himself as being torn between his "diverse places" before meeting Deleuze. He was a militant Marxist of the Trotsky variation, a Freudo-Lacanian at work, and Sartrean at nights when he was trying his hand at theory, Guattari, in Oury, Guattari, and Tosquelles, (eds), *Pratique de l'institutionnel et politique*, 47. Also see Guattari, *Les Années d'hiver*, 81.

3 Deleuze, *Réponses à une série de questions* (November 1981), in Villani, *La guêpe et l'orchidée. Essai sur Gilles Deleuze*, (Paris: Berlin, 1999), 129, and in 1988, PP, 197.

4 Deleuze, PS, 118–19, 156.

5 Ibid., 201; Deleuze is referring to Guattari's article, "La transversalité," in *Psychothérapie institutionnelle*, 1, (Alençon, 1965), 91–106, republished in Guattari, *Psychanalyse et Transversalité*, for which Deleuze contributes an important preface which discusses the theoretical import of transversality: Deleuze, "Trois problèmes de groupe," I–XI, reprinted in ID, 270–84.

6 Institutional psychotherapy, as we saw, took off in 1940 in the context of Nazi Resistance. François Tosquelles, the militant Catalan libertarian who evaded Francoism, and who was the first person to inspire Deleuze, accepted a position at the psychiatric hospital of Saint-Alban in Lozère, directed by the communist psychiatrist, Bonnafé, from 1942 and afterward. That is where many resistance fighters, patients, therapists, and intellectuals (notably, George Canghilhem) met one another . . . French institutional psychology is born in the context of the Resistance, and starts to think about the principles of a communitarian psychiatry that would enable the relations between the doctors and the insane to be transformed. The psychiatrist Georges Daumezon will give it this name ten years later. The Resistance inspires experiments in the psychiatric sector, and especially in the La Borde clinic in Cour-Cheverny, starting in 1953, where a militant Lacanian approach to madness was elaborated in the presence of Jean Oury and Félix Guattari. See above, 28.

7 Deleuze and Guattari, K, 7.

8 Deleuze, ID, 278. Also see Guattari, *Les Années d'hiver*, 291–2, and *Psychanalyse et Transversalité*.

9   Deleuze, PS, 202.

10 Deleuze, K, 7–8.

11 Ibid., 7.

12 Deleuze, F, 51. Deleuze takes up a declaration of Foucault's from *Nouvelles littéraires*, (March 17, 1975).

13 The neologism "alloplastic" is borrowed from Freud and describes the plane of culture in *A Thousand Plateaus* by insisting on the excorporeal production of the human mode of worldly habitation.

14 Deleuze and Guattari, K, 7.

15 Contrary to his usual method, Deleuze does not skimp on secondary references in the second edition of *Proust*, and he cites George Poulet, *L'espace proustien*, (Paris: Gallimard, 1963), reprinted in 1982 (P, 149); Roland Barthes, *Proust et les noms*, in *Essais critiques*, (1964); Gérard Genette, "Proust et le langage indirect," *Figures II*, (Paris: Seuil, 1969) (P, 147); Umberto Eco, *L'oeuvre ouverte*, (Paris: Seuil, 1965) (PS, 149, 147, 188, respectively)—an abundance of references, which is contrasted by the complete absence of secondary literature in the first edition. For Deleuze, it becomes a question of elaborating a theory of literature while taking part in the theoretical debates of the day.

16 Translator's footnote: Sauvagnargues is playing on the similarity between the words *machine* (machine) and *machin* (thing).

17 Félix Guattari, "Machine and structure" (1969): as we recall, the article is, in part, a rereading of *The Logic of Sense* and *Difference and Repetition*, republished in Guattari, *Psychanalyse et Transversalité*, 240–8.

18 Deleuze, PS, 175–6; Proust, *À la recherche du temps perdu*, Vol. 3, (Paris: Gallimard, 1954), "Bibliothèque de la Pléiade," 911 and 1033.

19 Deleuze, conversation with Michel Foucault, "Les Intellectuels et le pouvoir," in *L'Arc, Deleuze*, 49, (1972), 3–10, (5).

20 Deleuze is also interested in Joyce, Lowry, Faulkner, and Lawrence as much as he in Kafka, Blanchot, Artaud, or Mallarmé. The list is incomplete. Jean Paris highlights the importance of analyses dealing with Joyce and publishes a montage of excerpts from Deleuze's texts in "Joyce Indirect," in the journal *Change*, 11, (May 1972), 54–9, which he lifts from *Proust and Signs* (1970), and also from *Difference and Repetition* and *The Logic of Sense*.

21 J. Lacan, *De la psychose paranoïaque dans ses rapports avec la personnalité*, (Paris: Points-Seuil, 1980), 13–15; Blanchot, "La Folie par excellence," in Jaspers, *Strindberg et Van Gogh*, 10, n. 2. Lacan devotes his seminars to an exploration of psychoses: "D'une question préliminaire à tout traitement possible de la psychose," in Lacan, *Écrits*, (Paris: Seuil, 1966), reprinted in Lacan, *Écrits*, Vol. 2, (Paris: Points-Seuil, 1971), 43–102. Lacan's position is essential for Deleuze and Guattari.

22 Guattari, "Machine et structure," in *Psychanalyse et Transversalité*, 240–8. This
    formulation articulates the Lacanian "signifier" and the "differentiator" from *The
    Logic of Sense*.
23 Deleuze and Guattari, AO, 44.
24 The abbreviation BwO appears in *A Thousand Plateaus*: this new notation affirms
    Guattari's presence and his Lacanian training. Lacan liked to abbreviate his
    demonstrations in a quasi-algebraic form, and Guattari appreciates this explanatory
    method and uses them liberally in the works that he writes alone (e.g. Guattari,
    Cartographies schizoanalytiques, (Paris: Galilée, 1989), 104).
25 Deleuze, PP, 197.
26 Artaud, cited by Deleuze and Guattari, AO, 21.
27 Foucault, *Dits et Écrits*, 553–4.
28 This is a response to Laplanche's book, *Hölderlin et la question du père*, (1961), as
    well as Foucault's article, "Le "non" du père," *Critique*, 178, (March 1962), *Dits et
    Écrits*, 189.
29 Nietzsche, *Lettre à Burckhardt du 5 janvier 1889*; and Klossowski, *Nietzsche et le
    cercle vicieux*, (Paris: Mercure de France, 1969), 341.
30 Deleuze and Guattari, *La synthèse disjonctive*, reprinted in AO, 28.
31 Ibid., 20.
32 Deleuze and Guattari, K, 14–15.
33 Guattari, 'Machine and Structure' in *Psychanalyse et Transversalité*.
34 Deleuze and Guattari, MP, 10.
35 Deleuze, CC, 16.
36 Deleuze, D, 12, 54.
37 Deleuze and Guattari, MP, 17.

Chapter 6

1 Deleuze and Guattari, K, 33.
2 Ibid., 29, 30, 31, respectively. We find the same affirmation in *A Thousand
   Plateaus*, 130.
3 Deleuze and Guattari, K, 32.
4 Ibid., 48.
5 Ibid., 29. They rely on a letter to Max Brod from June 192. Kafka himself describes
   the situation of Jewish and Czech writers who find writing in German to be
   "universally impossible," calling it "gypsy" literature, connecting linguistic minority
   to the theme of nomadism: "Thus, it was a universally impossible language, a
   language of gypsies who stole the German baby from its crib and quickly dressed
   it in one way or another" (ibid., cited by Klaus Wagenbach, *Franz Kafka. Années de*

jeunesse 1883–1912, (1958), trans. Fr. É. Gaspar, (Paris: Mercure de France, 1967), 84–5). Deleuze and Guattari, then, characterize the "problem of a minor literature" by following Kafka to the letter: "How to become a nomad and immigrant and gypsy in one's own language?" (K, 35).

6 Deleuze, "Avenir de linguistique," the preface to Henri Gobard's *L'Aliénation linguistique*, (Paris: Flammarion, 1976), 9–14 (also published with the title "Les langues sont des bouillies où des fonctions et des mouvements mettent un peu d'ordre polémique," in *La Quinzaine littéraire*, (1–15 May 1976), 12–13, reprinted in RF, 61–5); the references appear in Godard, *L'Aliénation linguistique*, 9. Deleuze celebrates Gobard for proposing a tetraglossic analysis, which escapes simple binarism: the functions of language are multiple. Also see Henri Gobard, "De la véhicularité de la langue anglaise," *Les langues modernes*, 66, (1972), 59–66.

7 Wagenback, *Franz Kafka*, 25; the *Lettre* à *Max Brod* is cited by Wagenbach, 84.

8 Deleuze, PP, 182.

9 Ibid.

10 Ibid.

11 Ruyer, "Le psychologique et le vital," *Bulletin de la Société Française de philosophie*, (Paris: Armand Colin, 1939), 159–95.

12 Deleuze and Guattari, MP, 249.

13 Deleuze, D, 54.

14 Deleuze and Guattari, K, 29.

15 Deleuze and Guattari, MP, 127.

16 Ibid., 116.

17 William Labov, *The Social Stratification of English in New York City*, (Washington: Center for Applied Linguistics, 1966), 6.

18 Noam Chomsky, "Three Models for the Description of Language," *IRE Transactions on Information Theory*, 2, (1956): 113–24.

19 Deleuze and Guattari, MP, 117.

20 'Each grammatical transformation T will essentially be a rule that converts every sentence with a given constituent structure into a new sentence with derived constituent structure. The transform and its derived structure must be related in a fixed and constant way to the structure of the transformed stream, for each T," Chomsky, "Three Models for the Description of Language," 121.

21 Deleuze and Guattari, MP, 116.

22 Ibid., 116, 127. We will come back to these four postulates of linguistics a little later.

23 Chomsky, *Language and Mind*, (New York: Harcourt, 1968), 70. For example, "By a *language*, we will mean simply a set of strings in some finite set V of symbols called the *vocabulary* of the language. By a *grammar* we mean a set of rules that give a recursive enumeration of the strings belonging to the language," N. Chomsky and M. P. Schutzenberger, "The Algebraic Theory of Context-Free Languages," in *Computer Programming and Formal Systems*, (Amsterdam: North Holland, 1963), 118–61.

24 Deleuze and Guattari, MP, 117.

25 Deleuze, F, 63.

26 Deleuze and Guattari, MP, 95.

27 Translator's note: the author is highlighting the similarity in French between "insign" (*ensigne*) and "teach" (*enseigne*).

28 Deleuze and Guattari, MP, 109.

29 Ibid., 116.

30 Ibid., 127.

31 Ibid., 116.

32 Ibid., 129.

33 Ibid., 130.

34 Ibid.

35 Ibid., 119. The variable and optional rules allude to Labov. Labov, *Sociolinguistics* (University of Pennsylvania Press, 1973).

36 Deleuze, "Avenir de linguistique," the preface to Henri Gobard's *L'Aliénation linguistic*, also published with the title "Les langue sont des bouillies où des fonctions et des mouvements mettent un peu d'ordre polémique," in *La Quinzaine littéraire*, (May 1–15, 1976), 12–13. As the article's title indicates, Gobard's tetraglossic analysis is consistent with Deleuze because it allows for the connection of disparate, non-binary uses. But the "porridge," which is too cowardly, must be replaced by the notion of variable rule. The opposition does not bear on the existence or non-existence of rules, but on their status. Moreover, Deleuze always starts with constituted organizations in order to release lines of flight from them. See Deleuze and Guattari, K, 44, 48, 110, and Deleuze, F, 46.

37 Deleuze, S, 100.

38 Deleuze and Guattari, MP, 120.

39 Ibid., 130–1.

40 Deleuze, CC, 93–4.

41 Deleuze, S, 108.

42 Ibid., 107.

43 Deleuze and Guattari, MP, 123–5.

44 Deleuze and Guattari, K, 12.

45 Ibid., 149.

46 Ibid., 147.

47 Ibid., 103, n. 3.

48 Deleuze and Guattari, MP, 11.

49 Deleuze and Guattari, "Le Nouvel arpenteur. Intensités et blocs d'enfance dans *Le Château*," *Critique*, 318, (November 1973), 1046–54. Deleuze, "Écrivain non: un nouveau cartographe," *Critique*, 343, (December 1975), 1207–27. Deleuze, F, 46.

50 Deleuze and Guattari, K, 103, n. 3.

51 Deleuze and Guattari, AO, 235.

52 Deleuze, CC, 160.

53 Deleuze, F, 32–7, and Foucault, *Surveiller et Punir*, 31–3.

54 Deleuze and Guattari, K, 75–7.

55 Deleuze, CC, 13.

56 Ibid.

57 Deleuze and Guattari, MP, 51.

58 Deleuze and Guattari, K, 149–50.

59 Deleuze and Guattari, MP, 51.

60 Ibid., 134.

Chapter 7

1 "Artaud is the first person to want to reassemble the vast martyrological family
   tree of mad geniuses. He does it in *Van Gogh, le suicidé de la société* (1947), one
   of the rare texts where Nietzsche is named in the midst of other 'suicided' people
   (Baudelaire, Poe, Nerval, Nietzsche, Kierkegaard, Hölderlin, Coleridge, see 15),"
   J. Derrida, "La parole soufflée," *L'écriture et la différance*, (Paris: Seuil, 1967),
   253–92, (274, n. 1).

2 Blanchot, "La folie par excellence," in Jaspers, *Strindberg et Van Gogh,
   Swedenborg—Hölderlin*, (Paris: Editions de Minuit, 1970), 19.

3 Deleuze, F, 83.

4 "Strata" are borrowed from Hjelmslev's linguistics, but also from Simondon's theory
   of phases. They signal the turning point between *Anti-Oedipus* and *A Thousand
   Plateaus*, as Deleuze and Guattari say in *Rhizome*: we move from schizoanalysis
   to "stratoanalysis," from the rejection of psychoanalysis to a "geology of morals"
   (Deleuze and Guattari, *Rhizome*, MP, 33).

5 Deleuze and Guattari, QP, 164.

6 Ibid., 160–1; Deleuze, D, Chapter 2.

7 Guattari, *Les Années d'hiver*, 291–2.

8 This distinction is completely developed in the conference where Ruyer presented
   his work for the French Society of Philosophy in 1938. Ruyer, "Le psychologique
   et le vital," *Bulletin de la Société Française de philosophie*, Saturday session,
   (November 26, 1938), 159–95.

9 See Guattari, *La révolution moléculaire*, Paris, *Recherches*, "Encre," (1977), reprinted
   UGE, "10/18," 1980. Villani tells Deleuze that he should resume his theory through
   a re-articulation of microphysics and macrophysics, which picks up the opposition
   between molar-macrophysics and molecular-microphysics ("The world is double,
   macrophysical [. . .] and microphysical"). Deleuze responds: "The distinction

between the macro and micro is very important, but it belongs more, perhaps, to Guattari than it does to me. For me, it's more about the distinction between two multiplicities. That is what is essential for me: that one of these two types refers to micro-multiplicities is only one consequence. Either for the problem of thought, or for the sciences, the notion of multiplicity introduced by Riemann seems more important to me than the notion of microphysics," Deleuze, "Réponse à une série de questions," (November 1981), in Villani, *La guêpe et l'orchidée*, 106, 131.

10 Deleuze and Guattari, AO, 341.

11 On the relations of subjected groups and subject-groups, AO, 333, 417; Guattari, *Psychanalyse et Transversalité*, and Deleuze, "Trois problèmes de groupe . . . ," 281.

12 There is, then, a Nietzschean thesis of "herd pressure" that explains the "erasing of singularities." "'Culture' as a selective process of marking or inscription invents large numbers in whose favor it is exerted" (Deleuze and Guattari, AO, 410), as in Nietzsche.

13 Deleuze and Guattari, AO, 32.

14 Deleuze, *Lettre à Cressole*, (1973): Deleuze responds to Cressole who attacked him on account of *Anti-Oedipus*' success, accusing him of having become a "fame whore": "On one hand you tell me I'm trapped [. . .], that I've become a fame whore, [. . .] and that I will never get out of it. On the other hand, you tell me that I've always lagged behind, that I suck your blood and taste your poisons—you, the true experimenters and heroes, but that I remain on the edge watching you and benefiting from you" (PP, 11). Cressole's vindictive and honeyed criticism made Deleuze feel obligated to immediately explain the function of the Anomalous after the publication of *Anti-Oedipus*, as well as provide a detailed description of the schizophrenic situation. "Schizos, whether real or fake, have been giving me such shit that I am starting to see the benefits of paranoia" (ibid., 11) and "my favorite sentence about *anti-Oedipus* [*sic*] is: no, we have never seen schizophrenics" (ibid., 22). It is because *Anti-Oedipus* is "already full of compromises and full of too many things that are already known and that resemble these concepts" (ibid., 19), especially its binary oppositions.

15 This is borrowed from Michel Carrouges' *Les machines célibataire*, (Paris: Arcanes, 1954), which was inspired by Duchamp's work (especially the painting, *La mariée mise à nu par ses célibataires, même*). See Deleuze and Guattari, AO, 24, and K, 149–50.

16 Deleuze, D, 13. It is a constant theme in Deleuze to emphasize the artist's solitude.

17 Rémy Chauvin, "Récents progrès éthologiques sur le comportement sexuel des animaux," in Max Aron, Robert Courrier and Etienne Wolff, (eds), *Entretiens sur la sexualité, Centre Culturel international de Cerisy-la-Salle, July 10–17, 1965*, (Paris: Plon, 1969), 200–33. The expression is found on page 205.

18 Deleuze, D, 13–15.

19 Ibid., 13.

20 Deleuze and Guattari, AO, 160.

21 Foucault, "La Folie, l'absence d'oeuvre," cited by Deleuze and Guattari, AO, 157.

22 The Lacanian term, "schism," appears here and there in *Anti-Oedipus*, and Guattari
    uses it to name the fracture between the molar and the molecular. The schism is
    defined as "a system of divisions that are not only the interruption of a process,
    but also the intersection of processes. The schism carries within it new capital of
    potentiality," Guattari, *Les Années d'hiver*, 294.

23 Deleuze and Guattari, MP, 197.

24 Ibid.

25 Ibid., 13.

26 Ibid.

27 Deleuze and Guattari, AO, 46–7. Ruyer is the one who draws attention to the
    fecundity of Markovian chains for cultural theory, but also evolutional theories of
    living things: he uses them in the context of cultural vitalism. See: Ruyer, *La genèse
    des formes vivantes*, (Paris: Flammarion, 1958), chapter VIII, "Formations ouvertes
    et jargons markoviens." If Ruyer is not cited on this exact page, the argument from
    La genèse des formes vivantes is summarized in Deleuze and Guattari, AO, 340, and
    especially, AO, 344, n. 11, where Ruyer is even cited: "On Markovian chains and
    their application to living species and to cultural formations," see Raymond Ruyer,
    La genèse des formes vivantes, chapter VIII.

28 Deleuze and Guattari, AO, 46.

29 Ibid., MP, 405.

30 Ruyer, *La genèse des formes vivantes*, 171.

31 Ibid., 173. The "thematic" is a typical Ruyer concept that reveals a formative
    power to the living thing itself, or, more precisely, to the form itself. This power is
    irreducible to structural mechanism, such as finalism. Inspired by both Uexküll
    and Bergson, Ruyer compares this formation to "survey," almost anticipating its
    own development in music. Thus he discovers the Bergsonian relationship between
    duration and melody and Uexküll's developments in *Mondes animaux et monde
    humain* (Berlin, 1921), trans. Fr. (Paris: Denoël, 1965). Uexküll emphasized "the
    great fecundity of the musical analogy from the biological point of view" (150),
    by believing that "the melody of development obeys a musical score," (11) and
    that it belongs to the ethology restoring "the musical score of nature." With these
    Bergsonian elements, Uexküll stated: "bodily substance can be cut with a knife, not
    with melody," 156. Ruyer borrows his concept of the "thematic" from him, which is
    a "verticality" that is opposed to horizontal causal links and allows him to bring out
    a proto-subjectivity at the level of real form. This proto-subjectivity is irreducible to
    its function and develops its own melody, an important concept for Deleuze, which

he explores in *The Fold* and *What Is Philosophy?*, in particular. For Ruyer, form, in all its domains, is the product of an activity that is endowed with its own rhythm (*La genèse des formes vivantes*, 140).

32 On code scrambling see: Deleuze, "Pensée nomade," ID, 352; on Bernard Réquichot, 1929–61, the shocking and little known painter and author of poems written in jargon similar to Artaud and Michaud, see: R. Barthes, M. Billot, and A. Pacquement, *Bernard Réquichot*, (Brussels: La Connaissance, 1973).

33 Ruyer, *La genèse des formes vivantes*, 184.

34 Deleuze and Guattari, AO, 368. Lacan, "Remarque sur le rapport de Daniel Lagache," in *Écrits*, cited in AO, 46, n. 33.

35 This refers to Deleuze's analysis of the eternal return developed in *Nietzsche and Philosophy*, which he makes the third, non-chronological synthesis in *Difference and Repetition*. Mallarmé's dice throw corresponds to Nietzsche's eternal return in order to signal the non-chronological and intensive lightning strike in individuations (from thought to life). "To think is to throw the dice," Deleuze repeats (F, 93). This emission of singularities refers to the semi-random lottery that draws from the complex montage of Mallarmé's dice throw, Nietzsche's eternal return, and Jean Wahl's reading of the relationship between God and nature in Whitehead (Wahl, *Vers le concret. Études d'histoire de la philosophie contemporaine*, (Paris: Vrin, 1932), 207), and the semi-random drawing in Markov.

36 Deleuze, F, 92.

37 Deleuze and Guattari, AO, 46: "jargon" and "open formation" are textual repetitions of Ruyer, see Ruyer, *La genèse des formes vivantes*, 174.

38 Lacan, "La lettre volée," and Deleuze and Guattari, AO, 46.

39 Deleuze and Guattari, AO, 46–7.

40 Jacques Monod, *Le Hasard et la Nécessité*, (Paris: Seuil, 1970).

41 Deleuze and Guattari, AO, 343–4.

42 Deleuze, IM, 26.

43 Deleuze and Guattari, *Rhizome*, MP, 15.

44 Ibid., 16.

45 As we saw, the concept of territory comes from Guattari who already used similar concepts in *Psychoanalysis and Transversality*.

46 Deleuze and Guattari, MP, 273.

47 Translator's note: *Plan de Consistance* and *Corps sans Organes* in French.

48 Deleuze and Guattari, MP, 633.

49 Ibid., 247.

50 Ibid., 262, 264.

51 Ibid., 276.

52 Ibid., 271.

Chapter 8

1 Deleuze, D, 114.
2 The erasure of desire does not have to do with the fact that Deleuze returns to writing alone after 1980. *What Is Philosophy?*, the last volume of his collective opus with Guattari, contains the same disappearance.
3 Deleuze and Guattari, MP, 347.
4 Ibid., 342.
5 Ibid., 310.
6 Miller, "Hamlet," Correâ, 48–9, cited by Deleuze and Guattari, *Rhizome*, MP, 29. To be able to act as grass is a constant feature of the argument about the superiority of American literature, and Deleuze relies on Whitman's *Leaves of Grass* (published in 1855), in particular, of which he writes a lovely analysis in *Essays Critical and Clinical*.
7 Deleuze and Guattari, MP, 314 and SPP, 168.
8 Ibid., 343–4.
9 Chinese art—where poetry and painting, calligraphy, and art of the line are indiscernible and yet distinct—is a good reference example for Deleuze and Michaux. Furthermore, the contemporary expression used to say "art," *yishu*, is formed by two characters, *shu*, which means "technique or method," and had not yet had *yi* added to it until much later, is found in canonical texts from the third-century BCE and which is *graphically* broken down etymologically in Chinese as the following: "grass on top, a ball on the right, molding the ball; a lump of dirt on the left," Yolaine Escandre, "Grand art et hiérarchie en Chine: calligraphie et peinture," in Georges Rocque, (ed.), *Majeur ou mineur? Les hiérarchies en art*, (Nîmes: Jacqueline Chambon, 2000), 147–72, citation on 148–9.
10 Deleuze and Guattari, MP, 343.
11 Ibid., 12–13. Also see MP, 25, 35–6. The distinction between Anglo-American literature, worldy-historical and schizoid, and neurotic French literature so stuck in its illusory interiority has been crystallized since 1976, in *Rhizome*, the second chapter of *Dialogues*, and is found in the tenth plateau from *A Thousand Plateaus*, whose main point is completely developed in *What Is Philosophy?* and *Essays Critical and Clinical*.
12 Deleuze and Guattari, MP, 159.
13 Deleuze, D, 62.
14 Steven Rose, *The Conscious Brain*, (London: Weidenfeld and Nicholson, 1973), 78, cited in Deleuze and Guattari, MP, 24, and Deleuze, D, 50–1.
15 In 1953, Michaux writes his first text on ether ("Rencontre dans la forêt," in *La nuit remue, Œvres complètes*, 449–57); but the best examples are in *Miserable Miracle* (1956) and *Infinite Turbulence* (1957). The remarkable exhibit *L'Âme au corps. Arts*

et Sciences, 1793–1993, which took place in Paris at the Grand Palais from October 1993 to January 1994, presented mescaline drawings and drew a parallel between them and Santiago Ramon Y. Cajal's *Original Drawings of Nerve Cells* (v. 1890, Madrid, Cajal Institute) and photographic clichés of neural cartographies, which emphasizes the truly *rhizomatic* affinity of these projects (see Jean Clair, ed., *Catalogue de l'exposition L'Ame au corps. Arts et sciences, 1793–1993*, Paris, Grand Palais, October 1993 to January 1994, Paris, Réunion des musées nationaux, Gallimard/Electra, (1993), 384, 385, 487). On Ramon Y. Cajal and his essential, graphic contribution to neural networks, see Steven Rose, *The Conscious Brain*, 68.

16 Michaux, *Connaissance par les gouffres*, (Paris: Gallimard, 1961). "It was important that I wanted to completely consent. In order to enjoy a drug one must love to be a subject. I, however, felt like it was too much of a 'chore'," Michaux, *Misérable miracle*, in *Œvres complètes*, 621. Even if he dates his experiences back to 1956, a letter from Paulhan to Henri Michaux from January 1955 attests that they had already started prior to this date. See Jean-Michel Maulpoix and Florence de Lussy, (eds), *Henri Michaux. Peindre, composer, écrire*, Catalogue of exhibits organized by la Bibliothèque national de France, October 5 to December 31, 1999, Paris, Bnf/Gallimard, 1999,147, 154, where the letter is re-transcribed.

17 Michaux, *Misérable miracle*, with the foreword dated March 1955, *Œvres complètes*, 620–1. Deleuze writes these words to Michaux, dedicating *Difference and Repetition* to him: "you knew how to talk about schizophrenia so much better than anything I had ever read, and in only a few pages: the major ordeals of the mind, 153–62." Deleuze is referring to Michaux's text, *Les Grandes épreuves de l'esprit et les innombrables petites*, Paris, Gallimard, Le Point du jour, NRF, 1966. For a transcription of Deleuze's dedication see, Maulpoix and de Lussy, (eds), *Henri Michaux. Peindre, composer, écrire*, 157. On the importance of Michaux for Deleuze, see Bellour, "Michaux, Deleuze," in *Gilles Deleuze. Une vie philosophique*, É. Alliez, (ed.), 537–45.

18 Deleuze refers to Ferlinghetti and the fourth person singular: LS, 125 and Deleuze, "A Philosophical Concept . . .," translated in English by Julien Deleuze in *Topoi 7*, September 2, 1988, 111–12, republished in E. Cadava, (ed.), *Who Comes After the Subject?*, (New York: Routledge, 1991).

19 Michaux, *Misérable miracle*, 912–13. Carlos Castaneda, *The Teachings of Don Juan: A Yaqui Way of Knowledge*, (Berkeley: Regents of the University of California, 1969). Bellour, *Notice*, in Michaux, *Oeuvres complètes*, 1246.

20 Blanchot, "l'infini et l'infini," *La Nouvelle N.R.F.*, no. 61, (1958), republished in *Cahier de l'Herne Henri Michaux*, 1966, republished in Maulpoix and de Lussy, (eds), *Henri Michaux. Peindre, composer, écrire*, 170–4, citation on 174. Michaux, *L'infini turbulent*, (Paris: Mercure de France, 1957), 2nd edn, 1964.

21 Deleuze and Guattari, MP, 348.

22 Ibid., 346–8, and Castaneda, *The Teachings of Don Juan: A Yaqui Way of Knowledge*, "If the experimentation with drugs had marked everyone, even non-drug users, it is by changing the perceptive coordinates of space-time, and allowing us to enter into a universe of micro-perceptions where molecular becomings take over from animal-becomings," MP, 304. One must connect this use of drugs with what Minkowski says about schizophrenic space-time, see: Minkowski, *Le temps vécu. Études phénoménologiques et psychopathologiques* (Paris: J.L.L. d'Artrey, 1934; repr. Paris: Neuchâtel, Delachaux, and Niestlé, 1968). And consult the transcriptions of Michaux's lecture notes about his mescaline "experiences," edited by Bellour entitled, "Document," in Michaux, *Œvres complètes*, 1291.

23 Michaux, *Œvres complètes*, 617. For this "lyrical Esperanto," see the explanatory note from "Rencontre dans la fôret" by Bellour, Michaux, *Œvres complètes*, 1157–8, 1300, and 1297. The qualification of "lyrical Esperanto" is not very flattering: it lends toward a belief in universalization, an attempt to graft the universal onto language. According to Deleuze, it concerns a coefficient of applied foreignness to a given empirical language: to become foreign in one's own language.

24 Deleuze and Guattari, MP, 347. The citations come from *Misérable miracle*, 126 from the Gallimard edition and the *Grandes épreuves de l'esprit* . . . The same citation reappears in *The Fold*.

25 Faces and landscapes correspond to Michaux's work, which develops strips of landscapes, such as the series of watercolors from 1948, which involves an encounter between color and the shocking accident that cost his wife her life, and they create experiences of faceness and the proliferation of "heads" (see Michaux, *Émergences-résurgences* (1972), and Bellour, *Notice*, in Michaux, *Œvres complètes*, XVI).

26 Deleuze and Guattari, MP, 347. The citation is an excerpt from Michaux, *Misérable miracle* (Paris: Gallimard, 1972), 126.

27 Michaux, "Qui il est," *Peintures* (GLM, 1939). Michaux often returns to the difference between writing and painting, and the liberation that he thought represented the move from graphism, which was detached from the word. Klee is this movement. Michaux often comes back to the wonder of these "lines that dream." See Michaux, "Dessiner l'écoulement du temps" (1957), 371.

28 Deleuze and Guattari, MP, 349. The last text on drugs is found in QP, 156, and picks up this disqualification. "The question of knowing whether drugs help the artist create these beings of sensation, if they belong to interior means, if they truly lead us to the 'doors of perception' [. . .], receives a general response in the sense that compounds under the influence of drugs are more often than not extraordinarily unstable and incapable of conserving themselves [. . .]."

29 Deleuze and Guattari, MP, 349.

30 Michaux, like Artaud, never stops warning about being cautious (Deleuze and Guattari, MP, 349). "Mescaline, however, is not indispensable," Michaux, *Œvres complètes*, 1031.

31 Michaux, "Je peins comme j'écris," from the exhibit catalogue shown at the Daniel Cordier Gallery in Frankfurt (February 3 to March 15, 1959), not paginated. Daniel Cordier was the first art dealer to put Michaux under contract and promised him a huge individual exhibit (see Bellour, in Michaux, *Œvres complètes*, 1026). Daniel Cordier always insisted on his decision to focus on Michaux's painting, in order to counterbalance a writer's reputation for using writing as a cover for her plastic art, and this shows how annoyed Michaux was to be constantly reduced to his mescaline experiences.

32 Michaux, *La Ralentie*, *Œvres complètes*, 924. Perhaps Deleuze recalls this *Slowness* when he writes the following about science: "It is a fantastic *slowing down*, and it is through this slowing down that matter is actualized, as is the case with scientific thought that is capable of penetrating matter through propositions. A function is an instance of Slow-Motion" (Deleuze and Guattari, QP, 112).

33 Michaux, "Parenthèse," *Œvres complètes*, (1959), 1027.

34 Tachism consists of eliding the transfer of the paintbrush or hand and participates immediately in the viscosity of material. As opposed to the calligraphic *Movements* of the paintbrush, Michaux begins to produce ink paintings from 1952–6, where the medium is directly thrown onto the paper or canvas, and he seems to engage in Pollock's experiences, or Action Painting, as theorized by Greenburg. It would be naive to see a rupture with the modern at this point. Apart from Van Gogh's ink drawings, in the previous century, Leonardo da Vinci had already advised young painters to follow the haecceities of molds and cracks of old walls, which are able to give birth to forms.

35 Deleuze: "Bacon [. . .] thinks [. . .] that Michaux went even further than Pollock did when it came to irrational features and lines without contour," FBLS, 102.

36 Michaux, *Œvres complètes*, 1030.

37 Michaux, "Dessiner l'écoulement du temps" (1957), *Œvres complètes*, 372–3.

38 Michaux, "Parenthèse" (1959), *Œvres complètes*, 1028.

39 Deleuze, FBLS, 61.

40 Deleuze, RF, 200.

41 Ibid., 145.

42 Deleuze, FBLS, 55.

43 Ibid., 54.

44 Ibid., 55.

45 Ibid., 57.

46 Ibid., 55–6.

47 Ibid., 58.

48 Ibid., 25, 59.

49 Ibid., 60.

50 Lyotard, *Discours, figure*, (Paris: Klincksieck, 1971); see Deleuze, "Appréciation" by Jean-François Lyotard, *Discours, figure*, in *La Quinzaine littéraire*, 141, 1–15 May (1972), 19, reprinted in ID, 299.

51 Deleuze and Guattari, FBLS, 40.

52 Deleuze, RF, 194.

53 *Malerisch*, "pictorial," comes from the opposition between the returning line and the Baroque pictorial material, instituted by Wölfflin, in full, thick, marvelous, viscous clay. Deleuze makes a big deal out of this distinction in his reflections on painting and cinema, and reads Wölfflin through the great study that he writes on Maldiney, whom he introduces along with a study of Riegl and Worringer. See Maldiney's article, "L'art et le pouvoir du fond," in Maldiney, *Regard parole espace* (Lausanne: L'Âge de l'homme, 1975). Also see Heinrich Wölfflin, *Renaissance et baroque* (Munich: 1888), Fr. trans. Guy Ballangé (Paris: Livre de Poche, 1985; repr. Paris: Gérard Montfort, 1988); and *Principes fondamentaux de l'histoire de l'art. Le problème de l'évolution du style dans l'art moderne* (Basel: 1915), Fr. trans. Cl. and M. Raymond (Paris: Gérard Montfort Éditeur, 1992).

54 Deleuze, FBLS, 24.

55 Ibid., 26.

56 Ibid., 65.

57 Ibid., 48.

58 Ibid., 26.

59 Ibid., 48.

60 Ibid., 27.

61 Ibid., 30.

62 Ibid., 23, 25.

Chapter 9

1 Deleuze, CC, 176.

2 Ibid., 107.

3 Deleuze and Guattari, K, 40.

4 Ibid., 39.

5 Ibid., 40.

6 Ibid., 39–40. In 1975, the image designates the literary figure, not the image in the Bergsonian sense of an apparition and relation of forces.

7 Deleuze and Guattari, K, 24.

8 Deleuze, SPP, 161.

9   Deleuze and Guattari, MP, 461. The italics are from Deleuze and Guattari.

10   Ibid., 406.

11   Ibid., 314.

12   "Cf. the distinction between these two Planes in Artaud, where one is denounced as the source of all illusion: *Les Tarahumaras, Œvres complètes*, IX, 34–5," Deleuze and Guattari, MP, 327.

13   Nathalie Sarraute, *L'Ère du soupçon* (Paris: Gallimard, 1964), 52, 100; Deleuze and Guattari, MP, 327.

14   Deleuze and Guattari, MP, 311.

15   Ibid., 286–7.

16   Ibid., 291, 288.

17   The metamorphoses in the imagination refer to Bachelard, but also to Jung, an association that Deleuze makes regarding their treatment of archetypes ever since his first article on Masoch in 1961, see MP, 288.

18   Deleuze and Guattari, MP, 289.

19   Deleuze, *Spinoza et le problème de l'expression* (Paris: Minuit, 1964), 172. Also see D, 112–13; MP, 334, 325.

20   Deleuze and Guattari, MP, 290.

21   Deleuze, SPP, 171–2, and MP, 325.

22   Deleuze, D, 110.

23   Ibid., 63.

24   Deleuze and Guattari, MP, 315–16.

25   Ibid., 319.

26   Ibid., 229. Deleuze and Guattari cite Henry Miller's *Tropic of Capricorn* (New York: Grove Press, 1961), 121–3.

27   Deleuze and Guattari, MP, 230.

28   Ibid., 474.

29   Deleuze and Guattari, QP, 172.

30   Ibid., 156 and François Cheng, *Vide et plein, Le langage pictural chinois* (Paris: Seuil, 1979), reprinted in the collection, "Points" (1991), 63. The specification "if only through the variety of planes" expands the relevance of this definition, even to paintings that fill the entire plane and that do not appear to consist of empty space; the "empty space" is thus related to the interstice between planes and not the ground's presence.

31   François Cheng, *Souffle-Esprit, Textes théoriques chinois sur l'art pictural* (Paris: Seuil, 1989), 143.

32   Deleuze and Guattari, QP, 155.

33   Deleuze and Guattari, MP, 321, 474.

34   The expression "Mountain-Water" signifies an extension of the "landscape," Cheng, *Vide et plein*, 92. Pu Yen-T'U, cited by Cheng, 91.

35   Deleuze and Guattari, QP, 172.

36   Wilhelm Worringer, *Art gothique*, (Munich: R. Piper, 1912), Fr. trans. D.
     Decourdemanche (Paris: Gallimard, 1941), reprinted in "Idées/art," (1967), 86–7.
     Worringer comments liberally about Wölfflin, who opposes the fluid Baroque
     movement to classical enclosure, see Wölfflin, *Renaissance et baroque*, and *Principes
     fondamentaux de l'histoire de l'art*.

37   Worringer, *Art gothique*, 83, and in general, 61–115.

38   Deleuze, Pli, 20.

39   Ibid., 26.

40   Ibid., 26, Simondon, *L'Individu . . .*, 44–5. Also, Deleuze, FBLS, 124, n. 125.
     Modulation in the sense of a modulation of colors is an important concept in
     Gowing, *Cézanne: la logique des sensations organisées* (New York: Exhibit catalog,
     Cézanne, The Late Work, MOMA, October 7, 1977 to January 3, 1978), as in
     Maldiney, *Regard parole espace*, 61.

41   Deleuze and Guattari, MP, 470.

42   Deleuze, D, 114.

43   It's not that it would be more legitimate to oppose Beckett to Chétien de Troye, but
     when it comes to literature Deleuze is located in a creative position and enacts the
     implicit criterion with respect to current events.

44   Deleuze finds this theme of a completely invariant subject in Foucault and
     Nietzsche, which is not given as an anthropomorphic spirituality and is a
     surpassing of the great theme of the "Man-form." "Once again, there is no such
     constitution of a subject, but the creation of modes of existence, what Nietzsche
     called the invention of new possibilities of life, the origins of which he already
     found in the Greeks. Nietzsche saw it as the final dimension of the will to power,
     the willing-artist. Foucault will show this dimension through the way in which
     force itself is affected or folded [. . .]," Deleuze, PP, 160.

45   Deleuze and Guattari, MP, 321.

46   Ibid., 303.

47   Deleuze, IT, 18–19.

48   Ibid., 220.

49   Deleuze often stresses this aspect, for example, on p. 354: "It can no longer be said
     that one is better than the other, whether more beautiful or more profound. All that
     can be said is that the movement-image does not give us a time-image."

50   Deleuze, IT, 58–9.

51   Ibid., 7–8.

52   Ibid., 58.

53   Ibid.

54   Deleuze, D, 180–1.

55   Deleuze, CC, 44.

56 Ibid., 45.
57 Deleuze, IT, 220–1.
58 Ibid., 29.
59 Ibid.
60 Ibid., 31.
61 Ibid., 32.
62 Ibid.
63 Ibid.
64 Lawrence, *Éros et les chiens*, Bourgeois, 238–61, cited by Deleuze, FBLS, 85, and ID, 344.
65 Deleuze, FBLS, 83–4.
66 Deleuze and Guattari, QP, 192 (where Deleuze also cites Lawrence, "Le chaos en poésie," in *Lawrence*, Cahiers de l'Herne, 189–91).
67 Deleuze and Guattari, QP, 192.

Chapter 10

1 Montaigne, *The Complete Essays* (London: Penguin Books, 1987), 1197.
2 Deleuze and Guattari, QP, 26–7.
3 Deleuze, PS, 97; DR, chapter 5.
4 Deleuze, F, 29.
5 Deleuze and Guattari, QP, 204.
6 Ibid., 106, 108.

Index of Proper Names

Index